ONE DAY ON EARTH

A Third Eye View

To my beloved Ralph
and the fruit of our union

and

to my students, fellow writers
who enriched my life.

Dear Bonnylwin —

Enjoy your day on Earth!

Catherine Bauer

(proud to be a friend of Marcy!)

ONE DAY ON EARTH

A Third Eye View

Catherine Lazers Bauer

artist - Erika Jackson

Cosmic Concepts press
2531 Dover Lane
St. Joseph, Michigan

ONE DAY ON EARTH A Third Eye View
© Catherine Lazers Bauer, 1999

Library of Congress Cataloging-in-Publication Data

Bauer, Catherine Lazers, 1924-
    One day on earth : a third eye view/Catherine Lazers Bauer.
        p. cm..
    ISBN 0-9620507-8-4
    1. Life.   I. Title.
BD435.B39   1999
818'.5409 - - DC21   99-27397
                                                           CIP

printed and bound in the United States of America

15 10 9 8 7 6 5 4 3 2 1

published by
Cosmic Concepts press
2531 Dover Lane, St. Joseph, MI 49085

Acknowledgments

Portions of this book have appeared, sometimes in somewhat different form, in the following publications:

Spiritual Life, The Greatest Gifts Our Children Give to Us by Steven W. Vannoy (Simon & Schuster, 1997), *The Canadian Writer's Guide* (Twelfth Edition, 1997, Fitzhenry & Whiteside), *Childhood Is* (Carillon Books, 1997), *The Bloomsbury Review, Colorado Homes & Lifestyles, The Christian Science Monitor, Catholic Digest, 39 Plus, Senior Edition USA CO., The Milwaukee Journal, Chrysalis Reader, The Denver Post, The Rotarian, Mature Outlook, Creation Spirituality, Science of Mind, Midwest Roto, Unity Magazine, Canadian Author, Forefront, The Detroit News, The Creative Woman, Rosicrucian Digest, Exclusively Yours, Inklings, Art Times, Senior Beacon, Aging and the Human Spirit* (University of Texas Medical Branch), *Get Up & Go, Snowy Egret, Gifted Children's Monthly,* and *High Country News.*

The poems and prose by children used in the essay, "Children, Disciples of the Soul", are from *Miracles: Poems by Children of the English-speaking World* and *Journeys: Prose by Children of the English-speaking World*, collected and edited by Richard Lewis and published by Simon and Schuster, © 1966, © 1969 by Richard Lewis respectively. Used by permission of Richard Lewis.

publisher's preface

Publishing ONE DAY ON EARTH, A Third Eye View, by Catherine Lazers Bauer, is a rare privilege. She merits two shining credentials: for more than twenty years she has taught writing classes at the University of Wisconsin Extension, Ohio State University-Lima, the University of Denver, and the University of Colorado at Denver. From perusing the flood of letters that her students have written, we know that she was much beloved, and greatly missed when she moved on. She is a writers' writer, able to convince dubious beginners that digging deeply and writing honestly pays valuable dividends. Many of these students, including those who once doubted themselves, are now published authors.

Secondly, is the remarkable breadth of acceptance of her writing. One of the most common comments given to publishers and authors is that you can't expect readers with all different kinds of interests to want to read your beloved personal subject. Therefore, pick your little niche subject, see that your books are advertised to readers with identical interests and that's as far as you can hope to go. While this remark may be true for many writers, Catherine Bauer is an amazing exception with her wide acceptance in over 100 different national, regional and literary publications representing a wide variety of interests.

The subjects in this collection of Catherine Bauer's writing are not limited to particular ethnic backgrounds, regions or nations. Rather, she somehow touches the universal heart of all humanity through the everyday experiences we call life. A clue to the breadth of her vision comes from a letter she wrote to us September 14, 1998.

"Indeed, it occurs to me in this winter of my life that it is not nearly as important to grab the brass ring, as it is to clutch awe with all our might, while caught in the whirlwind we've labeled life."

Cosmic Concepts press is proud to be her publisher.

George W. Fisk

Table of Contents

SUNRISE

ONCE UPON A RAINBOW

I am a ghost in a lost world. The people are
strange creatures. They do not smile. They
never go out of this strange world. Sometimes
they look as though they are happy, but I never
know. The place they live in is just like a blank
space on a piece of paper.

Sandra Davis, Age 9
From Journeys, Prose by Children

Once upon a time, in the long ago and far away of the
mind of every adult there dwelt a fresh and splendorous
imagination. It allowed each of us to transform tricycles into
dirigibles and those we loved into fat, cozy bundles of comfort.
It created playmates for lonely days and sped us via land, air,
and sea to the capricious land of Make-Believe.

It was a time before you bartered with scientific reason,
trading the subjective genuine for the objective real. Anything
was possible, yet you questioned everything. Let's think twice
before we issue the time worn ultimatum, "Grow up!" Of
course, there's a lot to be said for maturity, but there's great
advantage, too, in keeping alive that child who is father of the
man.

Who else has a sense of wonder that is so magnificent?
A butterfly, a singing bird, or a field of grass was once cause
for celebration. A leaf, a rock, or a dandelion was a treasure to
be cherished and carted home. Every minute was a moment.

That's not to say tomorrow lacked splendor. Remember
what it was like to look forward to something? I mean *really*
look forward to something...with excitement and joy?
Nothing's very special anymore. My dad told me when he was
a kid ice cream was an annual treat to enjoy each Fourth of
July. The day was once special to me too. It meant a full day
of celebrating at Fireman's Park followed by a fireworks finale.

Sleep was hard to come by the night before.

In all your yesternights, was there ever one that was half as exciting as Christmas Eve? Every child makes Christmas Christmas. It was ever so.

What in the world happens to our senses as we grow older? The wearing out isn't nearly as sad as losing the keen edge of glee, that which Wordsworth called the visionary gleam. Kids taste, smell, feel, and see far better than you or I. And the sixth sense? It was never more finely honed. You can't hoodwink a child.

A friend told me she heard a six-year-old being interviewed on the local news after wandering from the family campground and being lost in the forest overnight. If the story isn't true, it ought to be.

In response to the reporter's question, the youngster said no, he wasn't afraid. "Not even a little?" The boy shook his head and said, "No, because God was there." Asked how he knew that, his answer was to the point, "Because *I* was there!"

Regarding the other five senses, I harbor in my brain some super-special smells that would hardly twitch a nasal hair today. Take watermelon...on a hot summer evening we carried thick, juicy slices to the old screened porch. It didn't just taste terrific, and feel wet and slurpy to the tongue; it smelled cool and clean—refreshing, like Mama's phlox after a shower, except you wouldn't want to eat rain-soaked flowers. I wondered why they didn't make watermelon-flavored ice cream, jello, candy, or pop. But then it might have lost its delicious distinctiveness. It could have become as ordinary as orange or strawberry.

When Mother tossed pork hocks and cabbage into a big kettle, the ambrosial aroma told me my favorite dinner was on the way. Now I cook cabbage with vent fan roaring, while spraying the kitchen with "Misty Glen" from an aerosol can.

As well as I remember carving the toothy grin in my jack-o-lantern, I remember the damp, earthy smell of fresh pumpkin, and the way the odor changed when smoke from the lighted candle blackened the pumpkin lid.

They say smell best triggers recollection, but there was no sound more comforting than the mournful whistle of the old steam locomotive each night around 10:00 p.m. I sank into my feather tick and listened to that wistful, faraway lullaby. As it melted into the stillness of the night, it left behind an all-is-right-with-the-world comfort and calm.

If we weren't so conditioned to what we label the ordinary, we would continue to marvel at trifles. Children see mysterious patterns in leafy branches, marshmallow clouds, and wood grain on a door. Color was never as vibrant as when you were four. That's mostly why kids love balloons, suckers, blocks, picture books, and fire engines. That's why they paint bright yellow suns, deep purple lions, and rainbows 'cross the sky.

Everything was bigger and better when you were just so high and even nicer then, than you are now. My grandmother's house, visited when childhood days had passed, had *shrunk*, I swear, in the ensuing years! When my son found his old stuffed rabbit in the attic, he insisted it could never be. "I remember well, he was much bigger when he went to bed with me."

Once you didn't run in and run out of the rain under a bubble umbrella. You welcomed it with open arms, head tipped to the sky, feet sloshing in a puddle. You felt its wetness, saw its crystalline beauty, smelled its freshness. The only way to improve upon it was to turn nature's thermostat down a few notches and catch snowflakes on your tongue.

One day when a storm threatened, my mother didn't buy my excuse for being late in getting home from school. I walked extra blocks just to feel the powerful wind pushing my back, lifting my feet, magically propelling me.

The wetness of worms on a fish-hook, the coolness of sand on bare toes, the mushiness of mud pies on stubby little fingers would never feel today as they did when the world was new and filled with wonder.

When I taught children's art classes, far more than I taught them, they taught me. Children are spontaneous, creative, filled with joy. (A paradox to ponder: sheer joy fires creativity in a child; when he matures, it takes pain to do the same.)

Kids have no hangups, no stereotyped notions of how it ought to be. They cut, paint, sculpt, and draw with sureness and vigor. If a picture doesn't look well right-side-up, they'll tip it sideways or upside-down. Newly inspired, they work from there. What began as a crooked house turns into a kite. Clouds metamorphose into flower gardens.

Third-grader Bobby, unhappy with his efforts, in a burst of frustration crumpled his painting. As I was about to comment, out of shame or curiosity, he timidly unfolded the sheet of Manila paper. The exciting explosion of melding colors was rivaled only by his smile of joy-filled surprise. A nubby textured area burst forth where paints pulled from one another, leaving tiny points of pigment. Marbleized blends filled one corner. Crinkles caused by crushing provided a batik effect.

"Whee!" he cried impulsively, and his creation held high was the center of attention. Everyone wanted to try. Why not? How many works of art and work-saving inventions do you suppose were born by happenstance?

We mounted the paintings on black construction paper. What a stir the hall display created. "How could they do it?" "Such expressions of delight!" "Third graders, incredible!" Teachers asked to buy the treasures.

When a little Jimmy or Marie thrusts forth a dandelion bouquet, I am moved to wonder if in all the world there is a wisdom as great as kindness. A child possesses a beautiful innocence that is not simply the naivete of not knowing, but rather a precious and rare kind of optimism, honesty, openness, and trust. If you fear frankness, you'd best not communicate with one who has not yet learned to worry about impressing others.

A kid doesn't try to keep up with the Joneses. Indeed, his plan of action seems to say, life is too exciting, exploring the earth too wondrous, to allow other people to live my life for me.

Yet how difficult it becomes to keep a sense of openness (it means remaining vulnerable); of freedom, fun, and laughter; of wonder and of joy...for inevitably, life is tragic. As we listen to the still, sad music of humanity, one day we come to regard earthly existence with stunned pity and silent awe.

How sad the poignant truth that adults must forcibly think in order to bring back, even in memory, that consciousness which is second nature to a child! I stand with Holden Caulfield. Of all the things that I could be, I'd like most to be a Catcher in the Rye. To keep the child happily alive in you and me...what greater calling could there be?

***

GRANDMOTHER MOST INFLUENCED ME

"We are our secrets."

...Frederick Buechner

Last Monday I attended a meeting of well-dressed, well educated women. Roll call was taken alphabetically and I was suddenly asked to name the most influential woman in my life and to explain why. Could you answer that question quickly without time to ponder?

"My grandmother," was my quick reply. Explaining "why" could pose some problems. She's all mixed up in my mind with sadness and gladness, with silly verses, songs, and superstitions.

Her house was a square white box with porches front and back. The parlor was never used; it was unheated in winter. The kitchen had cupboards with glass doors and a stove that was pot-bellied and black. A clock sat on a shelf. Its brass pendulum swung forward and back rhythmically, untiringly, measuring our days.

Grandma was not well dressed, nor articulate, nor well read. With no thought of impressing others, she simply "was." She'd seen fire, she'd seen rain. She endured this earth with grace. A quality of mercy was hers.

She wore homemade calico dresses with aprons to match and button-strap shoes. The sunbonnet she wore in the garden had a big hood made from cardboard pieces that were shaped like windmill fins and sewn between layers of calico.

My grandmother told me I came from the "Old Country" and was dropped from an 'aer-eo-plane', whereupon I landed on a lily pad in the 'crick.' "I left my kolaches in the oven and ran to pick you up."

One day while she was hoeing her garden, she overheard me telling the story to Matt Reamer's cows on the other side of the fence. Their big innocent eyes looked into my own.

Grandma laughed and that made me mad.

"Well, didn't I Grandma?"
"Deed you did, child."
"Then why did you laugh when I told the bossy?"
"I was just happy remembering."
"Tell me again, Grandma."

Grandma had rhymes for every occasion. When we sat under the big elm tree shucking peas from her garden and the rain began to fall, she shook her finger at the clouds:

"Rain, rain, go away.
Come again some other day.
Today Kotchie wants to play."

We dug angle worms from behind the chicken coop, put them in a coffee can, cut through Porter's pasture, and went fishing for crappies beneath the mill dam. I watched silver-blue darning needles light on our bobbers and Grandma sang a sexist rhyme:

"Fishy, fishy in the brook
Daddy catch you with a hook
Mama fry you in a pan
Kotchie eat you like a man."

Together we walked to the cemetery to visit Grandpa's grave and on the way, red-winged blackbirds whistled from cattail stalks. Telephone wires hummed in the still, warm air. I asked Grandma why, but she didn't know why. Grandma began to sing:

"Oh, the moon shines tonight on pretty Redwing,
The breeze is sighing, the nightbirds crying,
For afar, 'neath the sky, her brave is sleeping,
While Redwing's weeping, her heart away."

"Your Uncle Eddy used to play that on his accordion," she said. Uncle Eddy died of Hodgkin's disease when he was sixteen. Her eyes were sad, her laughter low, when I once asked her, then widowed and fifty-five, if she figured she'd have another baby.

When I pulled a wild daisy from the roadside ditch, she said, "Won't be long, you'll be pulling petals, 'He loves me, he loves me not.'"

"Uh-uh, not me, Grandma. I *hate* boys."

"Wait and see." She bobbed her head up and down. "It'll be sooner than you think."

Shuffling through the grass of the graveyard, we 'roused tiny bees. "Hope they won't sting us," Grandma said. She knelt near the big gray stone that said LAZERS. Next to it on the family plot, a smaller red stone had a lamb carved on it and the words "Our Darling." Mama placed a row of upended bricks around the tiny grave and flowers grew inside the jagged border.

I hated it when Grandma sat on her own headstone and rubbed a thick, curled fingernail across her date of birth. She'd cut off the tip of her finger while chopping wood as a child. "Wonder when the other date will be carved right here," she said.

On Tuesday evenings I huddled beside Grandma's kneeling figure in the damp incensed interior of Old St. Mary's. The brown beads of her rosary looked like withered beans. It sounded like one long word the kerchiefed old women sent echoing through the vast chamber. They struck their breasts responding to each priestly chant: "Havemercyonus, Hamercyonus, Amercyonus."

At Grandma's house, I slept in a brass bed in a bedroom off the kitchen. Sinking into a feather tick, I watched her undo her hair and comb the long black strands that fell down her back. She'd twist the fallen hairs together, then tuck them into the hole in the cover of a little china bowl on the dresser.

There was the night I put my nightgown on inside out and

began to change it.

"Sakes alive, child! Don't do that! Accidentally putting it on wrong-side-to is good luck."

"Aw, Grandma...why?"

"Just is. Same reason breaking a mirror brings bad luck for seven years."

I was in my teens when my grandma died at sixty-six. She seemed to me an old, old lady. Her passing was a hurtful sorrow, but it took me years to know what Grandmother meant to me.

I couldn't explain all this to the women I was with last Monday. It would come out sounding all wrong.

"Fishy, fishy in the brook," (?)
"He loves me, he loves me not," (?)
"Rain, rain go away, Come again some other day," (?)
"Don't break that mirror, We'll have bad luck for
        seven years," (?)
The Bohemian words she taught me. (It's why she
        called me Kotchie) (?)

How could I tell them of her plainness, her superstitions, the kolaches she baked, the quilts she made? Most of all, could I ever put into words her abiding, life-saving love for me when my mama was in deep depression after the death of her darling, golden-haired boy of three?

I only said, "My grandmother most influenced me."

***

LETTERS: A LEGACY OF LOVE

"Be mighty careful what you write in a letter," my mother used to warn. "It could come back to haunt you."

Although her intentions seemed more benignly mysterious, Emily Dickinson hinted at the same when she said, "A letter always feels to me like immortality...there seems a spectral power in thought that walks alone."

Those admonitions floated in my mind when my friend Teresa shared her story of letters from beyond the grave. Her Irish eyes, clear blue against her fair skin and raven hair, danced between joy and sadness as her words tumbled forth.

As a child, she said, she wanted desperately to see her parents loving and happy. More than anything, she wished for that—on every star and every wishbone. She pleaded in every prayer. "Mother and Dad never laughed together. They never touched. And they never touched us kids. I'm not talking about hugs—that was unheard of. I'm talking about a pat on the shoulder, a hand holding your own. It's hard to imagine that. It just doesn't seem natural, but that's exactly as I remember it.

"There you are," was all my father would say when he handed back a signed report card, even when the nuns had given me 4 A's and a B+ in Penmanship. It was the same with the boys. We were a robot assembly line. He signed each card. That was that. No reproach, no praise.

Teresa hastened to explain, "But there was no alcoholism, no physical abuse. Just an absence of love—at least none that I can remember, none that I felt. My parents were barely polite to each other and it got worse. As I grew into adolescence, they were hateful to one another. When we were grown, they finally divorced.

"When mother died, she left a key with a note explaining the location of a locked metal box. My two brothers and I went through the contents, a few legal papers, some rare coins, and a packet of letters tied with a narrow blue ribbon. When the boys wondered if we should open the packet, I said she would not have directed us to them if she hadn't wanted us to read the contents."

So the three read letters their father had written home when he was overseas in World War I. In perusing their legacy, tender loving parents were revealed. There was light-hearted humor, joyful exuberance, and a deep abiding love once shared.

Siblings who'd grown up not knowing how to express emotion were at once stunned and embarrassed by this peek into their parents' souls. "There was a letter Dad wrote home when I was two and my brothers were four and five. In it, we three were given the individual attention we never knew in our life together.

My well-disciplined brother, Tom, dropped his head toward his chest to hide his tears. His shoulders shook before sobs broke loose. "You're the man of the house now," my father wrote. "Take good care of your mother."

And Patrick, too, wept when father said he was returning the $1.00 Pat had earned gathering eggs and then sent it on to Dad. Although he appreciated the kind intent, Dad advised Pat to buy a well-earned treat. He asked both boys to take care of his little princess...a name I never recall hearing in our life together.

The grown trio was brought together in a kind of communion they'd never known before. We laughed through tears at the scrawled sketch Pat had sent to Dad of our new chicken coop. Dad added fenced-in chickens to the drawing he returned with cartoon captions above the talking birds.

All letters ended with expressed love, a prayer for their safety, and a request that they pray for an end to the war.

"It was eerie. I was meeting people I'd never known in

life." She shook her head and wondered aloud. "Something awful must have happened to change their lives—but they're both softer in my memory now. Mother wanted us to know that...once upon a time..."

***

FIRST LETTER TO AARON

Dear Aaron,

I'm seated in an airplane headed home. I'm writing on a napkin and the back of a ticket folder. I'd like to stand up and shout—"Hey! Aaron has arrived!" But these people might not understand, unless of course, they too have welcomed a grandchild onto the planet.

I won't see you again until summer, so I am carefully storing the sight, and sound, and feel, and sweet smell of you. The way you sigh, or frown and cry, your breath brushing my cheek, the feel of your solid little body in my arms, your head resting on my shoulder. I'm remembering your pursed lips, your dark blue eyes, and your Buddha belly.

We met and parted in the airport, you and I. I cried when I first saw you, but today I smiled when we parted. Your mother wanted to disturb your slumber and lift you from the car seat to see me off inside the airport.

"We need to introduce him to all the wonderful things in this world," she said. "We need to keep sharing the wonder with him, so that he'll never take the earth for granted."

But you and I won the argument and sent you both scooting back home to Dad. Besides, you and I know there are some things you can never really share. You have to live them yourself—when you're ready. What do you care now about a jet airliner? And the really special things, you have to *experience* in your soul.

For instance, just yesterday your mom was exactly what you are now...ten pounds of magnificent wonder in my arms. But could I have told her what she'd feel today? Well, I could have tried, of course, but it took you to make her live the miracle. Thank you for that.

The way your mother holds you, and looks at you, and sings to you, and naps with you on her chest ("He listens to my heart-beat, Mom")...and holds you and looks at you, and loves you, and feeds you at her breast...is something to behold. As old as the mountains, as new as the sunrise.

Your dad says he doesn't know why you have a cradle, you're never in it. He says we only let him hold you if he's good. The truth is the men in the family were your real welcoming committee. Mom says she could never have delivered their eight-pounder without Dad's coaching. And after you were born, Dad brought you to Mom in his arms.

Personally, I'm grateful you fellows so righted my daughter's life. She told me that herself, so I know it's true. She needn't have put it into words. I'm pretty naive, but even I could see that—plain as your mama's nose on your face.

I had my welcome plans all made, but you fooled us by arriving one month early. So Grandpa took time off and rushed to Wisconsin. Yes, Grandpa! Let me tell you a secret— Grandpa never takes time off; not *suddenly* like that, except for major miracles.

"Did you change diapers?" I asked when he came home.

"No, but I offered."

"Did you cook? Wash clothes? Clean the house?"

"It wasn't important," he said. Getting to know his grandson was important. Letting his daughter get plenty of rest was important.

Before you were born, I wrote a dear friend telling her my two childless daughters were having babies—late in life. I called it the coming of the Light. You might also call that the hand of God. Or you might call it Love. It's all the same thing.

Imagine my surprise when your parents' name book said Aaron means "the light." Listen Aaron, funny little exciting surprises like that happen all the time in everyone's life. Some people call them coincidences. I'm not so sure. A monk named Thomas Merton said such synchronicity (fancy word for joyful happenstance) is "God saying, Hi."

Pay attention to that stuff all your life. It means you must keep the kid alive within you. Magic is as easy as A-B-C (your initials!) when you're little, but it has a way of disappearing when you grow older—if you let it. Stay vulnerable and open and honest. Hang on tight to your splendorous imagination, for it unveils a very special kind of truth.

And for heaven's sake, don't let your name scare you. Sounds like a lot to live up to. Right? Hey! Not to worry. It's your nature.

Love,

Grandma

***

A SHOW OF HANDS

The sun and the moon and the stars would have
disappeared long ago...had they happened to be
within the reach of predatory human hands.

Havelock Ellis
"The Dance of Life"

Now there's a frightening thought, especially since space is our new frontier. One would hope the universe is well beyond our shortsightedness, our predatory grasp. However, there are those who feel we've come dangerously close to placing mankind among the endangered species and our planet on the expendable list. The first seems more likely than the second.

An awesome connection there is between hand and brain. Isaac Newton declared that, in the absence of any other proof, the thumb alone would convince him of God's existence. In 1758, Helvetius, in an essay entitled "The Mind," stated as an "incontrovertible fact that the structure of the hand is the sole cause of human superiority." He says the difference between man and other animals, is a direct result of the difference in their external form. Had our wrists ended in hoofs instead of hands and flexible fingers, he maintains man would have remained a defenseless wanderer of the earth, ignorant of art.

Antiquated thinking?

In 1980, John Napier, M.D. and professor in primate biology at the University of London, came to a similar conclusion. He credits the finger-thumb opposition for the emergence of man from a relatively undistinguished primate background. "Through natural selection, it promoted the adoption of the upright posture and bipedal walking, tool-using and tool-making which, in turn led to enlargement of the brain through a positive feedback mechanism....It was probably the single most crucial adaptation in man's evolutionary history."

Most non-primate mammals eat by putting their mouths to food, whereas primates lead a "hand to mouth" existence, lifting food to their mouths. Hence, there are accompanying anatomical modifications: the prehensility of the hand, shortening of the snout, and the migration of the eyes to the front of the face.

The hand works closely with the eye in translating our world to the mind. It is highly maneuverable and can "see" around corners and in the dark. For the blind, it *is* the eye. Jacob Bronowski, in *The Ascent of Man,* says "the hand is more important than the eye. The hand is the cutting edge of the mind."

How often when someone has shown you an enticing gadget, or a newborn kitten or pup, or a lovely gem of nature, have you reached for it exclaiming, "Oh, let me see it," when what you really meant was, "Let me feel it."

Like the face, the hands are highly individual and great expressers of personality or character. Think of someone you know well: a parent, spouse, son, daughter, lover, or teacher. Chances are you can readily recall the distinguishing characteristics of that person's hands. They may be graceful, delicate, slender, powerful, gnarled, or square. Texture may be coarse and callused, velvety smooth, or wrinkled and fragile. Color may be lily-white, brick-red, or mottled by brown spots of old age.

Although the chief organs of human communication are the vocal apparatus, the eyes, and the ears, no one would argue that hands play a major role in non-verbal communication. For the deaf, 'signing' via hand signals is the substitute for speech.

The face is well trained in self control. The hand is more honest by nature. It responds more unconsciously to mental states, often revealing what the face conceals. Opening out is apt to indicate pleasant emotions, while a closing up often accompanies unpleasant feelings. In raging anger, the hand closed into a fist becomes a battering ram.

Gesture enhances the effectiveness of speech. Without it, communication becomes sterile and mechanical. Mario, our Italian friend of twenty-five years, tells us that when he first came to this country he wondered about Americans. "Don't they *feel* anything? They act like a bunch of robots." He was accustomed to an unrestrained waving of hands and arms.

Dr. Napier lists the principal contexts in which man employs gestures: 1. As an accompaniment to speech. 2. As a substitute for normal speech. 3. As an accompaniment to professional activity, as with dancers, actors, or orators.

Desmond Morris says, "To study European gestures is to study the roots of American gestural communication." The crossing of one's fingers originated as a religious sign. It was a cryptic version of making the sign of the cross, a way of secretly warding off evil. The insult of thumbing the nose began in medieval times as a teasing jester's signal.

Winston Churchill's two-fingered V-sign means Victory everywhere (whether the palm is back or out as Churchill signaled), except in the British Isles. The V-for-Victory gesture with palm *back* has an obscene meaning in England.

In a 1998 study, Jana Iverson of Indiana University and Susan Goldin-Meadow of the University of Chicago discovered that hand gestures are not simply letting our fingers do the talking; they may be letting you talk. Twelve children, blind since birth, when given a reasoning test known to make sighted kids gesture, responded similarly. For example, hands were cupped and tilted in the air to indicate pouring liquid. After being told they were talking to a blind listener, they still gestured as they spoke. Thus the scientists concluded that if gesturing isn't learned from observation, and if gesturing persists even if the listener is also blind—it follows that the person being helped is the speaker. Moving the hands, they reasoned, helps the thinking process.

Pointing, clapping, waving, and back slapping are everyday communication gestures. Less familiar to the layman are the messages hands and fingernails convey to the physician who observes hands closely for clues to physical and emotional abnormalities.

Bulbous blue-gray fingernails (clubbing) often indicate chronic obstructive lung disease. Yellow skin color, telltale of smoker's hands, may also be indicative of cirrhosis of the liver, while moist warm hands with a weak grip signal rheumatoid arthritis. Cold dry hands go with circulatory disorders.

Hands are revelatory of vitamin and hormone deficiencies and anemia. They may indicate diseases of vital organs as well as malfunctioning lymphatic, cardiovascular, and nervous systems.

Changes in fingernail shape, texture, and color can reveal vascular diseases or disorders of the endocrine system. Three months after surgery a patient can expect peeling and chipping of fingernails—effects of anesthetic.

Restless fingers go with Parkinson's disease. The pill rolling motion decreases with voluntary activity. Conversely, with Multiple Sclerosis, a tremor accompanies voluntary activity.

A lively hand is the product of a lively mind—even vice versa, if we take to heart the observations of Helvetius, Napier, and Bronowski. I am reminded of another correlation of hand and mind. W.H. Auden says, "How do I know what I think until I write it?"

Hands pray. Hands blaspheme. While they touch with tenderness and mercy, they also strike out in anger. An open hand can be an invitation to friendship, a plea for a handout, or a tool for slapping.

We manufacture tools with which to shape, build, and

ease our lives. We steal, manipulate, and enslave. We soar to the moon, create works of art, and concoct weapons of destruction. Sadly, the most reprehensible repercussions seem to result from the predatory grasp of greed.

Makes you wonder if hands, like free will, in their propensity to work for good or ill, may be a gift too terrifying for humankind to handle. For better for worse, our prehensile faculties of hand and the ensuing effect upon the brain transform our world.

Researchers tell us only the playful porpoise has an intelligence to possibly match that of the human mind. I wonder, what might the porpoise have become with hands? And if that had come to be, I wonder next about the sea.

***

COOKIES AND TEA

Would you like milk in your tea? Sugar? Lemon? The questions are asked routinely, even though we each know the other prefers tea plain.

Immediately, conversation turns to important affairs of the day. "How have you been?" "Your husband happy?" "Your children well?" I look down at the stuffed owl sitting politely next to me. "Is this your youngest?" I inquire.

"Yes, that's my baby." She pats it with pride, takes a sip of tea—daintily—and then, "She has her father's eyes."

I muster quick self-control to squelch a smile, to keep the tone serious and the pretend party "real."

Whenever Nicole comes to brighten my life, we have tea and biscuits, or cookies, or crackers. She's all of seven now, and her visits to Grandma's house are not daily blessings but rare and precious occurrences. She comes from far across the land and the tea party is a ritual we always keep alive.

Tiny dishes are lifted from a box, water is heated, tea steeps in the pot, and cookies are cut into quarters to fit the miniature plate.

Invitations are issued. First to Nicole's favorite doll, Mary. Then we gather dolls from throughout the house—my mother's with lovely bisque face, my own "Baby Teresa" that I had as a child. We include the animals I keep in a box for just such visits, and of course, Nicole's menagerie of friends that she's brought along. There's Teddy Bear and Freddy Dinosaur, as well as Lambkin, Billy Goat, and Robert Rabbit.

We talk about the weather, favorite recipes, the neighbor's children, things that happened downtown or at school.

"I'm afraid I have some sad news," she reports with deep concern in her voice and eyes. "Benjamin was hitting Betsy, so my Mary tried to stop the fight. And do you know *what*?"

"No, what?" I'm all ears.

"Benjamin *bit* Mary!"

My hostess suddenly excuses herself to check Raggedy Ann who's napping and therefore had to miss the party. Returning, she explains, "She fights her nap, but she's such an active child. She requires that rest."

Long after the affairs of state and the politics of the world have been forgotten, these formal gatherings will be poems in my mind. Never underestimate the party where tea and cookies and conversation are served on a plaid blanket on the living room floor.

***

THE HOUSE THAT FRANK BUILT

I was born in the most favored spot on earth
— and just in the nick of time too.

...Henry David Thoreau

My sentiments exactly. I favor Marshall, Wisconsin, in the way Thoreau favored Concord, Massachusetts. I would not have traded my formative years with anyone on the face of the earth. The small midwestern towns of the 1930s are a lost phenomenon—often written about, frequently caricatured, and forever a part of one who grew up there. Something there is about knowing the first name of every person in a town of 441.

The time seemed right as well. Depression? The history books say so, but like so many children of that era, I was unaware of deprivation. It was an exciting, enchanting period when the visionary gleam of childhood colored my world.

Indeed, it may have been America's age of innocence as well as my own. In our town, the word depression meant a state of the economy, not a reason to visit the psychiatrist, or take anti-depressants. The only drugs I remember were the iodine pills to prevent goiter, which were doled out by Miss Hart, my first grade teacher, who had been the first grade teacher of several of my classmates as well.

My dad owned and operated the Chevy garage on Main Street for half a century. We lived just behind it in a small gray bungalow, which my father built. Dad was not a skilled carpenter. But, more importantly, he was a happy man, an optimistic Bohemian who chose to overlook "minor flaws" and celebrate the positive, whether in buildings, in people, or in the affairs of everyday life. "Life is what you make it," he used to say and he practiced what he preached by making his own life merry. My Irish mother, on the other hand, was feisty and pessimistic, ever convinced that doom lay just around the corner. "It's great if you can kid yourself," was her counter to

Dad's maxim for the good life. Amazingly, they made a lively go of it for 52 years. Our vine-covered house loomed asymmetrically into the low-hanging branches of box elder and evergreen. A white picket fence ran along the south lot line. Like the Maunesha River at the end of our street, the bungalow widened and narrowed in the most unlikely places. I once heard Thomas Moore say there is something very comforting in imperfection, something very human and humbling. That may well explain my empathy for the house where I was born. After all, in matters of the heart, who could live with perfection?

Even the back door was crooked. The top and bottom had to be sawed off slanting in order to fit the respective slopes of the summer kitchen floor and the slightly askew doorframe. This created a strange optical illusion. You wondered if the floor was sliding away from the house or if the door was sliding into the house. That topsy-turvy entryway reminded me of a wry, lopsided grin. You know—the way every house has a story to tell. This one shrugged its shoulder and knew the laugh was on it, but like the builder, who gave it life, it had the adroit talent of turning its wit upon itself. "Whatthehell!" it seemed to say as it opened wide to friends and family. Even tramps left marks on our picket fence, a signal for their cohorts who followed. Mother never refused a hungry transient.

In a quiet town, standing on a street that was quieter still, it was home in an era when people stayed put. They didn't leave even to be born or to die. My brother and I were born in the downstairs bedroom where my grandmother died. When Grandma could no longer navigate, I remember Dad carrying his mother-in-law from room to room.

The little "north room" upstairs was my uncle's bedroom before he married. Thereafter, it became a catchall for quilts, discarded clothing, Mama's hats, and Christmas paraphernalia. Cousins attending high school slept there winter nights when blizzards prevented their getting back to the farm. Aunt Elsie would bring chickens, ducks, eggs, or freshly butchered beef to repay the favor.

I can close my eyes, breathe deeply, and suck into my lungs that invigorating smell of cold, fresh air that permeated the house when frozen towels and underwear were brought in from the clothesline and bent across the rungs of a rack set on the big furnace grid between the living room and dining room.

While billowing heat thawed the laundry and perfumed the rooms, I huddled next to Mama and listened intently to "Hickory, Dickory, Dock," "Peter, Peter, Pumpkin Eater" and a verse about a man who built a crooked house. "He bought a crooked cat who ate a crooked mouse, and they all lived together in a little crooked house."

At the time I was too young to know I was growing up in a house every bit as crooked as the one in the nursery rhyme, but it wasn't long until I took notice.

When Irene and I played jacks on the kitchen floor, we shifted positions regularly because the floor slanted and it was advantageous to sit 'uphill'. Dad blamed the tilt on me. He'd point to the hook in the kitchen ceiling. "Your mama hung your canvas swing from that when you were just a tyke. You were a wild one. Jumped so hard, I noticed the floor was sagging. I had to put a post down in the cellar to hoist up this end of the floor." Chuckling, he admitted, "Still isn't quite level."

One side of the upstairs hallway bellied out. The wall rippled and swelled like the surface of a fun-house mirror. You had to keep your wits about you when descending the stairs. The second step from the bottom was shallower than the rest. Just as you hit a steady cadence, that narrow riser upset your physical and mental equilibrium. It wasn't nearly as disconcerting going upstairs because the jolt hit you early, before you were lulled into a false sense of security.

Dad wasn't into practical planning or traffic patterns. The living room was smaller than the dining room, you had to traipse through the kitchen to reach the basement stairs, and through the dining room to answer the front door. The wiring was hazardous and the heating system was inadequate...partly because so much heat escaped through loosely fitted windows.

But there were summer dividends. The vines on the outside of the house crept through the crevices and crawled across my ceiling making of my bedroom a private arbor.

Just as Dad added to his garage piece by piece as he could afford to do so, so did the jerrybuilt house "improvements" come to be. He put in a bathroom upstairs and the plumbing pipes crossed one corner of the kitchen ceiling. At Mama's insistence, small lean-to closets jutted from the corners of the bedrooms.

Eventually, he built kitchen cupboards of a sort. Dad put up shelves, then covered them with thin sheets of plywood, which he varnished. The "doors" were rectangular holes cut out of the panels. Narrow strips of dark molding covered the raw edges. Dime store hinges and latches completed the cabinetwork.

Pride in his handiwork knew no bounds. They worked, they provided concealed storage space, and they were inexpensive (more like dirt-cheap). Who could ask for more? He'd collar whomever he could to come have a "look see." With a dramatic flourish, he'd swing open the cupboard doors proclaiming, "A place for everything, everything in its place."

I watched my cousin squelch a belly laugh, then remark with a grin, "Yup, they're really different."

One of Dad's more successful improvisations was the cellar door. The basement doorway and a bedroom doorway stood at right angles. He installed a door that could be closed at the top of the basement steps, or swung ninety degrees and latched as a bedroom door. The only drawback—both areas could not have a closed door at the same time. His gloating was positively sinful as he swung that door back and forth, forth and back, amazed anew at his own ingenuity as he demonstrated before his goggle-eyed audience. A miracle, no less. A cause for celebration.

The porch swing placement was awry. Any kind of push set the thing banging into the windowsill, just a mite below the glass pane. Dad was philosophical—"An inch is as good as a mile." We never discussed philosophy in our house, but we lived it all the same.

Porches are often associated with nostalgia; some would say schmaltz since they're often depicted as synonymous with a friendlier lifestyle. However, if our 1998 Denver Parade of Homes is any barometer, they're coming back in favor.

I remember my son swaying to and fro with his little daughter on the old 'swing-chair.' "Grandma," he said, "this porch is the nicest part of your house."

He had a point. It was our winter ice box, the storage spot for our Christmas tree before and after use, my summer fantasy land as I cut paper dolls and read *Little Women, Anne of Green Gables,* and *My Antonia* while bumble bees bumped the screens.

On warm evenings it was the scene of courting for at least two generations. Ah! but on summer Saturday nights porch swings all over town squeaked and swayed to the rhythm of the village band, which played from 7:00 until 10:00 p.m. in a little gazebo situated on Main Street between the hotel and Sickels' service station.

Now listen, I'm telling you about a memorable house in a very small town...a lovable, if not so livable, disaster. It's important that you know I am not making fun. As Dad would say, we only 'josh' with those we hold in honor and in love. If Dad's level wasn't always straight, nor his square exact, there were nevertheless esteemed compensations. Walking on sloping floors beats walking on eggs—it's far less dangerous in the long run. *Feelings* determine whether you remember a place fondly or bury it, locked in pain.

We knew a deep mutual trust, that house, my family, and the people in our town. We never locked a door. Well, maybe now and then when we went on vacation. There wasn't much point in worrying about "locking out" because we didn't have much to "lock in." Our skeleton key was the kind that fit every door in town. When we left for the Black Hills or the Chicago World's Fair, we searched the house to find it, then put it under an up-ended flower pot on the porch rail, so it would be handy for Mrs. Hayes when she came to water the geraniums and the fern in the sun parlor.

Mrs. Hayes lived two doors away. She came from Wales and named her house "Bryn Tef" (Fair Hill), after her childhood home in the old country. "In Wales," she said, "you'd no more neglect to give a house a name than you would a child." And the name stayed with the house for all of its life even if the place was sold.

If I gave my gray bungalow a name, I'd call it "Sparrow"...albeit a lame one. A small gray sparrow has no great aspirations. It builds its nest in bushes, or even on the ground. It is ordinary and unassuming and found in great numbers all over America. Other birds may sing a more spectacular song, but the persistent chirp of the timid, yet dauntless sparrow, has a sustenance that lingers and will be remembered.

***

K-K-K KATIE, BEAUTIFUL KATIE

You're the g-g-g girl that I adore. From the moment you stepped off the airplane and rushed into Grandma's arms, you grabbed my heart and kept a good hold.

Your smile revealed a space between your front teeth. Aha! We share more than a name. Of course, that gap will no doubt disappear as your teeth grow along with you—but for now, it's a common bond. I'm entranced by your smile and I've never liked my own because...well, you know why, but Hey! I look at you and decide it's absolutely loverly. What's wrong with a gat-toothed grin. It's downright distinctive. It's captivating!

Grandma Lois told me you were adorable, bright, outgoing, and coy. "She'll wrap you around her finger," she warned. So why was I surprised and overwhelmed? Because I'd not seen you in several months and "experiencing" is a far cry from "hearing about."

For four days a blond pony-tailed pixie transformed our house to never-never land. A whirlwind went sailing down the halls and flew safely into Mom's outstretched arms. Squeals, sometimes glad and sometimes mad, ripped the rafters.

Between games of Candyland and Yahtzee, I taught you the song, "K-K-K-Katie," and you taught me "I Can Sing A Rainbow."

Red and yellow and pink and green
Orange and purple and blue
I can sing a rainbow
Sing a rainbow, sing a rainbow,
Sing along with me.

You ventured toward the railing on our deck that hangs in the treetops and Mom flopped on her belly next to you, showing you the safe way to peek at the distant ground. You found a huge fat spider on the folding chair and squatted to

31

watch it.

It reminded me of the time your mom, then about the size you are now, stood in the kitchen calmly unfolding the hairy legs of a huge tarantula in her tiny hands. Fortunately it was dead. She'd found it in a bunch of bananas. I screamed and she promptly dropped it, but her look said, "Why all the fuss?" Small wonder she's a veterinarian now.

Grandpa picked up the telephone and heard you chatting with a U.S. West operator on the downstairs phone. "What the heck is going on?" he asked. With perfect logic you explained you were only trying to have a chat with Dad.

When Grandpa saw you dancing in the living room, he wondered who turned on the stereo and the CD player. "I thought you did," says I. Turned out it was the littlest gremlin in our midst. I can see you now inhaling the rhythm, twirling tippy-toed, arms extended, hair flying. A ballerina lost in a pirouette.

The day you were jumping on the bed, Grandpa asked you not to. "One more time?" you asked. When he said no, you said, "I wish you didn't get so nervous around little kids, Grandpa."

I relive your excitement as you spied the squirrel, ran after it, and sent it scurrying up the tree. Puzzled by your reluctant playmate's disappearance, you turned to me and asked, "What happened?"

When Grandma skipped stones in Turkey Creek, while yours simply plopped to the bottom, you repeated your favorite question, "What happened?"

Grandma grabbed the back of your shorts when you reached down on sudden impulse to splash your hands in the water and almost lost your balance. "What happened?" you asked once more. I still feel a toddler hugging my leg—when Mom reprimanded and suggested being more aware of danger.

I remember the train ride at Tiny Town. Better still, the goodnight squeeze and the kiss that came after. Dancing hazel eyes invade my reverie.

Your voice still rings through the house, bouncing off the

walls and tumbling down the hallway. "What happened?" "What happened?" echoes everywhere.

It's a question we can scarcely answer. Now that you're gone, I ask myself "what happened?" How could a void so vast be filled by thirty-six pounds? For some of us, the world will never be the same again...now that you're in it!

***

CHILDREN: DISCIPLES OF THE SOUL

There are two worlds, one with eyeballs
facing out and one facing in. My eyes are in
and the world I live in looks pretty good.

.... George Semper, age 10
Journeys—Prose by Children
of the English-speaking World

We might all benefit if we could adopt George Semper's vision and focus on the inner eye. The trick may be to synchronize inner and outer worlds, to line things up properly in order to eliminate juxtaposition...much as I used to do with the stereoscope that belonged to my grandmother, and which still rests on my office shelf. The two eyepieces allow the observer to combine two separate images taken from slightly different angles. The result: a startling solidity and depth.

Speaking of solidity, depth, and inner vision, I'd like to share more of the writings of George Semper's peers. I have two favorite books: *Miracles* and *Journeys*, which I've used in many of my writing classes. The first is comprised of poems, the second of prose. The decision to write either (or something in between) was governed only by the children's desire to express something important to them in their personal style.

Richard Lewis, a New York elementary school teacher in writing and literature, collected the writings. Operating through the U.S. National Commission for UNESCO, Lewis worked with schools in eighteen countries where English was spoken and taught as a first or second language.

He requests the work be read as the children wrote it—carefully, openly, and seriously. Not samplings of precociousness, the writings are simply short, honest expressions of ordinary children. *"The quality of the work had more to do with childhood than with background or education,"* Lewis concluded. *"The writing revealed power, depth of feeling, understanding, and poetic consciousness far beyond my expectations."*

Youngsters who had not yet learned to write dictated their words to teachers or parents, as did Adrian Smith, age four, of New Zealand:

> The rain screws up its face
> and falls to bits.
> Then it makes itself again.
> Only the rain can make itself again.

Kids wrote of feelings, flora and fauna, nature and seasons, people they liked and people they puzzled over. They wrote about junked cars, a whirling cement mixer, and what it must feel like to be a hot water bottle. Robert Tanks, ten, compared wind in our world to yeast in a loaf of bread. An eight-year-old thought waves slapping the shore sounded like houses falling down.

A ten-year-old English lad named Dave wrote about how mean his brother treats him. At eight o'clock in the morning, Dave says, the yelling and ordering about begins. Although he fulfills the commands by delivering breakfast, picking up discarded clothing, and polishing his brother's shoes, he never receives his promised three-pence. Dave fears he would "get hung if I murdered him but I expect he will be better when he gets over being seventeen." All the commotion makes Mum go off her head. Mother, upon reading the piece, feels the young brother needs to see a psychiatrist and he should certainly cross out the bit about going off her head..."but it's my story so I'll leave it in."

Martin O'Connor, ten, rejoices in this song of self:

> I am a nice boy
> More than just nice,
> Two million times more
> The word is Adorable

Annabel Laurance, ten, of Uganda, might well be describing Emerson's concept of the Oversoul, or Teilhard's noosphere:

I have a little brain
Tucked safely in my head
And another little brain
Which is in the air instead
This follows me, and plays with me
And talks to me in bed
The other one confuses me,
The one that's in my head.

David Spiro, eleven, thinks of all the strange people he's ever met, his friend Joey is the most peculiar. "Nice boy, but dandruff. He is very creative which is both good and bad....In all what I'm trying to say is, well, Joey is kind of a sonic boom with dirt on it."

When I visited the USS Arizona in Pearl Harbor, Sara Maltz's words came to mind. The sunken ship still seeps oil. I remembered this eleven-year-old sage had written, "Mechanical things weep....They weep oil. Oil is the sorrow of machines."

Still another eleven-year-old wondered if there is a way to live without fear. Probably not, she decided, but it's important to keep right on trying.

Alissa Guyer, seven, describes her blue eyes, blond hair, freckles, arms, legs, and brain. "And I have a heart which I love with and lungs which I breathe with and bones and veins....But wait a minute! I *feel* something inside. I feel young and pretty and happy and nice to other people."

Every tidbit of poetry is an explosion of delight and wonder, emerging spontaneously—a sparkling enchantment.

A haunting, poignant message was penned by Sandra Davis, age nine.

> I am a ghost in a lost world. The people are strange creatures. They do not smile. They never go out of this strange world. Sometimes they look as though they are happy but I never know. The place they live in is just like a blank space on a piece of paper.

Haven't we all, at one time or another, shared Sandra's frustration? Much of what people say is not what they mean. What they espouse is not what they believe. What shows on their faces is not what they feel. Too often, what they do reveals not what they think, but that they do not think. Small wonder that something very sad happens to this simple profundity as these tiny prophets mature.

I'm leading up to the current hullabaloo concerning "Johnny Can't Write." Periodically, newspapers report abominable results of high school testing. A recent article stated, "Students did worse in writing than in any other subject." And get this—the piece drew an amazingly perceptive conclusion: "Writing problems are linked to serious shortcomings in communication."

Whose communication with whom? Listen to this comment from the National Council of Teachers concerning the grading of these tests in writing:

> While there may be a sense of sections within the piece of writing, the sheer number and variety of cohesion strategies bind the detail and sections into a certain wholeness.

What does that say? There are pages of similar gobbledygook. Hiding behind barricades of official jargon and educationese would be comical, were it not so insidious.

Here's but a portion of a note which a school administrator sent home with students, inviting parents to a meeting about a new educational program:

> Our school's Cross-Graded, Multi-Ethnic, Individualized Learning Program is designed to enhance the concept of an Open-Ended Learning Program with emphasis on a continuum of multi-ethnic academically enriched learning, using the identified intellectually gifted child as the agent or director of his own learning. Major emphasis is on cross-graded multi-ethnic learning with the main objective being to learn respect for the uniqueness of a person.

Make sense to you? Perhaps the highly educated pedagogues should step back a bit and listen to the natural language of the heart that children, in their innocent wisdom, know so well.

***

IT'S ALL RELATIVE

TO NICOLE, WITH LOVE
(Upon the death of my father)

Little girl, so precious to me, I want to tell you about your great-grandfather. He was my daddy and I wish you could have known as I knew him, and as your daddy knew him. But that can never be, because he died five days ago on August 2, 1973. In nine days, he would have been eighty-two.

Just above his head, where if he wakened he could see it, hung a white satin heart with yellow flowers and gold letters that said GREAT-GRANDFATHER. It was your goodbye to a fat, funny, laughable, lovable man you never knew.

Great-grandma is tiny and wiry (ninety pounds of feisty Irish tenacity). She sighed last night after the funeral, looked a little sheepish and said, "Well, tonight is Dad's first night out."

Her remark began to make more sense as she went on to explain, "How many times he'd come down to breakfast the morning after a funeral—and he was pallbearer for a good many in this town and always furnished a car for the mourners—he'd laugh so hard and say, 'Wonder how Billy Gibson (or Rudy Peckham, or Stuart Miller) slept on the hill. Last night was his first night out.'"

Mother related her initial response. "I said, 'Frank, you shouldn't say that and laugh so hard about it.'"

"Sam Fullert said it first about Mike McCann,' he explained, 'and I never forgot it.'"

And so we found ourselves laughing together just before going to bed on Dad's first night out. We felt a little guilty about that, but we agreed he'd rather see us laugh than cry, for he was truly a laughing man.

If a widow set a funeral date somewhat early, Dad would remark, "Boy, she sure got rid of him in a hurry. You gonna do that with me, Annie?" Dad died on Thursday and was buried on Monday. We didn't want to hurry him along. Funny, the things you remember in making funeral plans.

He was a self-made man—proud of being an automobile

41

dealer in our small town of Marshall, Wisconsin, for fifty-five years and building new additions to his place of business as he could afford to do so. Like a patchwork quilt, the garage grew in various directions, piece by piece. He was proud, too, of being village president for thirteen years, and commander of the American Legion for twelve years. He spent three months in the Army, but you'd think he'd won the First World War by himself; a more loyal Legionnaire never existed.

His last years of foggy senility transformed an alert, jovial man who had a merry love affair with life into a perplexed and befuddled stranger. However, even amidst his confusion, he usually retained his good humor and often brought forth unexpected smiles.

"Does he become sullen or vicious?" the doctor asked my mother.

"Oh, no, not Frank—not to me. He always thanks me over and over for waiting on him and says how easy I'd have it without him. He could never be mean to anyone—never in his life."

"Well, with hardening of the arteries, heart trouble and diabetes, a complete personality change would not be unusual."

In those last years, Dad would often ask my Ralph (your Grandpa Bauer) about his father, who died four years ago. Ralph would explain, but five minutes later, the questions would begin again. One day, Dad asked, "How's your dad, Ralph; how's Harry?" Your grandpa hoping to avoid the same tedious "go-round," replied, "Not too good."

I laughed and Great-grandpa said, "Katy, what are you laughing at?" When I answered, "Nothing," he said, "I know what you're laughing at, Harry's dead, isn't he?"

Ralph shot me a gloating smile for he always maintained that through his screen of befuddled confusion, Dad was often feeding his own amusement.

How he suffered his last few days in the hospital! On one of his better days he sat strapped in a wheelchair and as we left, he asked Great-grandma, "You going out tonight, Annie?"

My mother looked incredulous. "Why Frank!" was about all she could muster.

"Bet there's no boyfriend in Marshall good enough," he went on with his little game. She shook her head and smiled as if he were a mischievous child.

Through a toothless grin, he mumbled, "You notice she doesn't dispute that."

The pain transformed his merry blue eyes to glazed, lost beacons staring half-consciously at loved ones as he voiced a garbled wish to die. It was with relief that we viewed him in his final sleep. A comically vain man, he would have loved the comments of his friends who came to call: "How young Frank looks...so few gray hairs...no lines on his face," they said. He was severely burned by exploding gasoline twenty-two years ago and his new skin was as smooth and pink as a baby's. One lady, in honest innocence, leaned toward my mother and said, "Why, Annie, he hasn't looked so good in thirty years."

Dad was always proud of being taken for a much younger man. I remember the time he and I went to a carnival. Confident that an age guesser would never come near his sixty-three years, he stepped forward in smug satisfaction. Surveying your great-grandpa carefully, the man resolutely declared, "Sixty-two."

Dad was *furious!* He muttered to me, "That damn fool, I'd like to throw him in that river over there. He knows I don't look that old. What the hell's the matter with him?"

"How our kids loved him; he was such a jolly guy," was another remark well-wishers repeated at the funeral parlor. "When you gonna get married?" was the perennial question he posed to youngsters from two to twenty-two. Kids were always special to him—maybe because he never really grew up himself, but retained a joyful innocence, a childlike optimism, a perpetual smile around the heart. He was a big, roly-poly man, at one time weighing three hundred pounds. His body had to be huge to hold all that ebullient good cheer.

I remember the Halloween night he hid in the shadows and frightened the window soapers by tapping back at them from inside the darkened garage. How he chortled whenever he told the story. "This kid jumped back. 'Did you hear that?' he says. 'Yeah, I think so, what was it?' the other one says. Then I tapped again and awaaay they ran like scared rabbits."

Another Halloween he crept to the back of the garage and jumped out to scare me in my spook costume as I was on my way home. The ghost collapsed, screaming in fear, and then how solicitous he was! He held me and patted me, and whispered comforting sounds in my ear. Mother was furious with him.

Circuses were the great thrill of his life. For years we never missed the Ringling Brothers and Barnum & Bailey show that came to Madison each summer. E.B. White said, "The circus comes as close to being the world in microcosm as anything I know. It puts the rest of show business in the shade." My father may have agreed although I doubt he gave it serious thought. It was more a matter of being true to his nature.

The year I was in the hospital having my tonsils removed, he dropped my mother off to visit me and went to the circus alone. Afterward, seated on the side of my bed, he repeated his annual comment, "This was the best one of all—bigger and better than ever!" He went on to describe a favorite trapeze troupe or a new animal act. Mother only smiled and shook her head.

American Legion conventions provided another opportunity for the big kid to live it up. Mother and I always had to go along. He'd schedule trips months ahead. The only thing better than watching a parade was being a part of one. Everyone made jokes about his beer-belly. It shook and shimmered even when the laugh was on him.

How he loved to whistle at pretty girls! In heavy city traffic, he'd hurriedly roll down his car window and "Weet-whee-ooo" at a beautiful pair of legs or a pretty face. At home, the same shrill, appreciative sound sailed forth from the bench where he sat in front of the garage. When the startled girl looked his way, he loved to blame it on the fellow sitting next to him. Mother was philosophical, "With that stomach, I should worry."

Sensitive and idealistic by nature, I was many times acutely embarrassed by his earthiness. And then, because I loved him so much, I was ashamed for feeling embarrassed.

I hesitate to confess the memory I had during the dinner in the church basement following his funeral. I recalled a bingo game in that same basement. It was a night after Dad had eaten too much of mother's good bean soup. He had a few fellows pulling stacked chairs and tables away from the wall looking for a dead rat. "Must be something dead back there," they all agreed. "*What* a stench!" The tears rolled down his cheeks whenever he'd tell the story. "God! I had a hard time keeping a straight face." He'd shake with laughter.

Can you imagine a fat father stuffing himself into a tiny Austin automobile and driving it home for his daughter's *tenth* birthday—much to Mother's surprise and horror! His own driving lessons accompanied the gift. When a state trooper saw me driving around town at age ten, he followed me to the garage to investigate. Mother turned on him in fury. "Is that all you have to do—run around picking on little kids?" Her tirade continued until he retreated in silence. Don't try to understand that. I can't to this day.

Growing up as an only child, I was my father's frequent companion. He'd take me to Wrigley Field in Chicago to watch the Cubs play baseball. Or, we'd pack a lunch and spend a whole day fishing in a rowboat. He bought me a .410 gauge shotgun. How proud he was when I'd pick off clay pigeons and sometimes beat his cronies.

He was good at getting out of a tight spot. Once we quite unwittingly and innocently emerged from some fields after hunting pheasants and noticed a "No Trespassing" sign. An irate landowner was heading toward us from a car parked on the roadside. Dad went right up to the man. Extending his arm, he pumped the man's hand, declaring, "Well, hello there. Haven't seen you in years. How's the family. God, it's good to see you again!" The poor man assured us we could hunt on his land at any time.

"Who was he?" I asked when he left.

"Damned if I know, but I had to think of something fast. Wait'll we tell your mother!" He thumped his fat paw on the steering wheel and laughed all the way home.

There was the time we walked down the capitol steps in Madison. A panhandler stepped forward. "Got a dime, Mister?"

My father looked at him in mock seriousness. "Now whattya know about that? I was just going to ask you the same thing."

"Really?" The scruffy fellow jerked his head to one side. "Come on brother, I'll buy you a beer."

"Another time, for sure," Dad said. "I'm in a hurry today." They parted company with a smile and a wave.

And kind? Listen, he could not have been otherwise. I guess at that time, it was a given that men weren't supposed to cry. Well, I saw my daddy cry a good many times. When Mother was sick in the hospital, he sat on his bench near the garden and wept openly.

When he heard a man in a parking lot berating his wife, Dad walked up to the surly fellow. "You ought to be ashamed of yourself, talking to your wife like that," he scolded. The lady was so pleased; she kept thanking your great-grandpa.

He got after a neighbor. "I heard you yelling at your kids. I wouldn't treat a dog that way. What's the matter with you anyway?"

Yet he was a faithful defender of gossip targets. In a small town there's always talk. "There's always two sides to everything," he'd say, "usually more than two."

I never could see why, but Mother would get mad at Dad from time to time. Then he'd make constant trips from the garage to the house (sometimes ten in an afternoon), kiss her, hug her, and keep asking, "Are you still mad at me, Annie? Please don't be mad." He'd censure and upbraid himself, and how mad that made me because I felt his main fault was being too good. He had absolutely no temper with his loved ones. "I

46

hate fighting," he used to say. "It makes me sick inside."

Although he often ignored fast days and the numerous church rules and regulations, he defended himself vehemently. "I am a good Catholic. I'm just way ahead of them."

After a long absence from confession, he was prodded into going. Dad left the church fuming. "That priest kept asking me questions and more questions. 'Did I do this? Did I do that?' Finally I got mad, 'Dammit,' I says, 'I *told* you I got no sins. What the hell do you want me to do, *lie* to you?'"

He was sure that heaven existed and surprised the astronauts hadn't run into it. He was equally sure that he'd make it past the pearly gates. "It's how you live that counts." He promised me, "I'll put in a good word for you when you come along. I'll tell St. Peter, 'That's my Katy. She's been a good girl all her life. You let her in.'"

Your own daddy used to come out here summers and he slept in this small upstairs room where I am writing this letter to you. (He can tell you his own wealth of stories about 'Big Grandpa.') This was my room as a child. My parents lived in this house for fifty-three years. Few major changes have been made in the small gray bungalow that my father built. The box elders in the side yard were planted the year I was born. Now the trunks are huge, the branches twisted and mighty. From my window, I can see the limb that held my swing. It has a jagged scar from a summer storm. Vines still grow over the windows. In long ago summers, they used to crawl under loosely fitted screens and creep upward across my bedroom wall and ceiling.

My parents' room is just down the hall. When I was a kid, I'd hear Dad getting spiffed up for business trips to Madison or Milwaukee. Knowing he was alone, I'd often call when I could hear him talking and laughing. "Who are you talking to, Daddy?"

Always the answer was the same. "I'm having a special conversation with a very intelligent man." He'd go on chuckling and chattering, dabbing oil on his hair and splashing his terrible lilac toilet water on his face and neck.

Once he left a note in the bathroom. In an almost illegible scrawl, he penciled, "If someone doesn't get some toilet paper, I'm going to have to go out in the garden and use pie plant leaves."

The memories roll and tumble in my brain.

My daddy used to squeeze me, hug me, rattle me around in his lap, and then declare to Mother, "It's the mixture, Annie. A pretty little Irish girl like you and a big fat Bohunk like me—we sure turned out a winner." Planting a horrible, sloppy kiss on my cheek, he'd say over and over, "Won't that be a lucky guy that gets you!"

Of this I am sure: he influenced me as no one else ever has or ever will. Maybe his antics spoiled me rotten. I like to think that instead his faith in me gave me what I hope is a healthy love of self. I want his goodness to instill a tenderness where bitterness might sometimes dwell. May his deep charity plant a faith and understanding where otherwise despair might creep from time to time. He used to say, "Life is what you make it, Katy." His zestful love for life should make me remember there *is* joy in the world.

As the framed adage in your bedroom says, "Children learn what they live. Children live what they learn." Sometimes I think I was not a good learner, but I think my daddy was a good teacher.

***

THREE GRANDMOTHERS

With her foot she pushes the fork deep into the ground and turns over great clumps of rich, black earth that fall apart and crumble. I squat on the ground, the better to reach out for flesh-colored angleworms before they slither back into the soil.

The dirt feels cool and moist to my fingers as I partly fill an old coffee can into which I drop the worms. When Grandma and I have enough, she turns the fork over and rakes the ground to make it level once more.

We set our poles, pail, can of worms, and braided rug situpons through the barbed wire fence, then climb the wooden gate and cut through Porter's pasture on our way to the creek. Long, wobbly bamboo poles are pointed skyward and twirled to untangle lines and bobbers. We thread our fishhooks with squiggly worms.

"Doesn't hurt 'em a bit, Kotchie," Grandma says. "Worms can't feel like you and me."

We sit on the bank of the Maunesha just below the dam and when the fish are slow in biting, there are plenty of happy distractions. Enormous rocks bulge out of the water—stepping stones. Even if I slip on a mossy spot, no matter. The water is warm and nowhere more than chest high.

The small, flat stones along the shore are just right for skipping. Grandma shows me how to hold the stone and line it with the river's surface. "Bend over like this. Then swing your arm and let 'er go." One-two-three, sometimes five or six skips before it sinks.

I huddle next to Grandma on the shore and get a sunburned nose. Silver blue darning needles light on our bobbers. Sunlight dapples the Maunesha. Water bugs glide, then jerk-jerk along the surface.

And Grandma recites a sexist rhyme:

> Fishy, Fishy in the brook
> Daddy catch you with a hook
> Mama fry you in a pan
> Kotchie eat you like a man.

It's a bigger pond some twenty summers later and my kids splash in the water at my parents' cottage on Lake Namekegon. Grandma, carrying a styrofoam container filled with snacks and cold drinks, motions the kids into the boat while I sprawl on the pier to soak up sun.

"That's bad for your skin," my mother warns. But I am young and foolish and know that Bronze is Beautiful and that I shall never really grow old.

The boat is anchored about one hundred feet from shore. I hear their voices drift across the lake. With witch hazel pads covering my eyes, I can, nevertheless, tell whenever a fish is landed. The kids clap and shout, and then it's back to business.

The fish get cleaned on a board nailed between two trees at the lakeshore. My children gag and giggle when heads and innards are tossed into the water.

"Fish will eat it," my father says.

"Aw, Grandpa—that gunk?"

I help mother dip the fish in flour and cornmeal. Pickerel and bass sizzle in the pan while the delicious smell fills the kitchen and floats outside. The kids come in from swimming and puddle footprints on the linoleum kitchen floor. We gather round the drop leaf table near the window and eat until our stomachs hurt. Boats with fishermen drift by and we hear kids squealing and splashing from way up at Kravick's cabin.

My granddaughter, Nicole, comes to visit me each summer. I tell her stories about when her daddy was a little boy swimming and fishing in Lake Namekegon in northern Wisconsin; and when I was a little girl skipping stones on the Maunesha in our Wisconsin village, while fishing for crappies with my grandmother.

I live in Colorado now on the banks of a mountain stream. It gossips and gushes in spring and summer, but has little to say in autumn. In winter it freezes over, but when I walk its edge, I hear it gurgle. Winter dyspepsia, no doubt, from swallowing rocks too large in size and number.

My granddaughter and I jump onto those rocks, thinking to cross into the woods on the other side. On our backs we carry small packs containing sandwiches, fruit, and cans of soda, as well as bird book, wildflower book and games for playing. The day is ours.

A leap or two, a look around—without thinking why, we hunker down, removing our shoes and socks, dangling our feet in the clear, cold water.

They tell me, and I tell her, that once upon a time trout filled Turkey Creek. The wild turkeys, too, have disappeared—flown away, leaving only their name behind them.

We spot tracks of elk and note that firs grow on the north hillside, while ponderosa pine populate our sunny slope.

From the rock upon which she sits, my child's child leans toward the water to peek at her reflection, but the mirror is too fast moving. Her sleek, blond hair falls forward like a scarf veiling her lovely face, hiding it from me. She puts her hand in the water. Slowly, carefully, she swishes it back and forth, like a mother testing her baby's bath water. Then her hand is still. She lets the liquid slither round her graceful fingers, sifting the wonder, as if to ask which is now, which is then, which is yet to be? Wise beyond her years, she makes no attempt to stay the magic in her hand.

***

IN PRAISE OF TREES

Did you know trees talk? Well they do. They
talk to each other, and they'll talk to you if you
listen. Trouble is, white people don't listen.

...Tatanga Mani, Stoney Indian
Touch the Earth, T. C. McLuhan

With me, it's trees. Trees have always been special. If
you pay close attention to life, I'm convinced there are
uncanny patterns and phenomena (individual affinities) that
speak to us in strange ways, awakening us to the
interconnectedness of all things. I don't know if that's inborn
or acquired.

Perhaps my grandfather, in planting two box elders in the
side yard the day I was born, also implanted my love for trees.
First trees, like first love, may awaken awareness. Members of
the solid and respectable maple family, box elders are yet
considered poor relations—soft skeletons in a hardwood closet.
They're known as the dandelions of the tree world. Box elders
grow too easily and too well; they never learned to play hard to
get. Maybe a depression baby rated depression trees.

Did you ever see a box elder for sale in a nursery? Blue
spruce, mountain ash, Russian olive, Norway maple; but box
elder? Never! It doesn't grace the manicured lawns of a
pretentious estate. Any self-respecting landscape architect,
once he heard the name, promptly forgot it. Neither is the
afterlife of this lowly tree impressive. Whoever heard of a box
elder armoire or solid box elder paneling in a drawing room?

Nevertheless, my birthday trees were like the lovable
mongrel that wags its tail, follows a kid home from school and
becomes the faithful family pet. Like a deft puppeteer, the
biggest box elder maneuvered my motions at the end of a rope
that held a tire. From heavy chains slung 'round their waists,
the trees held my hammock. They set a worthy example.

Simple, honest, sturdy, and unpretentious, they grew into fine shade trees that didn't believe in putting on airs.

Over the years, essays, journal entries, and sketches grew from trees. I can get corny and carried away at the sight of a magnificent oak, or the sound of wind murmuring in a stand of pines. Old drawing books bulge with trees I grew up with. As a campus war bride, I crept under the slanted eaves of our tiny apartment, peeked through a wavy glass pane, and immortalized a stately elm. A wild cherry in Indianapolis, I sketched in full summer regalia and sans leaves in autumn. I made watercolor sketches of Wisconsin evergreens, white-barked birches at our summer cottage, and a crimson maple at our Illinois farm.

Speaking of the farm, how I loved the pine grove, a temple no less, that lay beyond the corn and soy bean fields. In summer, I made my way cautiously trying not to disrupt the sacred quiet, crouching to avoid low hanging branches. But still I sent owls flapping noisily from their perches in the treetops. In winter, chunks of snow slipped from laden branches; craters made eerie moonscapes in the ground snow.

And when the pine boughs waved in the wind, the wind "om'd" deep and low. A mantra or a Gregorian chant was never more holy. Other times a casual observer might have insisted there was no wind. But when I sat on the forest floor, my back against a trunk, I felt that solemn seer move to an unseen rhythm. Wordless parables it breathed to me.

A big black walnut tree grew near my country garden. "They're becoming scarce," my neighbor said. "Why don't you sell it? It shades your garden." Then the clincher, "It would bring a right good price."

But I make friends with trees. How often I'd wished I could press my ear to the trunk of the walnut tree and listen to its secrets about our antecedents who chopped the same black earth and gathered corn and tomatoes from the garden plot. You'd no more *sell* a friend than you'd neglect one in time of need.

When our locust tree in Ohio was desperately in need, we

moved swiftly, taking an ailing branch to the county agent. He prescribed an antidote.

It was an evening in late June while I was working in my vegetable garden that Ralph got out the chemicals and spray equipment and proceeded to treat our locust. He sprayed it top to bottom, saturating the leaves, before discovering he'd used weed killer instead of the antidote.

Then he walked toward my garden where I was weeding squash and beans. The last streak of pink was slipping behind the world when I heard my name being called ever so softly. I saw Ralph's shadowy outline in the dusk. "Katy, come here and tell me you love me," he said.

With hoses, we soaked and doused and flooded that tree until it wept waterfalls by starlight. Nevertheless, the leaves browned and fell lifeless to the ground. We had high hopes that it would come back the following spring, but only the topmost branches gave any hint of life. The effect was bizarre—a skeleton wearing a feathery tufted toupee of yellow green.

Ralph took as a personal affront the few allusions I made to the sad tree, so we both sort of looked the other way when we were near it. But in midsummer, we noticed snippets of green popping out on lower branches, and by September, our full-leafed locust laughed and called it spring.

Eventually, the tree forgave us our trespasses and got back on schedule, budding in springtime, dropping leaves in autumn. A patient silence had been our only recourse. It's like that with people sometimes. When you want to say the most, you ache inside and say the least...and wait.

Now we live in the Colorado foothills, a land of scenic wonder compared to the gray industrial flatlands of Ohio. Depending on the season, Turkey Creek rushes, or trickles, past our door. Doubleheader Mountain monitors our days.

Everywhere there are Ponderosa pines. Beautiful, tall, proud pines. Twisted, skinny, scraggly pines. One harbors a tree house, another balances a swing. They fill our six acres to the north, south, east, and when we came, to the west.

Our good neighbor, a forester, reminded us soon after we arrived that there were many beetle-infested trees on the south slope west of the house. "They'll have to come down," he said. "The beetles start flying in late July."

He marked the trees, tying scarlet ribbons in their hair (ugly strips of plastic). From the house I heard the roar of the chain saw, the loud cracking of splitting wood, the crashing thud of tall trees hitting the ground. Three days it took to fell thirty-three trees that took 60 years and more to inch their way toward the Colorado sky.

My husband, our neighbor, a lad we hired, and I pitched into the task of stacking piles of cut wood. The gray cross sections got sprayed with insecticide. The battlefield became thick with felled trunks and severed limbs.

There's something sacrilegious about replacing what was once a forest with black-plastic-shrouded mounds. One is tempted to place a wreath of the prolific Rocky Mountain wildflowers (columbine, penstemon, cutleaf daisy, and Indian paintbrush) atop the brittle burial mounds except that, too, would be a kind of added desecration.

Some say it's nature's way. Only man wants trees to live forever. There is, after all, a ruthless unconcern to the scheme of things. There is also universal calm and order. Rather than contemplate, I chose to fill my wheelbarrow with small young pines that grew in the leach bed. "They'll need transplanting," the former owner had said, pointing to the thick new growth, "or the roots will cause trouble."

I hauled the saplings to the barren slope along with gallon jugs of water. The hose would never reach that far. I wheeled my barrow across a narrow footbridge, but couldn't push it up the steep slope on the other side. Back and forth I went, emptying my vehicle of its contents, slinging young pines and a spade over my shoulder, carrying jugs of water in my free hand, then reloading my vehicle. I laughed aloud comparing myself to pioneers who'd met mountains and emptied their Conestoga wagons so the beasts could haul them up sharp inclines.

That's not all I laughed at. I remembered how smug we were. "No yard work!" we boasted to incredulous friends in Ohio. "In the mountains the terrain is *as is*...trees, wildflowers, rock outcroppings, and natural ground cover. No grass cutting!"

"None at all?" There was envy in our neighbor's eyes.

"Nosiree! Not in the mountains," Ralph echoed. And to a hallelujah chorus, we sold two motorized mowers, a rider and a push model Toro.

But in the mountains of Colorado, my husband has been sleeping with a heating pad tucked beneath his back and pillows stuffed under his knees.

Lying in the dark stillness of the night, I heard Ralph groan as he shifted position. "Your Majesty," he said to no one in particular, "these peons have no grass to cut."

Then in a falsetto, he paraphrased the insensitive Marie Antoinette. "Aha! Then let them cut *trees!*"

I smiled, but only a little.

Monarchs of the tree world figured prominently in our lives in the summer of 1998. We camped with our son and daughter-in-law in Prairie Creek Redwoods State Park on the coast of Northern California. It happened to be the 75th anniversary of the park. We learned that in 1769, mammoth redwoods covered two million acres. "Save the Redwoods League" managed to save just under 40,000 acres of ancient forest.

In the age of dinosaurs, redwood species dominated much of the Northern Hemisphere, including today's Arctic. Due to climate change over the millennia and ruthless logging, the redwood habitat was reduced to a narrow fog-bound corridor along the Northern California coast.

At an evening campfire program, it was exciting to learn that our very campsite, Number 64, was used in the filming of *The Lost World*, the second Jurassic Park Movie. It's not hard to imagine an enormous tyrannosaurus rearing in the foggy mist among the towering redwoods.

Ferns grew five feet tall along the stream that edged our campsite. The water was clear; every pebble, rock, and moss-covered stick was visible. But the surface danced and winked as I sat and watched from my perch on a fallen moss-covered fir. A redwood tree drops 500 gallons of water each day. I wondered if that accounted for the mysterious dimpling?

I tipped my head straight up but couldn't see the top of the tree where the needles grow more soft and fine. Squinting at the sifted sunbeams piercing the stubborn fog, I was reminded of an Ansel Adams photograph.

It would take at least six adults to encircle the redwood that stood next to my fallen tree. Redwood trees grow beyond 350 feet tall, taller than the Statue of Liberty. Tannic content and thick bark make redwoods impervious to killing diseases, insect and fire damage. Coastal trees can live more than 2,000 years, averaging 500 to 700 years.

John Steinbeck called them "ambassadors from another time." He pinpoints the sensation of sitting in the hushed quiet among the redwoods when he reminds us they "leave a mark or create a vision that stays with you always."

Gentle giants with delicate, feathery foliage, cones less than an inch long, and seeds the size of tomato seeds, they are God's houseplants; also a timeless sanctuary for the human soul.

***

MAMA'S SOLUTIONS

Eighty-eight in years and pounds when she died, Mama was independent as a jay-bird and just as sassy. All persons are different, but Mama was different from most. Her solutions to life's perplexities in no way resembled the methods of the majority.

Inflation? They say it's hardest on the elderly. Mama found it a challenge, a skill she honed carefully over the years. Appliances, furniture, and rugs lived for eons in our house. Her 1928 Maytag was the washer in use when she gave up her house in 1975. She could depend on it. "More than you can say for the newfangled contraptions they build nowadays."

Our gas stove perched like a bowlegged crane in the kitchen corner for 25 years before being moved to the north cottage. The burners wheezed, the oven door was warped, but it was "family."

Our GE was the first refrigerator in town; it knew the added distinction of being the last refrigerator (of its kind) in town. The square box with cylindrical drum top merited a historical marker. Worn rugs and tattered oilcloth became pads for their replacements.

How mother loved a bargain! There was the Christmas we bounded into my parents' living room and did a double take at the scrawny broomstick tree tucked into a niche.

Ralph and I tried to squelch our laughter, but our son, who was 5, blurted, "It has branches only in front, Grandma."

"It's a corner tree, honey. That's what the man called it. How much do you think I paid?" she asked.

"Twenty-five cents?" I ventured.

"Exactly! And a corner tree was just what I needed."

Her self-satisfied beaming was rivaled only by the brilliance of the two strands of lights draped among the sparse branches.

Once Mama discovered Goodwill and St. Vincent de Paul, department stores were never-never land. Even then, she checked items for flaws to warrant further markdown.

"These buttonholes show wear," I heard her mumble while examining a coat in the Goodwill store.

"But Mama, you *know* it's been worn."

"Five dollars is too much." I ducked behind the racks as she marched toward the checkout counter.

"Is $4.50 OK?" the lady asked.

Later, when I chuckled and shook my head, she scolded, "You needn't laugh, fine lady, the Hart, Schaffner & Marx suit Dad wore to your son's wedding I got at St. Vincent's for $4.00. It looked lovely. Some old man must have bought it and then up and died—you could tell it had no wear to speak of."

Her bargain cashmere coat with real mink trim got *lots* of wear. Years after its purchase, I was walking behind her when I noticed a gouge in the fur collar. "Mama, there's a chunk missing in the back of your collar!"

No response.

When she took too much aspirin, she said she got "deaf as a beetle." I thought it was one of those days. I began to repeat, this time louder.

"I HEAR YOU!" she mocked. "You needn't shout."

"Well, what happened?"

"Just don't get so excited." Turned out the collar was beginning to show wear beneath her chin. Cutting a hunk from the back and gluing it atop the bare spot in front solved everything.

Maneuvering for markdowns got a further workout in the grocery store...a tomato with a blemish, a can with a dent, a box with a tear. Plastic cups, dishes, and forks were carried home from fast-food restaurants to be re-used again and again. They got washed like regular dishes. "Mama, what are you saving?" I asked. "Time? Money? Work?"

"They're too good to throw away. Ask Prudy."

Prudy lived in the apartment across the hall. They exchanged empty boxes, jars, container covers, and old magazines.

Speaking of Prudy, one day mother smugly announced, "Just today Prudy said, "Why Anna, you've lost your front tooth! And she's lived across the hall for five years."

You see I'd been after Mama for years to have her missing front tooth replaced. She'd been wearing the same plate for 30 years when she sneezed, sending it flying to the garage floor, breaking out a front tooth and cracking the roof. She wore it for fifteen more years before it went to heaven with her.

The dentist refused to paste it together when she carried in the remnants in a paper bag and she refused to replace it. She patched what she could with super-glue. It felt fine. "I may kick the bucket next year," she reasoned. "I'm not wasting good money on a new plate that might give me nothing but grief. Besides, you're the only one that notices it."

Then the clincher: "I can smile so it doesn't show. See?" She stretched her lip over her front teeth as if about to apply lipstick. She even talked that way for ten minutes, until she forgot about it.

Throwing "good money after bad" via trips to the dentist was the epitome of frivolous waste. When she learned repair to my teeth might run over $100, she was taken aback, but just for a moment. "I'd have them all pulled," she said. "You could get a good plate for that kind of money."

M.D.'s didn't fare much better. One day Mama slipped on a rug and twisted her foot. It was so swollen, I insisted she see the doctor. "It's all right," she said while smacking her swollen and feverish ankle with her cane. WHOMP! "Now could I do that if anything was broken?"

Prudy and the two young nurses who lived upstairs finally convinced her she should let me take her to see Dr. Thompson. In the waiting room, she hobbled up to the counter with a pained expression, asking if she could get in past the roomful of waiting patients. "Mama," I whispered, and tugged her arm, but by that time the nurse was ushering her into the doctor's office.

Immediately she went into her act. Whomp! with the

60

cane. Bang! on the swollen ankle. "Now if anything was wrong, could I do that? Of course not. My daughter made me come."

Dr. Thompson laughed. He felt her ankle, pressing this side, then that. "I guess you're right," he agreed. No mention of X-rays. That little woman could be overpowering. Ushering her out the door, he announced, "Anna, you've made my day."

"Yes, to the tune of $12," she said, but she was smiling. To me she explained, "He's used to the old complaining biddies running over here and pestering him constantly. Melva and Doris and Tressie are here half the time and telephoning the other half. What can he do? They oughta take us all out and shoot us after we hit seventy-five."

It was her spontaneous reactions to situations that startled the observer. Like the time we were at the cottage and Dad yelled from the pier, "ANNIEEE!" We were washing dishes, and she flew like lightning. She knew Dad was landing a big one. White hair flying, she leapt down the embankment, sprinted along the dock, then belly-flopped upon the twenty-pound Northern that was thrashing about the pier. When Dad had the head mounted (preserving the whole thing would have cost too much), his typed caption beneath the trophy read, "Landed with the help of my wife, Annie."

Another time, she was walking home from the store near our cabin when she heard the cry. Dropping the grocery bags in the road, she dashed to the pier and scooped the flailing fish into a net, but lost her balance and fell into the lake. Holding the net high, she saved the fish and Dad was shouting, "Good job, Annie!"

There was the day she doubled for a hunting dog. She lit out across a field chasing a wounded grouse. Dad was cheering from the sidelines, "Faster, Annie, faster!"

We learned of another hunting incident when we went out to visit my folks and found mother with a bandaged hand— the size of a boxing glove. On a trip home from the cottage, Dad saw a deer heading into the forest beside the road. He

61

stopped the car, grabbed his gun from the trunk, and rushed in pursuit of the animal (who, fortunately out-maneuvered the hunter). Mother, left standing near the open trunk, slammed it down on her hand. Her screams, "FRANK! FRANK!" were in vain. When Dad finally wandered back to the car, he found Mother in dire pain, her hand still caught in the trunk door.

His apologies, understandably, were not readily accepted. "You must have heard me screaming," she said.

"Well, how was I to know this time it was something really important?"

Chasing hornets roused shouting of another nature. While inside the cottage, we noticed hornets hovering about the eaves. Mother grabbed the aerosol can of insect spray and ran outside. She would shoot the nest, then run backwards when the hornets were flushed from their haven. In a moment, she'd renew the attack. It was like one of those comedy scenes from a silent movie when the film was speeded up and figures were set to rushing forward, then back in mad chaos.

"Annie, stop it. Get in here." But my father's warnings went unheeded.

My son stared open-mouthed. "That's the *bravest* thing I ever saw."

"Brave, hell! That's plain nuts." Dad was as mad as the hornets.

Only when she considered her task completed did Mother come inside.

The day she observed me trying to remove a staple from a sheaf of paper, she rushed to my aid with a pair of pliers. It reminded me of the time I was defrosting the refrigerator. She had a brainstorm and disappeared to the basement of her apartment building. She reappeared brandishing what she thought was just the tool I needed for loosening ice from coils: a three-foot long, three-inch thick plaster of Paris sword; one of those fake things people hang over fireplaces in recreation rooms.

Whew! was she mad the day I scrubbed her kitchen floor.

"This is *my* house. How would you like it if one of your kids took over and scrubbed your floor?"

"I'd say, 'Fine, go to it.' When I'm eighty-seven, I'll expect it."

"You think I'm dirty? I'm surprised you'll eat here." She drummed her fingers on the arm of her chair. "You're driving me crazy."

"I'm not, Mama. You are, and over nothing." Then I laughed and told her she was cute when she was mad. She swooped down on me like an angry bird and swished away my scrub bucket. Dashing the dirty water into the toilet, she flushed it away.

"WAIT! I'm not through!" I raised my arms, my scrub cloth dripping.

"Goddammit, you are now!" she screeched.

***

ONLY A BIRD

It was a red and gold and green day of October's Indian Summer. I fastened three ears of Indian corn to the front door knocker. The soft breeze that rustled the locust leaves would soon be sharpening its edges.

Ralph cut the grass for the last time. I brought in tomatoes, beans, onions, carrots, and squash from my garden. We cut the heavy blossom from atop the bowed sunflower plant that grew near the garden fence and set it out back for the hungry birds.

In late afternoon, while Ralph watched the football game, I went for a walk. I met a couple about our age riding a tandem bike. They waved and smiled. That's something we must try, I decided as they sailed by.

I saw several children huddled on the lawn with a brand new puppy. "What kind?" I asked.

"A beagle," a blond boy of about ten replied, peering at me from under the beak of his baseball cap. "Her name is Tammy." She was beige and bouncy and beautiful.

I walked the high ridge along the reservoir and saw a boy sitting on the stones along the shore, launching mighty battleships that resembled broken branches.

Crossing the golf course, I tipped my head skyward to follow birds in flight. Two swallows (I'm guessing, but the tails were forked) were soaring and swooping as they chirped to one another and piped a hymn to life and to the setting sun.

Nearing my own door, I took the long way around the house and stopped at the corner, startled to hear a loud chirping and twittering, then a fluttering of wings, followed by a scratching sound. A bird had fallen in the downspout. I ran and told Ralph and he got the ladder. I steadied the sides as he climbed to the top step. Immediately, the creature grew silent, no doubt in added fear and terror. The pipe angles from the eaves before it shoots straight down at the corner.

"It must be a very small bird," Ralph said, peeking down

the dark and narrow opening. He tapped the spout gently and we heard a weight suddenly go swishing down the pipe.

"Oh, good! It will fall out at the bottom," I said, running to the corner and peeking behind the shrub.

"No, I'm afraid not," Ralph said. "The pipe travels underground for some distance and then protrudes out into the ravine."

We listened at the pipe's end, but it was far from the downspout. The pipe lies diagonally under the ground. Ralph and I looked at each other, felt helpless, walked back and forth from the house to the ravine, and finally—wordless—went inside.

I thought about the bird in the evening and again after getting into bed. At breakfast the next morning, I said, "You know Ralph, I couldn't sleep. Kept thinking about that little bird. We should have flushed the drain with the hose. What would we have had to lose? Either it would have killed the poor trapped creature or flushed it safely out to open air."

A soft laugh burst from Ralph and his glance met mine. "Funny, I couldn't sleep either, and I was thinking exactly the same thing. If it were a person, we would immediately rip up the ground, but..." his gaze grew soft, "we tend to think—it's only a bird."

***

ON MOUNTAIN CLIMBING AND WRITING

Much madness is divinest sense
To a discerning eye;
Much sense the starkest madness.
'Tis the majority
In this, as all, prevails.
Assent and you are sane;
Demur, —you're straightway dangerous,
And handled with a chain.

...Emily Dickinson

On my morning walk, I noticed the mountain climbers are back once again honing their skills now that the ice and snow have disappeared. About two miles from my house, a sheer rock face shoots up a few hundred feet. The climbers scramble up with their picks, spiked shoes, backpacks, and dangling ropes. Now and then one will wave a greeting, but usually they're too busy concentrating on the task at hand.

I was reminded that not long ago I saw a handsome young man being interviewed on "60 Minutes." This fellow is an attorney; he is also a mountain climber. He's going to undertake another big climb—maybe Everest, I don't remember. At any rate, a famous and formidable peak was mentioned. The man has five young children and a wife who never voices opposition to his intrepid spirit.

On one of his climbs, he fell into a deep crevasse. His partner had fallen first, and so he found himself atop his friend. Somehow he was able to get up and out. He tried in vain to rescue his companion, but the man died trapped between walls of rock.

I wish now I had paid more attention to this man's story;

66

I hadn't realized I'd be writing about it. His story seemed, at the time, to be something distasteful and foolish which I wanted to ignore, yet it also exercised a delicious and menacing fascination.

Although this young professional had survived the fall, he required surgery, and a portion of his lung was removed. Pictures taken at the time of the tragedy showed a thin, haggard, bewhiskered, young man who could speak only in a husky whisper. God knows he needed his voice as a practicing attorney. The road back to health was long and arduous, but, now, healed and hearty, this once battered soul is preparing for yet another climb.

That triggered a strange personal reaction. I didn't know whether to scorn him, pity him, admire him, or simply dismiss him from further consideration. It seemed inappropriate to react in any one of those ways. An admixture of all those emotions gnawed at my mind.

To complicate my dilemma, a few days later, I happened upon a similarly perplexing conundrum. I rarely watch television. I've seen "Real People" about five times in my life. Yet there was Sara Purcell on "the tube," huffing and puffing while climbing the perpendicular wall of a mountain. She was following a young master climber—of *eighteen*, mind you— who was praising her progress, urging her on. Of course, he reached the top first and scrambled to the plateau as gracefully as a mountain goat. Stretching his neck over the precipice, he shouted encouragement and told her how great she'd feel once she reached the top, which she did.

Afterwards, she explained that the young man had artificial legs. You know how he lost his legs? Right! An accident while mountain climbing. And get this, now he sees certain advantages because he can screw on and off various feet depending which are more adaptable to particular terrain. With great fanfare, the curtains were lifted aside and out stepped the young man onto the "Real People" stage...a good looking, happy-natured lad. But once again I had to wonder— Good Grief! What is it with mountain climbers anyway? Isn't ordinary life exciting enough? Are they curious or crazy? Bored or balmy?

How about writers? In *The Writer and Psychoanalysis*, psychiatrist Edmund Bergler states that he has never encountered a normal writer, not in his office nor in private life nor in examining the life histories of writers. "Normal people just don't feel impelled to write." In *The Act of Creation*, novelist and scientist Arthur Koestler devotes a full chapter to the archetypal experience he deemed of special significance to the act of creation. Some overwhelming catastrophic event plunges a being downward and backward to the tragic plane. After a fall through the manhole from the trivial to the tragic, life is never the same. In *Dynamics of Creation*, Anthony Storr states that an artist does not turn to creative activity simply because he possesses a particular skill. Like Koestler, he defines creativity as an actualization of surplus potential, the tapping of dormant capacities under exceptional or abnormal circumstances: a kind of redemption, even a defense mechanism against anxiety, boredom, or depression.

For whatever reason, one who writes well must be perfectly true unto himself, even though he risks censure in stating his truth. Indeed, risking censure is often not a matter of concern to him. Carl Jung asserts that man, in his painful search for liberation, learns that it can come only from within. "Man must acknowledge his dependence upon forces within himself which are neither rational nor under the control of the will."

The mountain climber is often asked incredulously, "Why?" The standard stereotyped response is, "Because it's there."

The writer, too, may often ask *himself* why he chooses to

constantly suffer the silent, lonely, frustrating battle that is yet an ecstasy akin to prayer. Perhaps the most honest answer is, "Because I cannot *not* write."

Mountain climber and writer—at first glance, an unlikely pair. But deep down perhaps they are blood brothers, hooked by a nagging compulsion to keep on climbing, wrestling their daemons in order to recreate and recapture the exultation that defies description and transcends understanding. Neither, it seems can solve the mystery that baffles self as much as the observer. At best, one can only restate the paradox. That alone seems possible on this plane.

***

WHAT'S A GRANDDAUGHTER?

A granddaughter is for asking "Whassat?" "Why?" and then "Why?" some more! She's to show leaves and caterpillars and butterflies to...and rocks and clouds and a crooked stick too.

She's a blond, pony-tailed, hazel-eyed beauty to push on a swing, to slide down a slide behind, and to sit across from on the see-saw. She's to build sandcastles with, and her toes are to tickle your toes under cold wet sand.

Her smile is Valentine's Day, the 4th of July, the Circus, and Carnival time. She makes Christmas Christmas. Her birthday calls for star-spangled celebration. She blows out her candles, then whispers in my ear, "I wished for a diamond ring for you, Grandma."

During a game of "Let's Pretend," she takes my picture with a cracker box, hands me mewing kittens to hold, and drives me to Chicago in her Chevrolet. I have to squeal in terror and cover my face with outspread hands when she "be's a monster."

She's to lie down with at nap time and tell stories to...about when I was a little girl. She listens as if my words were spun from gold. When it's her turn, she begins, "Once upon a time," and hurries breathlessly with a lengthy tale. Frustrating sighs soon follow as her mind races ahead of her ability to put thoughts into words.

When I sing songs to her, she *never* says I sing off key, even though I always do. After singing her song to me, she says, "Now you clap, Grandma," and she claps too.

I save all my pennies and she lets me drop them in her piggy bank. When we play some dumb old game I just made up, she shrieks in glee, "Let's do it again, Grandma. Please, just one more time."

On warm days, we toss dried bread to hungry ducks and imitate monkeys at the zoo. On rainy days, we peek-a-boo through bubble umbrellas. On snowy days, we catch snowflakes on our tongue and build a snowman in the yard. Later, on the carpeted floor, she has me sit against the wall, then rolls the ball across the room. And when I miss, it's herself (in gales of giggles) that she rolls upon the floor.

We have tea parties and invite the dolls. We line up chairs for a choo-choo train. ALLLL-'BOOARRD! Toot-toot! Clang-clang! Dolls and suitcases, tigers and teddy bears get stacked in "cars" and we "chuga-chuga" down the track. She flies by jet when I hold her on the rail as we sail down the steps in stores.

She prefers my lap to any chair and hugs so tight when she kisses me. "I *love* you, Grandma,"...music to my ears! The words echo and bounce through empty days.

A granddaughter is to spoil Grandmother rotten!

***

WHAT'S A GRANDSON?

An eye-opener, that's what he is; a fix for frailty, failing eyesight, or faulty hearing; an antidote for apathy, boredom, a case of the blahs. Seeing the world through his two-year-old eyes is nothing short of revelation. How blind we become to unselfconscious wonder as we grow older.

When his mother announced the impending trip from Wisconsin to Colorado to visit Grandma and Grandpa, wide-eyed and laughing, Aaron made one succinct statement: "Wow-ee!" Turned out it was as much prediction as proclamation.

Just yesterday he sucked in his breath and pointed his finger more times than I could count. "Look, Grandma, a bunny!" Sure enough, I hadn't spotted it camouflaged among the gray-brown rocks and scrubby foliage of our mountainside. There it sat, eyeing us cautiously, inspecting two human creatures who stood very still and stared back.

Aaron thought he spied another rabbit when a squirrel crossed our path. Our Rocky Mountain squirrels are black and they have what look like long bunny ears, but are really extra long hairs that shoot up behind their pointed ears.

"Duck?" He tilted his head and listened to distant quacking. Could be. Ducks populate our Turkey Creek. Yes, very likely, I agreed as I listened carefully.

"Airplane?" He heard a dull roar and sought verification. "I think it's a truck on Highway 285," I said. Throwing our heads back, we checked on high. (Right again!) A jet chalked a line across the sky.

Another swoosh of air intake and a fat little paw extended. A bright vermilion butterfly on a dandelion leaf. A brave one, too, for the tiny finger almost anointed the stained-glass wings before they fell open, flapped, and carried their magic on up the hill. "Butterfly, butterfly," he screeched, imploring the creature to stay a while.

But disappointment is short-lived, for each departing

72

wonder leaves in its wake—another. I picked a dandelion and put it under his chin to see if he liked butter. We picked several more of the bright yellow flowers for Mommy and for Grandpa...a bright bouquet for the kitchen table. No one told him there are those who dub these golden treasures weeds.

Picking up a pine cone from the drive, he held it up for me to see. "Pine cone," he said. I'd told him *once* the day before. It's downright reassuring to realize that one of us can remember It's disconcerting too. I thought two-year-olds were for asking questions like What? and Why? and Why? again. And I thought grandmas were for pointing out nature's little miracles, not once, but twice, and then twice more.

When we spied a lady bug, we let it crawl on Grandma's finger. This creature, too, he recognized for it was in the book Grandma made for Christmas. The rhyme, old as time for his grandmother, was new to Aaron.

> Ladybug, Ladybug
> Fly away home
> Your house is on fire
> Your children will burn.

We hunkered down on the grassy bank of Turkey Creek and launched ships galore, fragile crafts that resembled sticks and leaves and long blades of grass. Grandma had to grab the back of his pants when Aaron leapt forward, squealed, and pointed. Aha! a water bug. Not just one, but four among the reeds near the shore. The sight of them took me back. As a child, they used to fascinate me when I went fishing with my grandmother. The creatures glide, then jerk; float, then stagger.

Aaron called them spiders. "Waterbugs," Grandma said. "Waterbugs." He shook his head in confirmation.

On our walk back up the hill, we shared toting the mail. We had to stop and sometimes squat—the better to watch ants on the driveway. One was dragging a bug. "Why?" I wasn't sure but, "For food," was the guess I made.

It's a long driveway, so we played games. When Aaron stood still, I circled 'round him several times, then hurried on ahead to take my silent stance. He'd paddle up to my spot and trot around me, giggling and squealing all the while, unaware that it was Grandma's ploy to avoid carrying him after he'd stood begging a "ride" with outstretched arms.

We never make it past the propane tank without mounting the monstrosity and together chugging along in our steam engine, or if he grasps his imaginary steering wheel, I know it's a truck he's maneuvering down the busy highway. This time, Aaron spurred his wild steed down the trail. "Giddyap, horsie."

Thereafter we crossed the yard to watch the neighbor's real horses. When the collie barked, Aaron leaned against the fence, tilting his head against the post, and began to sing in a wee voice. I crept closer, ear cocked. "Old Macdonald had a farm, eei-eei-o. On his farm he had a doggie. Woof-woof here. Woof-woof there...had a horsie. Neigh-neigh here. Neigh-neigh there. Neigh-neigh everywhere."

Later his mother verified, yes, he had learned the song in nursery school.

Can you believe all those marvelous wonders exploded on one round trip from the house to the mailbox at the foot of the hill?

Miracles his grandmother just took for granted.
WOW-EEEEE!

***

WHY I WON'T WORRY (TODAY)
ABOUT WASTING TIME

Time present and time past
Are both perhaps present in time future
And time future contained in time past.

...T. S. Eliot

Harry Golden said he never bawled out a waitress because he knew there are at least four billion suns in our single galaxy of the Milky Way (and there are billions of galaxies in space, each a million light years from another). Millions of these suns have planetary systems, including billions of satellites. The entire she-bang "breathes" as an enormous, ever-expanding and contracting, whirling pinwheel revolving at a million miles an hour. Our sun and earth are on the edge of this oval-shaped wheel.

Why don't these billions of revolving and rotating suns collide? Because space is so vast that a mathematical ratio would depict planetary bodies as specks of dust 4,000 miles from their nearest neighbors. Bearing this in mind, Golden felt it was "silly to worry if the waitress brought string beans instead of limas."

New technologies are unveiling ever more amazing secrets about the cosmos...and at the same time revealing inconsistencies about the age of our universe, the evolution of life, and the nature of consciousness. As my father-in-law used to say, "The more we know we know we know, the more we know the less."

Surely fine minds that foster breakthroughs require hefty dollops of time to do nothing—as well as feverish brain activity—if for no other reason than to allow unhampered space for the intervention of inspiration.

When in a quiet, contemplative mood, I find it absurd to regard time as so exceedingly precious a commodity that not a moment is to be wasted. Delmore Schwartz calls Time "the school in which we learn, the fire in which we burn."

Ben Franklin is a little less dour. "Dost thou love life?" he asks in *Poor Richard's Almanac.* "Then do not squander time; for that's the stuff Life is made of." He also maintained "Time is money," thus allotting it ultimate value. But Franklin's credibility suffers when one realizes the *Almanac* main themes of thrift, self-discipline, moderation, frugality, and the work ethic were rarely a part of Ben's lifestyle. A womanizer who sired illegitimate children, he retired at forty-two, and in his early years, regularly overdrew his bank account.

Exactly what do conscientious, self-righteous do-gooders mean when they say time is golden and should never be wasted? Reflection or rumination never seems to count as time well spent.

A practical-minded writer friend sold an article, "Ten Ways to Use Ten Minutes." Lists are hot how-to items. Busy people love self-help material that is clear, concise, condensed and categorized. While standing in line or waiting for an appointment, she suggests working crossword puzzles; reading (always carry a book or magazine); handwork, if you're so inclined—like whittling or knitting; making lists of incomplete tasks in order of priority; writing letters; naming state capitals; or doing isometric exercises like squeezing your gluteus maximums (which, incidentally can be done while driving your car). The message is clear. At all times keep mind, or body, or both, well occupied.

How about the spirit? What better case can be made for "time to do nothing?" Now and again I question the American work ethic. Must every act be associated with doing something constructive, honing the intelligence, challenging the mind, improving the memory, or perfecting the physique?

I'm sure you've observed that recreation and physical fitness cost a fortune and are tackled with a vengeance. Folks young and old mentally flog themselves to jog highways and byways and psyche themselves through painful gymnastic rituals in exclusive health spas—hell-bent on losing weight and strengthening heart and body muscle.

It brings to mind Thoreau's observation concerning "young men whose misfortune it is to have inherited farms, houses, barns, cattle and tools...How many a poor immortal soul have I met well nigh rushed and smothered under its load, creeping down the road of life, pushing before it a barn 75 feet by 40...". It was also Thoreau who advised throwing away a whole day for a single expansion of air.

The most holy, intelligent, and wise who walked the earth saw value in silent, solitary communion with all that is. Jesus went into the desert. Buddha sat beneath the Banyan tree awaiting enlightenment. Socrates stood transfixed for hours. Einstein achieved the same trance-like state sitting in his rowboat gazing at the water. Asked what equipment he'd require upon assuming a new professorship, he replied, "Paper and pencil."

I'm inclined to believe (although I constantly fight the "do something worthwhile" syndrome) that the business of "doing nothing" is now and then as good for the least of us as it has ever been for the greatest among us.

Forever is now. Eternity is this hour. So why not clover chains, sandcastles, and woolgathering? Dreams are an elixir to the creative imagination. They evoke Eureka's and clear cobwebs from the brain.

I'm convinced (at least for today), that it's downright silly to chastise ourselves for wasting time, for sitting and thinking ...without even a holy book in our lap. If you think infinity instead of time, jogging that extra mile or hustling that added buck becomes as inconsequential as being served string beans when you ordered limas. Ranks right up there with honking when the light turns green.

***

WHO SAYS I'M LUCKY?

"You're so lucky! It could have been worse," seems to be the universal refrain when human beings comfort their peers. It seems people just can't leave well enough alone when calamity strikes. It was brought home to me anew when I visited a friend who'd just undergone a mastectomy.

Barb yanked the sheet to her chin when I entered her room. "Now you don't have to look at my butchering."

"C'mon, Barb, cut that out," I scolded.

"They just did." Her wry sense of humor was left intact.

"Look," I said, "I know there will be lots of tough battles you'll have to fight alone." I decided I'd made a real boo-boo when I saw her look of shock.

"You don't know how glad I am to hear you say that," she said. "Do people think my brains were in my chest and I've been left a half-wit? Every other person comes in here telling me it could have been worse. Ellie Carter informed me a mastectomy wasn't bad. Did I read about the little girl with the cancerous eye, and the doctor removed the wrong eye?

"Dammit! I know other people have worse troubles, but that has nothing to do with what I'm going through. Those peddlers of canned sunshine can take their good cheer and shove it."

I had to admit I've often shared Barb's disgust. There's always someone around to point out how lucky you were to have broken only one lens when you sat on your glasses. Providence was looking after you.

When your new car gets smashed in the parking lot and you don't know who hit it, and your own insurance won't cover it, you're reminded how much worse it could have been if you'd been inside it driving down the highway. That you would have been ten miles from the point of impact is not the point they're making.

When Frank Clark was 'listing' to the left, his landlady asked if he'd hurt his back. "Nope, got arthritis," he explained.

"Arthritis," she gasped, then on second thought, "Well, I expect you're lucky."

"Didn't know it was a blessing," he said.

She pointed out nobody dies from it. "You could have heart trouble, or it could have been your lungs, or brains, or pancreas."

By the time the good woman was through cajoling, Frank felt he'd been complimented on an astute decision, although he'd had no choice at the smorgasbord of woe. Matter of fact, he felt obliged to jump for joy, but his sacroiliac just wouldn't take it

Know someone grieving over a severed relationship? The usual observation is: "Thank heavens it was before marriage." It was after marriage? "Thank heavens there are no children." There are children? "Who needs that constant fighting? The kids are better off without the bum. Good riddance!"

Ever notice how cheer runs rampant in the funeral parlor? Someone dies in his sleep—"What a wonderful way to go. I should be so lucky when my time comes. Be glad he didn't suffer. Or, when long suffering is finally terminated—"How lucky she is to be out of her misery. Give thanks." A friend gazing into my father's casket told my mother, "Why Annie, he hasn't looked so good in thirty years."

My mother-in-law calls that looking on the bright side. She says it's better than being a crepe hanger, which is what she calls a perpetual pessimist like my mother. Even crepe hanging has a bright side when, with my foot in a cast, I am forced to listen to my mother-in-law's comparisons between my minor mishap and the plagues of poor Mrs. O'Banion. She has "sugar diabetes," a child in the hospital, and a drunkard for a husband. "Now there's a woman with a peck of troubles, but she's always smiling. You call a broken ankle trouble? I say count your blessings." When I twisted my foot on the curb, I could have fallen and fractured my skull. I should thank my lucky stars.

On the other hand, my mother knew all along that it was bound to happen. "You should wear more sensible shoes...you're just lucky you didn't break it long ago."

When it comes to calamities, is late really better than never? Is half a disaster better than none?

When a friend looks at my sunburn, my hangnail, my crumpled fender, or my broken ankle, and says..."Gee, I'm sorry," and let's it go with that, *that's* what I call being lucky.

***

IMMEASURABLE MOMENTS

Have you noticed that you can't flip through a newspaper or magazine without facing a quiz? You can rate your mental dexterity or answer queries that facilitate self-evaluation, or—far more likely—help explain the eccentricities of family and friends.

Sets of questions appear under miscellaneous headings: How happy are you? Are you well adjusted? How's your sense of humor? Should you own a pet? Can you handle money? Do you like yourself? Do you prefer cabbage or candy, and what does this mean?

Everything gets analyzed to death: fairy tales, hair length, eye movements, color choices, choice of pets, nightmares and dreams. Everything is scrutinized and interpreted as representing something else...deep and dark and hidden. Sometimes I think psychologists are dedicated killjoys.

Feelings, God bless them, are to enjoy, not to analyze. Watch a kid go bouncing down a yellow brick road, then tell me how the whimsical "why" around his heart gets twisted into the weary, worrisome, diagnostic "why" of adulthood.

When we put emotions under a microscope in order to dissect every thought, itemize every action, and categorize every insight, we lose that joyful spontaneity that is the effervescence of life. It's fun, at least once in a while, to simply lap up the icing, ignoring the color, calories, and consistency.

Thoughts and feelings make me me, and you you. Wouldn't you hate to gauge on a scale from one to ten the intensity of your reaction to those meaningful moments that plop into your lap at unexpected times? For example:

Outfoxing a blowhard.
Teaching a kid to tie his shoes or tell the time.
Having a friend write a poem—just for you.
Trusting a hunch and finding it right.

Doing your best, surprising yourself. (Damn, that's
    good!)
Finding what you've been searching for.
Living and loving the fantasy you've read to a child.
Experiencing the shock of reading something true.
Following that with insight into you.
Sharing a secret and entering a soul.
Realizing your unique experience is universal.
Having your kid fill the gas tank after using the car.
Enjoying communication with your dog.
Experiencing the mysterious communication of the eyes.
Listening to birdsong.
Watching a bird take flight.
Watching a living tree cut down.
Watching your world turn green,
Or brilliant yellow,
Or rust,
Or white and silent.
Seeing a slaughtered deer at the edge of the road.
Dancing to the music, singing in tune.
Solitude in your quiet room.
Falling, falling—then suddenly being given wings.
The first, last, and in-between times that someone said, "I
    love you."
Laughter. A happy smile.
Tears.
Being appreciated.
Being at the right place at the right time and knowing it.

Being suddenly interrupted while working—as I was just
now—by someone you love, who wants to know, "Hey, can
you spare a minute?" The call was to "Come real quick and
look at the sky."

***

82

SCHOOLING

HOW I FEEL WHEN I'M ALONE AND WRITING

"All my friends and most of my acquaintances are writers of one sort or another...but it's remarkable how little I know of what happens to writers when they're actually alone and writing." So says Rust Hills, fiction editor of *Esquire Magazine* and author of *Writing in General and the Short Story in Particular.*

I knew a deep empathy and a comforting relief when I read Mr. Hills' own lamentations concerning the writing process. I was not a unique freak after all. When he has the time to write, Hills complains, the ideas are not there—or if ideas are abundant, the words won't come. Forcing himself to place words on paper helps not at all: "Insights become platitudes as when phrased under duress."

These are honest assessments with which I can identify, and yet in my heart I believe that writing is an apprenticeship that leads to soul, to Self. For me, it is akin to prayer, so why the accompanying pain, anguish, and frustration? Perhaps it is an attempt to bring compatibility to inner and outer worlds.

As Hills points out, it helps not at all when you're ready to entrust your writing problems to your wise subconscious, but it's more concerned with "sex, carpentry, or tennis."

How exasperating to glance at the clock and realize you've been dawdling for hours. Might be a good time to check the mail. Aha! a letter from a friend. An interesting cover story in the weekly news magazine beckons. It's an infuriating dilemma.

Back to work. A sentence comes out really fine. Maybe you'll get rolling before the day has disappeared. The day does disappear leaving you with worthless fragments? There's no describing the terrible feeling inside. On the other hand, if you turn out work with which you're satisfied, there's an inner elation, sometimes a downright disbelief that asks, *Is that me?* Chances are it's more truly you than the social self you peddle about your daily world. Writing is a magnificent way to learn to know self, to hear one's own voice, perhaps for the first time—to tap the music that dwells within each of us.

Joyce Carol Oates says creativity can never be fully explained in rational or scientific terms. She calls it "one of the most mysterious of human endeavors." I agree.

Writing cannot really be taught! Someone has said it takes talent, energy, and self-confidence. It also involves risk taking. If it is to be meaningful, writing must be honest. It involves digging deeply into territory which we keep hidden, not only from others, but even more dangerously from ourselves. As any writer knows, rarely are all these necessary attributes perking simultaneously. The aforementioned mental bugaboos intercept, interrupt, and deaden whatever talent or energy spurts forth—and any fool knows what that does to self-confidence.

Exactly what is self-confidence? Perhaps you don't have it or know what it is until you've moved past it—beyond self-concerns to open innocence.

I teach writing. No, I preside over classes and occasionally if I'm lucky, and if the atmosphere is right, good things happen. I become very excited over student writings and I know emotional and aesthetic catharsis vicariously, to the point where I neglect my own work.

That's what happened when "Rust Pandora Hills," with his observations concerning writing, gave me a cracker-jack idea for a writing exercise. I asked students to jot down their thoughts and feelings on the subject: "How I feel when I'm alone and writing." I was astounded and delighted with the results.

Many admitted it was one of the few times they were really being themselves. As one person put it, "When I talk with others, I find I tamper with my ideas and feelings. They become consciously or unconsciously warped into what I feel the other person wants to hear."

Another said, "I feel good when I write. I even enjoy writing lists to organize my thoughts, my shopping, or my projects." A young photographer echoed these feelings: "I know I'm not a great writer, but I feel worthwhile when I'm writing. I feel as good as when I wash all my windows." One young woman said she writes "to say I—to announce and to hold a day, a feeling, an understanding, the look of morning light....I saw and heard and felt the currents of my time on earth."

Erma Harper, who has published a book of Appalachian stories, had so little confidence that her voice wouldn't function to read her initial efforts in the first class. She had this to say:

> I write best when my arms ache and my fingertips tingle. Is that crazy? I can't write the things that come into my head...they need translation into another language and that's the hardest part of all.
>
> The songs of the universe dance through my head when I sit me down to create. Every child's whimper, every bride's delight, every soldier's victory is *mine.*
> When I am alone with my thoughts *I know* the fear behind snobbery, the courage behind tears, the sadness masked by a hollow laugh.
>
> ...When I write, I feel like a Kristopherson song. From deep within, I relate to the lyrics blaring from my kids' record player..."They're only words...but words are all I have."

Jim Jones, hydraulic engineer, surprised me with this:

> Everyone is alone when writing. There's no way I can imagine another soul's entry into this temple without ravaging. I feel holy, detached, separate from the world, moving in a different plane among entities who exist for themselves. I empathize with every fiber. I bleed, I cry, I laugh, I celebrate, I mourn, and I'm exhausted when I quit.

Joan Palmer, farmwife and secretary, writes:

I feel the time of reckoning has arrived. I've cleaned the house, washed the dishes, paid the bills, taken my bath, washed my hair, done my nails, completed every chore and exhausted every excuse, so I sit at my desk, pen in hand.

I feel inadequate, illiterate, stupid. Doggedly I write, one sentence at a time. Then it's done. With a sinking heart, I read my work. Before I finish, my heart is thudding in my throat and I think, *damn, that's good!*

Jo Anderson, award-winning poet, says:

I'm very good at making metaphors, building tones and textures with words. They're beads I can string together in a necklace. Words are jewels. I like to make them my own, turn them, hold them to the light, toss them in the air, roll them on my tongue. Pity it's such a lonely hobby. Most people are not interested in words and so I come to writing class to share the miracle of language.

Rose McClure, secretary, made this observation:

Creative people have always been accused of being different. Everyone has idiosyncrasies. Creative people express theirs. This frightens people who know only how to work and how to propagate.

Sara (not her real name), now a professional writer, explored her need to write:

Not to write would be to cease to exist. In Hebrew, the name of God is a tetragram, four letters that are unknowable, ineffable, and never to be pronounced. Three of the letters occur in the verb "to be." I take from this that if we are truly fashioned in the image of God, we must strive to be—to be whatever we are. "I will be" sounds like "eh-hi-ye." Hear the liquid vowels, the rush of air, the breath? When I write, I am allowing that breath to be. The trick is to get out of the way so it can be heard.

Novella Davis had been writing poetry for years which she kept in boxes beneath her bed before being named "Ohio Poet of the Year." She writes because she says she cannot not write.

I write because I have a lot to learn, particularly about myself. There is nothing that transcends the surprise of self discovery.
...It is in learning to tap the unconscious that we come to understand ourselves and others...This is the source, perhaps more correctly the force, from which we write. To the religious, it is the ground of being, or God. I believe there is no creative power in our work without this force.
This inexhaustible treasure mine is not reserved for the chosen few. It is there for the tapping. Through writing, I draw upon the substantive power of this creative force in my life.

A University of Denver sociology professor called writing the magic carpet of the growing-up years...a means to write through problems, record hurts, and develop ideas.

...When I read what I'd written, I felt validated, real. Somewhere along the way I stopped writing....There was work with its own style—constraining, limiting, draining....I had publications, but I had never become a writer. I have rediscovered buried treasure, found that lost magic carpet for my soul.

A writer of poignant and powerful short stories confessed that writing began as escape and outlet, then became a looking glass of all her distorted reflections. As she dared to become braver and more objective, she waited tremulously for providence to smite her, to punish her insolence.

That heavenly hand played a whimsical trick on me. For the first time, I could view my life and family with a more objective eye...."Mine enemies" were no longer simply perpetrators of the hell in which I lived. They become human to me. I felt some of *their* fears, and *their* frustrations. Pen on paper! My minor miracle.

Grace Grant, a practical nurse, clipped a note to her final assignment. In part, it said:

Listening to my fellow writers pour out their ideas and feelings has made me realize what gems we humans really are. It has given me greater depth of insight into the people I encounter daily. I want to promote more understanding, love, and happiness. How about that?

How about that indeed? That's reason enough for me to feel the inner path is a road well chosen. These bits of writing gave me such a high that I didn't feel the need to write for seven days. When I did, I wondered why I had to again suffer that silent, autonomous, frustrating battle before I was finally lost in my work.

You may well ask...and you still choose to call that painful process prayer?

Let me put it this way. Not too long ago I saw slides of a friend's trip to China. Two ferocious beasts guarded each side of the entrance to a magnificent house of worship. Paradox and Confusion were their names. The idea was you had to get past those devil-dogs in order to reach the temple.

Until we *think* and *write* (and I'm not sure of the proper order, there's a circuitous pattern involved), we live on the surface of things. I should amend that and substitute "live creative lives" for "think and write." All persons are creative, but talents vary. Penetration isn't easy, but once you've plugged into the deepest, most secret rhythms of life (even accidentally)—into that generative force which is a part of us and apart from us—there's a resultant elation. Some become hooked by a nagging compulsion to reactivate, rekindle that exultation.

When a writer knows the desperate bliss of having successfully transmuted a special moment—a feeling too deep for human tears—so that another can, in his own way, experience it vicariously, with the result that both writer and reader gain insight into who they are, that's like participating in an act of magic. Even more than magic, it resembles prayer.

***

WRITE ACROSS THE GENERATION GAP

A few years ago I taught a writing class in which students from an alternative high school and senior citizens came together to explore the past, examine the now, and speculate about the future. The rapport was heartwarming and spontaneous.

Perhaps that should come as no surprise. Both groups have much in common—they exist on the fringe, the young awaiting their debut, the old making curtain calls. Living on the edge means being nearer the sublime mysteries of birth and death, farther from the "etiquette" of the world.

On the first day, they paired off—two by two, young and old—and interviewed each other. "Capture essence," I reminded. "Write honestly."

A young girl wrote, "First I noticed her deep-set eyes. I once read that's a sign of a sensitive person. I decided the theory was true regarding Carol." The student confessed she wished she weren't so shy, "but I knew as Carol told me of her pain, she was reaching out to me, helping me ever so gently, to talk about things I often hide. 'Communication is a life-line,' she explained. 'Humor gets you through the rough times.' She'll die with smile-creases in her cheeks. I hope she never complains. They are a gift."

Carol, the older woman, blinked back tears as she read, "I find I love this girl. I asked what thoughts impress her most deeply, what experiences most affect her writing. 'Death,' she said to my surprise. She's only seventeen. She told me of the day her mother died. And then I felt a warm, comforting presence enveloping us both. Her mother?"

The day they videotaped our class, members lingered afterward to watch the replay and were astounded at all the laughter. "We were so busy every minute," someone observed. "I didn't realize we were laughing so much of the time."

I tossed a canceled stamp on the table as a warm-up writing exercise. Ice, the handsome smooth-faced boy with spiked hairdo of ebony and white, wrote a poem about a love letter as sharp and cutting as the jagged perforated edges of the canceled stamp.

His listeners smiled, cajoled, and sighed. "That's so beautiful. May we each have a copy?" At break time, he played the piano and everyone clapped. Encouraged, he brought his guitar to our next meeting and set his poem to song.

Young and old shared secrets, many rediscovered through writing. Running away from home at fifteen (an oldster wrote it), first loves (a lifetime ago and just last Tuesday), loneliness at any age...and what it means to pick up and go on when you feel like giving up and lying down.

On the final day, an exchange student from Austria announced in her charming accent, "I liked this class. It's very good to be with the older generation. I like to think about the ideas the seniors gave me."

"Ha! You found out we aren't all grumpy, stodgy, old crabs, didn't you?" Mary laughed.

"I liked everything fine," a septuagenarian said, "except when you all talked at once and I couldn't hear anybody." That happens when people get excited and have important things to share. Spontaneity spans the generation gap.

"I hate to see this end," Ruth admitted. "I'm so glad there was no preaching. I tried to be honest with the kids and I tried to listen carefully to what they said. I'm not always good at that but I am getting better." She confessed, "Writing came easier than I figured. The class opened me up and drew things to the surface." Ruth smiled and looked straight at Ice. "The young people added light to our lives."

As for Ice, he simply wished more people had written poems.

Months later, Ruth telephoned me when her husband died. "I got the nicest letter of all from Ice," she said.

***

S IS FOR SMITH IS FOR SALESMAN

There was that day in October, right here in Lima City, Ohio, when the Music Man walked into my classroom. Harold Hill wasn't the only rootin'-tootin', rip-roarin', yessir, dyed-in-the-wool Musician-Salesman with a Capital M and a Capital S.

With brass, buoyancy, and bounce, a spiffy, sport-coated Vaughn Smith breezed into writing class. He brushed his wiry reddish-blond hair into a wavy pompadour and blue eyes spit fire behind wire-rimmed spectacles. He answered my initial roll call: "My dear, how old are you?" I guess he figured a trim man of seventy-five who looked twenty years younger, had outgrown the posings of protocol.

I soon learned that it was fruitless to make the same written criticism ("wordy and repetitious") on all of his assignments. "Honey, there's just no use telling me not to *re*peat. I've been a salesman all my life, and in sales, yessir, in sales, that's the name of the game! I gotta crank 'er out the way she comes, dearie. That's just me, and I gotta be me. If I cut out what you call extra words, I'm being somebody else, don'tcha see?"

Whatever the class assignment, Vaughn turned in lengthy chapters about his sales experiences. This bell-ringin', drum-beatin', everytime a bull's eye traveling salesman hit the road when he was eighteen and covered most of the states in the USA—hitch-hiking, bumming rides on any moving vehicle, and walking till he wore holes in his shoes and blisters on his heels.

In Amarillo, Texas, in the false hope of relieving sore and aching feet, he put his left shoe on his right foot and his right shoe on his left foot and kept right on walking.

The true test of a salesman, he says, is making a go of it in a buyer's market. "In the days of the WPA, I promised myself I wasn't going to lean on a shovel. From early morning till late at night, I was going steady just to make enough to *live* the next day."

He sold magazine subscriptions ("'working my way through college'—we were the guys that originated that"), second-hand watches, specially tailored suits, vacuum cleaners, roofing, real estate, washing machines, water softeners, paint, pots, and pianos. Regarding the latter, he says, "I sold pianos, but it's one instrument I never learned to play."

Watkins products? Fuller Brush man? "Never! You're stuck with the same territory." Used cars? He's insulted at the question. "Cars are the bottom of the line in the sales game— the least prestige. Didn't you know that?" Like Harold Hill, he rarely knew the territory, and he never worried about his line. "All selling is the same. You sell the story and you throw in the goods." He stresses an exception to the rule. "You don't *sell* your friends. You explain it to 'em and then let them make up their own minds. Not long ago, I sold some insurance to very good friends. Few months later the wife got very sick. They've already got an $800 return on a $38 investment."

Vaughn insists his earliest memory dates back to his third year when he tried to beat his mother's washtub with a live drum stick. His mother rescued the cat Vaughn was swinging by its tail and he still remembers the licking he got as a result.

However, it never quelled his love for music. Growing up in a musical family, it was ever an integral part of his life. He has played banjo, bass fiddle, and slide trombone; he also sang with the family combo which entertained at weddings and celebrations. He still plays in a small dance band called The Rhapsodiers, and proudly presents a business card picturing a silhouetted dancing couple.

In the 20's, Vaughn played in the five-piece band perched on the upper deck of a riverboat. Their popular dance tunes entertained the guests floating on Indian Lake at Russell's Point Amusement Center in Logan County, Ohio. "Guess you're too young to remember the Charleston?" Whenever the other musicians rested, Vaughn grabbed the microphone and began a lilting spiel describing the panoramic scenery. It meant added tips from the pleased tourists and it delighted the boat owner.

When the season was over, he sold advertising in Dayton. When material products were hard to come by, he was not above selling manual services. He convinced an amusement park operator in Sarasota, Florida, that his buildings needed a fresh coat of paint. The pay wasn't much, but it was enough to get him off and rolling. "Figured I'd head for Dallas, but I got a ride with a fellow in a Pierce Arrow who was heading for Memphis. Immediately my plans changed from Texas to Tennessee."

He'll never forget the time he sold a suit to a handsome black fellow who gave him a ride across the cotton fields of Mississippi. "I'd just come across on the ferry from Helena, Arkansas, and I walked several miles along the levee. Middle of the night it was. Didn't know it then, but they told me I was takin' my life in my hands. It's plumb fulla wild animals. Really. Well, anyway, it's a long, drawn-out story, but finally I got me a ride to the next town with this young fella and his girlfriend. She crawled into the back seat and didn't have much to say as I remember. But let me tell you when he says, 'What's your business?' Aha! my ears perked up. Got out my plaid swatches. Gave him my spiel and instead of giving him my last 65 cents which I'd offered him for the ride, I ended up giving him a $3 discount on a new suit, thereby saving my 65 cents! He pulled over and stopped the car. The light from the dashboard was kinda dim. When he got out and looked at them swatches in front of the headlights, I was surprised how tall he was. No time at all, I had my tape measure hanging around my neck. 'Be sure and tell your friends,' I says. After all, even Jesus Christ had a front man in John the Baptist, right?"

He explains, "My whole life has been one of promotion. When I got one thing rollin', I moved on to something else. Ain't that awful? Probably shoulda stuck to one thing. If I had, I mighta been a rich man today."

Now Vaughn feels a man with all this selling know-how ought to *sell* it, so he's written a book about his experiences. He has absolutely no doubts concerning its publication. "Why of course it'll be published. It's got a lifetime of valuable selling experience in it."

The first thirty-two pages, he feels, are the important ones. They'll be printed on colored paper...pink, he thinks. "That's the meat. The real secrets. I can just see the guys on the podiums at sales conventions all over this country waving my book overhead. 'Get Smith's book today! Read the pink pages! To Hell with the rest!'" Anything following the pink pages, he admits, is chaff... filler... stuff so a publisher will print it. "Thirty-two pages don't make a book, don'tcha see?"

Now let me say those precious pink pages are eye-openers. He counters my questioning, my incredulity. "Of course, I'm serious!" he declares. He was not in the least annoyed at my laughter. "Gave it to a teacher friend of mine to read." He threw his head back and roared. "She called it hogwash; said I was plumb crazy. But listen," he grew serious, "it works. I spent fifty-five years selling. I oughta know. My wife was an invalid for twenty-three years. She required lotsa care. I had to make every minute count... couldn't fool around wasting time. I will guarantee any man who is looking for a workable gimmick that he will find it here and double his sales if he reads this seriously."

In the pink pages, Vaughn categorizes wide foreheads, small chins, squinty eyes, high cheekbones, narrow faces, and large noses. "No sense in the world wasting time on a pinched narrow face," he says. "Aim your pitch to fat faces. They love a bargain. You can only annoy low foreheads if you talk too

much, they don't like running chatter. Heart-shaped faces—
now that's your artistic type."

"Vaughn, it only worked for you because you believed
it," I said.

No siree! My brother's entire sales career was based on
my system. He was top salesman for his company. He's the
one's been after me to write it all down.

"Listen, honey, I told some of those secrets to the real
estate lady in this writing class and she came in all excited the
next week. Her eyes were this big, and she says, 'Vaughn,
Vaughn, it works!' I says, 'Well, *course* it works!'"

Vaughn believes himself to be on the side of the angels.
He sold me. I believe it too. I can just see those sales
managers shouting from podiums all over this *en*tire nation,
*"Get Smith's book! Read the pink pages! To hell with the
rest!"*

***

THE HAVES AND HAVE-NOTS

I went to another state to conduct a writing workshop in 1988, and an interesting fringe benefit emerged when the County Director of Gifted Education read the newspaper announcement and invited me to speak to a couple of fifth grade classes. She picked me up and we drove to an affluent northeast suburb on a Thursday afternoon. We cruised winding streets lined with sycamores and enormous houses before reaching the low rambling "Open School."

Thirty kids ambled in at lengthy intervals. We were situated in a partially screened section of a very large room. Some students sat on chairs, others settled themselves on the floor. Some had pen and paper, some did not. We passed out paper and writing utensils to the have-nots.

"Oh great! you're gonna have us write. Think I'll leave," said a young boy with spiked bleached hair. While others were not so outspoken, their bored faces brought to mind a feeling I had experienced in, of all places, Disney World. During a lively parade down the avenue, I noted the apathy of onlookers and was reminded then of something I'd read. Some famous wit had remarked after viewing can-can dancers at the Folies Bergere that he had never seen so many sad faces and happy bottoms.

It wasn't even a challenging "Show me" that I read in their attitude, but rather, "I could care less." Boredom can be far more insidious than belligerence.

We did a clustering exercise—about people and about objects in their lives. "Write honestly," I said, "or don't bother to write at all." Some didn't bother making me a little sorry I'd appended my ultimatum. I asked for volunteers but no one wished to share, so I suggested I gather the sheets, shuffle them, and read the writings without revealing names. They were agreeable to that approach.

One person wrote, "My dog is the only 'person' I can talk to." Another wondered about a dad he had lost track of. He tried to recall his face, but couldn't bring it to mind. "Were his eyes blue like mine, or were they brown?" Still another complained about her step-siblings who were hard to get along with and called her names she hated. There was a touching tribute to a grandparent who offered stability in a crazy, mixed up world. Anger was vented in several instances—"all kids want is to be *free*." It was pointed out that teachers and parents, adults in general, just don't understand that.

Objects they chose to cluster included allowances they wanted increased, dirt bikes, suntan parlors, guns, cars they hoped one day to drive, even drugs—to my surprise. One kid, with friends who used them, wondered if one day he might try drugs. "Probably," he concluded.

"You'll see an enormous difference in the group we visit tomorrow," the lady director said as we left the school. She was glad that I'd gathered the papers to read. "They were certainly honest and revealing, but weren't they *sad*?"

On Friday we drove several miles across flat farm country dotted with white frame houses and red barns. We passed rich black fields planted with soybeans and corn. The school building was old and large, a red brick square with metal stairways on the outside wall. My companion called it a consolidated school, which drew farm kids from surrounding areas.

The gifted class was in a small cramped room that seemed like an overcrowded closet. I scarcely had room to stand and talk to the group, so I clambered atop a low cabinet and perched there, to the delight of the kids.

The director was so right. What a difference a day made! Kids beamed and smiled, asked disarming questions and plunged eagerly into every exercise. Hands perpetually waved as they asked about my life and openly shared their own. The young teacher, too, was bright-eyed and enthusiastic. She had long red hair that fell down the middle of her back making her look like a princess who'd stepped out of a fairy tale.

I showed them a blown-up cartoon I'd brought along. Yesterday it hadn't seemed a fitting thing to share with such a pseudo-sophisticated, somber group.

I told these youngsters that when my husband heard I was planning to work with gifted children, he handed me the Gary Larson drawing of a boy pushing hard on a door clearly marked PULL; the door to the "Midvale School for the Gifted." "Show this to the kids." he said.

They laughed and at one girl's suggestion, it was passed around so they could sign their names. Some scribbled messages, like, "Glad you came through our door," and another wrote, "My dad must have a sense of humor like your husband's. He showed me this cartoon before."

As we left school that day, my chauffeur reminded, "I told you you'd see a world of difference in this group. Aren't they a delight? I'm going to recommend that their teacher take my place when I retire next year." (Peter Principle in action?)

It was exhilarating and fun, I agreed. "Did you notice what most of them wrote in the Bio-Poem when I asked each to list three wishes? Nine times out of ten, they asked for more money, riches, bank accounts in order to buy 'things.' I thought to myself God Forbid!"

She laughed. "You know you're right. They did list those things." She shrugged, "I guess the grass is always greener..."

Now I know it's dangerous and downright ridiculous to draw stereotypical conclusions. All rich kids and all kids from broken homes aren't spoiled and bored, just as all farm kids aren't wholesome and happy. I'm only relating a quick overview of an experience I had one Thursday afternoon and one Friday morning.

The second group sent me thank-you letters after I got home. They said warm and funny things about our visit. It wasn't often, they pointed out, that a gray-haired lady sat like an elf, cross-legged atop a cabinet and laughed with them and helped them share important feelings.

I wrote back and said I'd already stored that morning among my mental treasures. I told them, too, I hoped they'd always remain as rich as they are and be wise enough to know it.

Nevertheless, it's the know-it-all, couldn't-care-less, Thursday faces that float across my ceiling and haunt my dreams.

***

TEACHERS I HAVE KNOWN

We think we learn from teachers, and we
sometimes do. But the teachers are not always
found in school....Sometimes what we learn
depends upon our own powers of insight. Our
teachers may be hidden.

...Loren Eiseley

Indeed, those teachers that work the greatest
transformation in our lives, are often not only hidden, but are
themselves unaware of teaching. Their influence may therefore
be the greater, for it is our inner eye which brings them into
focus. They are catalysts motivating, fomenting curiosity and
change.

Has it ever seemed strange to you, as it has to me, that
neither Socrates nor Jesus wrote a word? No how-to books.
Via irony and parable they illuminated lives in deeply
individual ways—ways, which like the great truths of life, are
incommunicable. Both were rebels, accused in their lifetimes
of being mad. A divine madness that everlastingly impacted
Western civilization.

But let us begin with classroom teachers, many whose
influence is lasting. Fred Millet describes the born teacher as
one who achieves something of the artist's creativeness in his
skill in bringing about a vital relationship between student and
subject. He describes such a teacher as part actor, part
preacher. Sensitive to the reactions of his audience, he is yet
less self-centered than the actor and feels a moral responsibility
to his subject matter as well as toward his concern with
bringing light to his charges. "Like the pastor," says Millet,
"he is a cure of souls."

To an extent, that describes a high school English teacher
who left a permanent impression on me. She opened doors and
awakened insights. Unfortunately, she and I were each too

young to have reached full potential as teacher or student, she being a slightly arrogant, but brilliant new graduate of a prestigious university, I being a starry-eyed junior with an insatiable appetite for reading and an affinity for the language arts. It was a symbiotic relationship. She added enrichment to an area I loved. I, in turn, must have filled certain needs of a fledgling teacher...hanging on her every word, while exerting every effort to do my best work.

At that point in my life, I was unready to recognize a "cure of souls." I'm not sure one ever becomes that wise or free, but if the old are not always wise, at least one goes on learning with every victory and every blunder.

I find that I may discover hidden meanings after much time has passed. An image, a word, a remembrance—an unexpected linkage pops forward from behind my mind and nudges my consciousness.

Among my finest teachers: children of all ages. When I work with youngsters, every day becomes a learning experience. I remember the summer I conducted an art workshop in a city park for the children of migrant workers who came up from Mexico to pick tomatoes in Ohio.

One little soft-eyed child motioned me toward his face. "Ees that your mawther?" he asked, pointing to the little white-haired lady sitting in the folding chair beneath the sycamore.

Indeed it was. I apologized for not having introduced her to the children and quickly made amends.

Once again, the youngster motioned me close and almost whispered, "Then how's come you're *both* so old?"

I'm not exactly sure what that "teaches," but the sudden and unexpected joy of it lingers. Kids possess a beautiful sense of openness, wonder, and surprise. Keeping that openness means remaining vulnerable, taking risks, banishing fears. And so keeping the child alive beyond the age of innocence is never as easy as it ought to be.

Each summer my granddaughter's visit is a learning time for me. When she was very small, we took her to the circus. She watched the elephants and trapeze artists perform small miracles while she ate cotton candy. At the fair, she and Grandma rode the ferris wheel and waved to Grandpa waaaay down there. At home, she rode with Grandpa on the power mower. When she frosted two hamburger buns for Grandma's birthday—one was for the birds, one for us. Grandpa made a bad joke about Nicole decorating Grandma's buns.

When she returned to her home, Nicole's mother asked, "Of all the things you did, what was the most fun of all?"

"The bestest?" She thought long and hard.

"The *very best!*" her mother said.

She was sure it was when the big ball grew small from sitting in the sun. Grandma threw it on the garage roof, like she always did, so Nicole could catch it when it came rolling down. "But you know WHAT?" Her eyes grew large. "It stayed there!" Wonder of wonders! Did her mother really understand? "It just *sat there*, Mom!"

"And that was the greatest thing of all?"

"Uh-huh." Amid gales of giggles, she bobbed her head up and down. "Grandpa got it down and pumped it up and then *he* played ball with me—and mostly he never does."

Serendipity comes alive...with a dollop of wisdom from the heart of a child. How often we demand the thrill of the ferris wheel ride, overlooking those small surprises which yield the richest dividends.

Inevitably, family members teach one another. I raised two feisty daughters and a steady, even-tempered son. When someone is hurting, I try to remember Anne's compassion and deep caring. She has a beautiful way of saying just the right thing to make a hurting heart feel lighter. I think the trait has roots in her ultra-sensitive nature, her own deep capacity to feel.

When pride rears its ugly head, I try to remember the day daughter Beth came home from school with a gorgeous ceramic horse she'd made in art class. It had the fragile quality of a Japanese seascape. Mane and tale resembled frothy flowing waves—the kind you see in Oriental paintings.

"Beth, it's exquisite." I was quick to praise every facet of its being—the perfect form, the vibrancy and action, the unusual glaze she'd ground herself. I placed it on the table and pranced around, viewing it from every angle.

"Gee, you're as bad as the kids in class. It made me mad," she said, "the way they all gathered 'round. 'Oh Beth, I didn't know you could do that.' 'That's awesome.' All that garbage. People who hadn't said Boo to me all year... all of a sudden I was 'wonderful Beth.' I'm the same old me inside. How come throwing some clay together makes me a different person in their eyes?"

Even-tempered John seemed to know who he was ever since he was a toddler. He is his own person; he is his father's child. Always I've envied his steady-as-a-rock demeanor. Once when I laughed aloud at the warning, "If you're a perpetual optimist, you're just not paying attention," he reminded me he regards himself as a realist, who is yet an optimist.

From my husband I have learned to take myself less seriously. When I begin beating myself for acting the fool, he offers an unexpected twist of humor that makes me laugh and suddenly see that too much self-scrutiny can become a kind of pride that smothers spontaneity. "Besides," he points out, "people are too wrapped up in themselves to really give a hoot."

Because my father and his mother before him kept alive that child who is father of the man, those two progenitors I cherish. Giving little thought to "ought" or "should," they were, in their naturalness, simply able "to be." Often I was not a good learner, but each day that I live, I learn they were great teachers and those times I like myself most, I realize they are what I am.

Too often, I remember the perpetual anxiety that was the essence of my mother's being. Once she explained in desperation, "I wish you could live inside my skin for one day, no, for an hour. Then you'd know..."

But today I recall a time when I was grown and married with children of my own. I was broken-hearted and I went home to confide in my mother. She said very little. Instead, she walked over to a big stuffed chair, sat down and opened her arms. Then she, who seemed half my size, held me on her lap, cradling me, rocking my body with her own as she must have when I was a child. I always knew my mother loved me, but I never felt it more than I did that day.

We moved to the Illinois farm exactly when I needed it. I knew no one; hence no telephone calls. We lived four miles from town and the farm house was set back some distance from the gravel road. Walking the fields with my dog was an antidote for pain. I remember Anne Morrow Lindbergh writing something to the effect that gazing at a flowering bush was as good a way as she had found to bring peace to a troubled soul. I knew exactly what she meant. But, as Loren Eiseley says, it's not something you would report to the academy.

Insights are forceful hidden teachers. Elusive intangibles, emotionalized ideas resulting from experience provide personal truths to live by.

I recall laboring over a piece of writing which I concluded was really fine. An editor wrote, "It has lots of charm if you can get past the irritating first page. Why irritating? It comes across pretentiously."

That startled me. Pretentious? I felt I hadn't the where-withal to *be* pretentious. I've always thought of myself as a very simple soul. So I grinned and regarded the comment as a kind of backhanded compliment.

Some time passed before I connected the incident with a quotation a TV news director brought to writing class. He said it kept him on target in writing news releases. It was from *Alice in Wonderland*, and it went like this:

"The question is," said Alice, "whether you can make words mean so many different things."

"The question is," said Humpty-Dumpty, "which is to be master—that's all."

The quote took on deep personal meaning when I associated it with the writing endeavor which had been labeled pretentious. Aha! the word had indeed become master. I had been reading my favorite essayist, Loren Eiseley. I suspect that I had, perhaps even unconsciously, been attempting to imitate his erudite style. I had tried to impress rather than communicate my own "crown of feathers," my own truth. I rewrote the piece and the same editor accepted it.

I wish I had more vivid dreams. My poet friend tells me her poems often come to her in dreams. My pencil draws forth things I never knew I knew and introduces me to a me I never met, one I might add who is more truly me than the facade that often walks the world.

Speaking of truth and social self, my daughter-in-law was chatting animatedly with our young neighbor whom she'd just met. Patrick is about her age and they had both recently returned to college. "I flunked out 15 years ago," she said, "but now I'm doing great."

Patrick looked startled, then laughed aloud. "I flunked out several years ago too, but this is the first time I could say it out loud to anybody." He grinned like a kid landing a sunfish. "Doesn't hurt a bit, does it?"

My dog, Duchess, was a singular teacher. Is it silly to say a *dog* brought out the best in me? To be loved and appreciated is to be a better person. To Duchess, I had no faults. She had a remarkable way of making me feel good and loved and needed.

This mongrel terrier was supposed to be my daughter's pet, but from the day she arrived, she and I knew instant rapport. Duchess knew she was no ordinary dog, and it was no time at all until I knew it too.

I was bereft when she died. The hurt is deep when you lose a friend. Diligent to please, she'd given so much and asked so little. Few folks know the art of living. Duchess knew it well. There was no hidden reality behind the outward show. Hers was a hardy soul at peace with itself and its fellow creatures.

The hardest task is to talk about the most terrible teacher of all. Pain is perhaps the greatest hidden teacher of man. It was F. Scott Fitzgerald who said:

> We have two or three great moving experiences in our lives—experiences so great and so moving that it doesn't seem at the time anyone else has been so caught up and pounded and dazzled and astonished and beaten and broken and rescued and illuminated and rewarded and humbled in just that way ever before.

Pain changes vision in a way no other experience can. Into the emptied mind and the bludgeoned heart comes deliverance through the awful grace of God. Inexplicably, against one's will, it comes—a rebirth, thrusting one like a seed shot from a bursting pod, beyond one's self into the One Self.

A dear friend lost a son who overdosed on drugs; later a daughter was killed in an automobile accident. She confided, "I am overwhelmed and mystified in positively *knowing* my two children played a part in my soul's growth."

I was able to relate completely. The greatest paradox? How different *experience* from all you thought before!

Such "cures of soul" remain inscrutable poems in my mind, precious stones dropped into still water, whose ever widening circles continue to take on new and unexpected meanings if I take the time to pay attention. To listen is to pray.

***

A CIRCLE HAS NO END

My business is Circumference.

...Emily Dickinson

Not long ago, in a "School for Creative Learning," as well as in life, I, too, was about the business of Circumference. A challenging, uneasy task, for examination reveals the line bounding a circle has no beginning and no end. Small wonder, a quick twist turns it into a symbol for infinity.

I presided over a writing workshop for 12 and 13 year olds. Youngsters have a beautiful attitude of openness and curiosity that says anything is possible, yet questions everything. The younger the person, the truer that is. To my delight, the magic was still alive and well in the group I visited.

I tossed a circle of string around each student's neck. "Drop it anywhere," I suggested. "and embark on a safari. Fling it on the ground, a desktop, or around a picture in your room. Encircle an object, the neck of a person, or the footprint of a pet. What do you see? Look long and hard and write. You've tossed a pebble into a puddle. Read the rings and ripples that grow in number."

Music of the earth rang out in heart songs about a cluttered table-top, a slinky, green grass, animal friends, and grandfather's hands.

Mike encircled a patch of grass. "It has seen a bit of what we all have in common: Change. Winter to spring, clean to dirty, baseball to parades and parties....As night turns to day, we see ourselves grow older and wiser...change separates this day from the next. It is the void that turns good to bad and right to wrong. It is the one thing the world can rely on." The "spirit of the grass," he says, "ever changing, evolving, and surviving, *knows* that is just the way it is."

Jordon says "I love it, I hate it," when he writes of grass. How good it feels in summer under bare feet, how bad the cold, wet shock of it in winter. "I hate mowing the lawn with the old piece of junk that barely works. Grass flies out from under the mower hitting my legs. I love grass, but sometimes I can't stand it."

Ben says he's always wanted a blanket made out of grass. He sees "each blade as a slender isosceles triangle ...something small and simple that I've looked past every day." Stopping to look pays dividends. "When you do that—the grass is greener on *your* side of the fence."

Two students wrote of a favorite backyard tree. Kellyn says she and her oak tree "grew up together. 'the tree and me'—pals!" She climbs her old friend, even in winter—to knock snow off its branches. Lately, she hasn't had time to climb her tree. "Homework has taken over." She decides she may steal time from her work "to go visit an old friend and sit in the boughs while watching the sun set over the mountains in the west."

Matt compares the roots of his elm to family ties and fears the day he must leave his own roots ("a sobering thought, growing out of my protective shell and going into the world"). The forked branches remind him of life's choices, even of political parties. But then analogies fade: "I am caught up in how beautiful the tree is and I am shutting off everything else. I barely notice the breeze cooling, the shadows growing longer, the light dimming."

"What is a slinky for?" asks Robert. "In stretching itself, it sends us a message to stretch our imagination." He puts one end in each palm. "Maybe it can be a spiritual passage between exterior surroundings and the slinky inside us all. Maybe true joy is becoming completely in tune with our inner-slinky." He says he'd rather think of it that way than as "a marketing scam to drive poor people like me insane trying to understand it."

Melissa, Beth, and Claire wrote of animal friends. A cat, a horse, a dog impart lessons for living about friendship, trust, and sharing.

Melissa recalls the first time she put on her horse's bridle.

"It is necessary to reach into the horse's mouth....He was so gentle and patient. He just stood there waiting. Ever since, I have thought of him as one of my greatest teachers."

She recoils at the fear some trainers instill in horses in order to win medals. The beasts "stand like beaten children with frightened eyes, heads hanging low.". Her tactics were more gentle. "Sometimes I'd notice him growing impatient and unresponsive. Then I would walk him at a pace he liked and leave work behind." A mutual trust blossomed. "I dismounted and led him out of the arena. He lowered his head and gently touched me with his nose. We were a team and a good one."

Molly feels chagrin upon circling objects on the coffee table: cans of V-8 and diet cola, wrappers from the Subway sandwich shop, a necklace, a game, homework, and clean towels she hasn't put away. "I see objects, but I also see my lazy afternoon and memories of time spent with my good friend, Heather."

Erica spun an imaginary circle around grandfather's hands..."steady with tools, piecrust edging, and those he loved....When he died, the man who moved the refrigerator found (in it) 18 different kinds of open pickle jars."

Danny zeroed in on the letter H on his keyboard. "First used in the Middle East by ancient tribes, it began as the drawing of a loom with three threads stretched between two crossbeams." Although "abused and punched, the letter H remains proud of its ancient origins. It endures to serve future generations."

There were musings on red shoes ("I can fly when I wear them"), a bulletin board ("six years of memories"), the forest ("Wind music lets the trees call you to them"), a mantel clock ("Whose eyes picked it out brand-new? Who chose the wrapping and the bow? What did the greeting card say? Was it a wedding gift, a neighbor's thank you, or a just-because?").

Finally, a string on a counter surrounds a cup splotched with chocolate pudding and grape juice that belongs to the infant brother of the writer. The young writer listens as he writes: "In the living room a radio drones on endlessly about politics and death. Tossed beside Tommy's cup is a computer disk with secret thoughts and poems...a disk that holds a mind and heart, a cry for help that no one hears."

Strangely, I am suddenly reminded of a hand-stitched banner my granddaughter crafted for our fiftieth anniversary. It says, "Our family is a circle of love."

When will we ever learn? Our family is the world.

***

ON WRITING

The Almighty is a writer...
God's main attribute is creativity.

...Isaac Bashevis Singer

While Singer maintains that humans, made in God's image, possess the divine spark of creativity, this modest Nobel Prize winner yet holds no lofty illusions. "Writers were not born to change the world. We cannot even make it worse."

Chekov agreed it was not a fiction writer's mission to solve questions of God and pessimism. "His business is but to describe those who have been speaking or thinking about God and pessimism....Only stating the problem correctly is obligatory for the artist."

Stating a problem "correctly" or truthfully—that is in accordance with one's own voice and vision is not easy. One must put aside all questions of modesty or shame. "Shame is not for writers," says John Updike. Philip Roth agrees. "It's not that one doesn't feel shame or that one is shameless, but it's to be struggled against." Roth maintains it's the things you don't even say to people you trust most that constitute a major portion of your real life. "I think fiction—at least my kind of fiction—is about that."

Each book, he says, throws up its own problems. In that sense he believes writing is a singular profession. Dentists, engineers, teachers, and physicians are more able to draw upon their years of experience. "In writing you get little help from all you've done in the past. You discover anew as you go along."

Flannery O'Connor saw a metaphysical bonus of delight in that tough truth. "If a writer is any good, what he makes will have its source in a realm much larger than that which his conscious mind can encompass and will always be a greater surprise to him than it can ever be to his reader."

If any writer's fiction leans away from typical social patterns toward mystery and the unexpected, it is the work of Flannery O'Connor. She bristles when her intentionally grotesque fiction is said to portray a world that is unbearable and without hope. "People without hope do not write novels. Writing is a novel experience during which the hair falls out and the teeth decay." Rather than an escape from reality, she calls it "a plunge into reality and it's very shocking to the system."

Likewise, O'Connor was shocking to the systems of the writing students she addressed when she proclaimed too many people are interested in publishing, in making a "killing," in being a writer...rather than in writing.

True perhaps, but as a teacher of writing, more often I agree with Joyce Carol Oates's observation: "I believe the average person is deeper, more talented, and more intelligent than he probably believes."

All writers are different because all people are different. They write for many reasons. The most serious writers are compelled to communicate the inner voice of self and beam the light by which they see. Life's major decisions are not made in the mind.

Whatever the motivation, the deep digging of writing pays valuable dividends. It unveils inner secrets and introduces us to a self we keep buried much of the time.

I stand with Flannery O'Connor when she strips the high-falutin' grandeur from the word, and suggests that 'art' is "writing something that is valuable in itself and that works in itself. Its basis is truth....the person who aims after art in his work aims after truth in an imaginative sense, no more, no less."

It's a worthy ambition. Any noise can make us look, but art can make us see.

***

115

PUSHING SIXTY ON THE FAST TRACK

I'm almost 60 years old. I don't know why I always say that. Anybody asks me my age, I say, "I'll be sixty on my next birthday. Why don't I just say fifty-nine—especially since I was fifty-nine two months ago.

Well, I do lots of strange things. For instance, here I am in a log cabin in the Rocky Mountains near Fairplay, Colorado, sitting in on a drug bust...with about 20 kids and two young married teachers, Jim and Millie. The kids are their advisees. This is a "Beginnings Trip," part of an orientation program. Jim and Millie's eighteen-month-old son, Jeremy, came along on this trip.

It's at times like this I feel a little funny working part time in an alternative high school. I read an article in our mountain paper written by an exchange student at the school. He described the goings-on in laudatory terms—the emphasis on self-knowledge, complete honesty, and community service. It all sounded pretty revolutionary and meaningful...kids being challenged, rescued you might say, from the boredom of rote feeding of information. I decided I'd like to be part of this exciting approach.

But listen, you wouldn't believe the kids today. Maybe you would. I'm probably the one behind the times. This new generation is into sex and drugs, and these kids can't seem to complete a simple sentence without a four-letter word.

At first that shocked the living daylights out of me and I let them know it. They'd spot me coming down the hall and say loud enough for me to hear, "Cool it, watch your language. Here comes Catherine." Now I tell them they'll have to think of some new words. The old variety has lost all impact.

I'll bet you my second-hand bicycle that at least ninety percent of our kids come from what my generation calls 'broken homes.' I don't nose into the case histories, but I know there are some doozies. One that comes to mind is tiny Jennifer. Lived with her dad, because her mother was in a mental hospital. Now her dad is in prison for burglary. Because she's so small, she'd crawl through basement windows, go through the house and open the front door.

You know how they say a prophet doesn't swing much weight in his home territory. It's supposed to be worded in a more biblical way, but anyway that's kind of the way our school is looked upon in our immediate vicinity. "Hippie High," they call it (even though the days of the hippie are long gone)—the school for dropouts, druggies, and freaks.

Sure *freaks* me out from time to time. However, a lot of good things happen, amazing things really...complete turnabouts for problem kids. There are no grades, no credits, and they don't clamp down on poor attendance or laziness. Lots of kids seem to be majoring in sloth. The theory here seems to be that it takes a while to adjust to being able to shoulder responsibility for your own education. In my opinion, we're pretty short on consequences around here. So who's asking my opinion?

The school operates on the walkabout program. Kids have to complete six passages to graduate. We've had visitors from all over the USA who come to observe...members of national and state committees on education, and a nun from Edmonton, Alberta. She's principal of a Catholic Alternative High School (pretty traditional by our standards). She stayed with me the four days she was here.

I figured the language, the lax attitudes, and the weird get-up the kids wear, would really joggle her rosary, but she took it all in stride and had lots of good to say about the school. Matter of fact, the night of our Open House, she stood up suddenly amid the gathering and introduced herself before praising the school and the students. Said she'd talked to the young people and felt our country's future was in good hands. Sam, our principal, quoted her at the graduation ceremony in May.

And there was a professor from Ontario who's writing a book and a teacher from Buenos Aires who was getting his doctorate in Boulder. They both interviewed students and staff members and cooked meals for us in Munchie—featuring food typical of their respective areas. Munchie is what we call the school lunch program that's run by the kids. They even built and operate a solar greenhouse where much of the food is grown.

So you can see, experiential education is emphasized. Boy, they sure *experience*. Trips like this one are a major part of the curriculum. They travel to the wilderness, the inner city, even to other countries to get a taste of different cultures. This particular trip is a way to acquaint students with each other and how the school works.

They're getting a pretty darned good idea right now. It's hotter than Hades in here. The heat sizzles, intensifying the moment which is already electric.

"Some of you have been using drugs. Who wants to admit it?" Jim asks the question of the 20 students seated in front of him in a semi-circle.

"No hands, hmmm?" Jim's tone is as soft as the look in his steady gray eyes which are scanning the kids, stopping now and then to mirror a steady gaze, moving on to meet uneasy glances which occasionally shift to the floor or to their own reflections in the wall of windows.

Jim is 36 and bearded. Brown hair almost touches his shoulders. His legs are long and skinny, his knees bony...tinker toy sticks held together with round knobs. He wears khaki shorts and a tanker top that says "No Nukes." His teeth are straight and white and when he laughs, it's a kind of understatement that never makes much noise. His smile is slow and easy, like his wit which often ignites bursts of sudden laughter in staff meetings.

There's a soft and careless gentleness about Jim. It's typical that he'd take turns with Millie, taking a year off to care for their infant Jeremy so she could return to teaching. Now they're both back at school and Jeremy is in Day Care, but he often turns up at school. The kids love having him on this trip.

Actually, Jim looks a lot like the pictures we hang in

churches and assign to the messiah. Maybe that's why his ravenous appetite, as well as his loud and frequent belching is a little disconcerting.

He's scanning the group, looking for raised hands, but sees none. "Figures. It's about what I expected." The silence is crackled by the pine logs burning in the big wood stove. The heat and the silence are shuffled and shoved nervously into corners by restless bodies shifting about on benches and on the floor. A light bulb with a metal hood is tilted to shine down from the loft...not unlike a spotlight focused on a suspect in an old Grade B movie.

The uneasy hush is partly a result of the sudden shift of mood from raucous fun and games to third degree grueling. Moments ago, the log walls of the lodge were bulging with explosive laughter. Jim attempts to recapture the camaraderie.

"This'll loosen ya up," Jim is waving a wooden spoon in his hand, motioning the group to gather round. Millie slaps a palm to her forehead. "Oh no! don't tell me he's gonna do *that*!"

Kids cluster in the circle of light. "After this, nobody's going to feel like a fool—or at least not as big a one as I am." From center stage, Jim waves his arms as if in flight, periodically bending his knees, dodging about, bobbing up and down. "What bird am I?"

"Duck," the cry rings out.

"Right! And now? A sudden flailing of arms is followed by a quick jutting forward of his hips and a glance backward.

"Goose!" Several voices shout as one.

"Right again." And so the star keeps performing. The Arctic Tern, on to the spoon bill, and finally while one arm winged it, the other free hand pointed the spoon outward from his groin.

"Woodpecker!" Some kids fresh from traditional school look askance while others are convulsed with laughter. Carl, a Mexican boy who's a senior and favorite of the group, turns to the girl seated next to him, "Jim did that in physics class one day when we came back from break."

"Aha, no wonder you had all the right answers."

The demonstration worked its intended magic and loosened up even the shy kids for a game of charades. Diminutive Patty does a highly personalized interpretation of a strip-tease artist while another kid hums "The Stripper." She bends forward in an awkward motion pretending to pull panties down over her hips, guides them to the floor, and gingerly steps out, as one might in preparing for bed rather than performing in a girlie show.

The guess, of course, is on target and Patty warms to her audience's laughter. The game continues until Jim interrupts and calls a group meeting. They're a regular occurrence on Open School outings so it was assumed this was a usual wrap-up of the day's activities and a look at the next day's schedule.

"Back to the matter at hand! As I stated earlier, some of you have been using drugs. Who wants to admit it?" No hands. Instead Jim's proclamation meets with a silence which falls abruptly, like one of his wild birds felled by a hunter's bullet.

Jim looks straight at Chuck, a new kid sitting cross-legged on a chunk of wood just outside the circle. "Carrying drug paraphernalia is not allowed, Chuck. I happen to know you brought a pipe along."

Chuck is short and wiry. He has a jerky bounce to his step. All week he's been saying, "This is a really neat school and I've been in and out of more schools than I care to count." His straight blond hair hangs to his shoulders. ("I just cut it— used to be down to my waist.") A rolled kerchief circles his forehead. His earlier smiling, aberrational "Yes sir, No sir, Sorry about that, Ma'am," shifts to sullen stillness. In this school everybody—kids, teachers, principal, secretary, janitor—is on a first name basis.

"You have nothing to say?" Jim gets no answer. "We can't follow you everywhere. We don't want to be policemen, but we do not allow this stuff at school or on school trips.

Above all, there is no pushing, no involving others. You all know it. The county says drug use means a five-day suspension. I'd rather deal with it in more helpful ways. After all what does five days off mean except one big trip? An opportunity for more of the same. Doesn't make sense to me, but we have no choice in the matter."

Kids begin to comment. Carl, the popular Mexican boy, is more clean-cut looking than most with short, neatly combed hair and a tiny alligator on his knit shirt. Often the kids call him "Preppy," but it's in good-natured fun.

"I'm really disappointed," he says. "This seemed like a great group of new students. At first when I saw Evie's punk-rock get-up and Phil's Mohawk, I thought, Oh, no!" He looks at each of them, "But when I got to know you, it was different. You were really OK and I felt ashamed of myself for making judgments. Now all this. I'm no narc or nothin', but..."

Before he can finish, other students echo disappointment, then look at Jim as if to say, "What now?" Jim looks at Chuck and waits. The boy mumbles something about *always* carrying his pipe.

Jim says he knows there were others. He waits.

"OK, I was stoned this afternoon." The admission comes from Phil, another new kid, the one with the Mohawk. He's tall and quiet and his big brown eyes seem to spell trust when they look directly into your own.

No one reacts to the confession with more intensity and surprise than Millie. But that's Millie's nature. She reacts to life with joy and spontaneity and honest feelings. Her brown eyes fire-dance like fourth of July sparklers and her whole face takes on the excitement of a kid on his first carousel ride when she brings in unusual rocks or pieces of bone she's found in the woods, or explains a new game, or shares sketches from her journal. She's an art teacher. Has a Master's degree in Art, but it hasn't hurt her a bit.

When she has the kids participating in a walking race, her eyes gleam, her face turns red, her hands roll into fists and her bent arms work back and forth as swiftly and mechanically as her racing legs—heel, toe, heel, toe. She sets a rapid pace. Her laughter rings loud and full. Her enthusiasm and energy are boundless and contagious.

Now she looks at Phil. "How *could* you? You mean even after our talk this afternoon, the five of us sitting under the pine tree?" Her voice wavers but resumes steadiness as she recalls, "At least I'm not quite as naive as I was seven years ago when I came to this school. I remember we had such a warm, wonderful talk with the new Beginnings group and all the teachers...and that very afternoon, *that very afternoon,* thirty-five kids went out and got stoned. *Thirty-five!* I cried. I out and out bawled.

Carrie, a second year student cuts in angrily. "I'm really pissed. I really am. You guys knew better than to mess up like this." She talks about some of her former problems. "I had to have beer. Drank it all the time. Tried to sneak it along on trips. And, Oh brother, how I lied to Millie. I'm trying to tell you guys it's not gonna work. Don't lie to her and waste as much time as I did. I'm doin' better now, but it took a whole year."

Others have their say. Chuck mumbles and stares at his crossed bare feet. "I've been busted so many times, I don't give a shit. I've had school up to here."

Millie is mad. "Now you listen here. I don't care how many times you've been busted or thrown out of schools. This is different. Do you hear me? *This is different!*" Her words are exploding bullets.

A bright and pretty girl named Julie, who has spent years in psychiatric treatment, speaks up. "It's true. My folks tried everything, but I made my life hell and theirs' too. I didn't want to come here. Nothing else helped. Why should this school? Believe me, it does help if you give it half a chance."

Millie looked straight at Phil. "How do you feel right now? That's what I want to know."

"Ashamed."

Ann hops over on Julie's bench, whispers in her friend's ear, and they begin to sing, "We love you, Chuck and Phil."

The display adds to the uneasiness. "Oh, well," Ann shrugs and both girls laugh nervously.

Jim says, "I think enough has been said. We'll have to work out your suspension with Sam when we get back." Sam is the principal.

"I just hope you guys heard the caring." It's Martin, a new boy, whose remark capped the whole sordid affair.

The group dispersed and went outside for cigarettes and talk. That's what fooled me. It was 11 p.m. and I thought they were crawling into sleeping bags in the loft, so I crept into mine. Suddenly, here I am zipped into a sleeping bag on the hardwood floor of the big downstairs room and 20 kids are crawling all over the place, talking, playing cards, eating. They step over and around my prone body and I look straight up at their wide grins. "G'night, Catherine," they say. "Sweet dreams, Catherine."

I tossed my jeans over in the corner, so here I am, trapped in my underpants feeling like some kind of nut. I can't crawl out now and get dressed again. Little Jeremy is sleeping on the far side of the room. Apparently only the very young and the old feel nighttime was made for sleeping.

The floor is hard and I roll on my side. I can see Chuck's head silhouetted against the light shining through from the kitchen. Bits of light glow through his long blond hair. He's seated at the end of a big picnic table with Jim and Millie. His voice is soft and inaudible, but I hear Jim say, "No, I don't think you're burned out. I've seen plenty of kids who are and I don't see it in you."

Millie says something, then puts her arms around Chuck.

"It was hard for me to come and talk," he says. He tells of being shifted from one foster home to another. Right now he lives with an uncle. "I used to be more open, but I stopped talking. I didn't want people feeling sorry for me."

"I don't," Jim says. "There are kids here who've had it a helluva lot tougher. Some easier. We take what we get in life and work with that."

His biggest worry, Chuck repeats, is that he's already burned out from acid.

Come morning, Phil asks that everybody be present for something he wishes to say. "I'd just like to thank you all and I want to promise every one of you, I will never do a thing like this again on a trip or at school." Later, he repeats his promise to Jim and Millie. "I will never do it again." He looks them in the eye.

"Never is a long time," Jim says. Millie hugs Phil.

As if on cue, to break the solemnity, an irate Kathy comes screaming from the loft. "Somebody put their shit all over my sleeping bag and we're supposed to be packing up to leave. What the hell am I supposed to do?"

I feel instant shock, something between alarm and genuine horror, in all those cliché-ridden places like a knotted throat and a queasy belly. How was I to know that human excrement is a synonym for paraphernalia?

Cleanup crews leave the place in better shape than we found it. The kids and Jim pile into the yellow school bus that came out for pickup. I ride home in the van with Millie. She drives. Between us, Jeremy sleeps in his car seat

Millie says she's satisfied with the trip. "First time out you expect trouble with drugs. But aren't the kids just great? The way they step in and take charge and don't let the offenders get away with that stuff?"

We were both embarrassed, we admit, the day we climbed the sheer cliff and sat atop the narrow plateau overlooking the valley. We couldn't help overhearing the two girls spelling out their sexual exploits.

"I sometimes wonder if they talk like that in front of Sam? He seems so perpetually proud of the kids and always praises their behavior."

Millie says she doubts it...him being principal and all. It has a bearing.

Three weeks later at Staff Meeting, Millie breaks down

and cries. The kids in her class are so bored and apathetic. "And I'm not a boring person. We do *interesting* things." Chuck is in trouble again because of drug use in school. Julie is back to her wild fabrications, and Carrie wants to quit school—or, for sure, change advisors. Phil seems to be doing fine. "One, one, out of how many?"

Last week, Janet was the teacher in tears. She caught two of her advisees having sex on a school trip. "We had a group meeting and I hope it was handled in the right way. It seemed so at the time, but now I'm not so sure." She expressed misgivings. "In a way, it's as if they've become some kind of folk heroes."

"Folk heroes?" There was a smile in Jim's voice and a leer in his eye.

Blair is reporting on his twelve advisees. Only three live with both parents, and one has an alcoholic father. "Just one kid is growing up as I did in what we tend to call a normal home. Sometimes I get to wondering what a normal home is."

Dave laughs and compares their plight at "Open High" to a Mash triage. "We keep doing meatball surgery."

Millie can't laugh. She says it's getting to her. Maybe she's too selfish...with a little boy to think of, she says she may be losing patience and understanding.

Sam jumps in, "If it's affecting your relationship with Jeremy..."

"No, no. It's exactly the other way around."

Millie will be OK. They'll declare a "Staff Day," or a retreat and give sustenance to one another. Support is the name of the game around here. This staff is phenomenal. They're not simply well prepared professionally, they are beautiful human beings.

One day when I said as much to my smart-aleck husband, he said, "I suppose you figure that's why you got hired?"

"Pffft," I said. Stuck out my tongue for good measure.

And what a mix makes up this faculty. A couple of Jews, an Irish Catholic who began this staff meeting by making the sign of the cross and imitating the Latin spiel of a priest while dispensing a blessing. He's gung-ho on nuclear disarmament and has a group of activists at school who go around talking to organizations or anyone who will listen. There's a beautiful ex-nun (married to an ex-priest), and a free spirit who looks like a 1960 flower child. She's a favorite with the kids...*loooves* them all to pieces. There's also a prematurely gray-haired fellow who looks like a solemn judge and has a fiery temper. He's Hispanic and will vent his frustrations by ranting and raving in rapid Spanish, knowing he'll not be understood.

But the staff is all alike in that they're open and honest and caring...maybe to a fault? One day in staff meeting I told them they were like Shel Silverstein's "giving tree"—giving of themselves until there's only a stump left and *even then,* they invite, "Come sit on me." Blair, the biology teacher who knows my stint is temporary says, "Catherine, one day we're going to miss that Harry Truman approach."

Well, anyway, Millie will take her turn at getting new steam, stamina, and strength from her colleagues. Next week Millie will be smiling and optimistic and enthusiastic.

It's not Millie I worry about. It's me. All these teachers are about the age of my kids. Where do I get new steam? I'm sixty-years-old—well, almost. And for crying out loud, things are so *intense* around here.

***

AROUND AND ABOUT

A DAY IN OLD CONCORD
(With Henry David Thoreau as our guide)

Less than thirty miles west and slightly north of the heart of Boston lies Concord, Massachusetts. Early one morning in mid-October, a bracing tang in the autumn air and a golden canopy of elm leaves extended an invigorating welcome to this historic town. The streets were exactly as Thoreau described them on October 9, 1857: "The elms are now at the height of their change. As I look down our street which is lined with them...they remind me of yellowing sheaves of grain, as if the harvest had come to the village itself." And then, as was his habit, a caustic clincher, "and we might expect to find some maturity and *flavor* in the thoughts of the villagers at last."

My husband and I decided to "rise early and fast" taking to heart Henry's admonition, "Only that day dawns to which we are awake." We vowed "to spend one day as deliberately as nature and not be thrown off track by every nutshell and mosquito wing that falls on the rails." (Strange warning from one who was constantly set *on* track by carefully observing just such microcosms.)

If humankind suffered his disfavor, nature and his brute neighbors were esteemed teachers, and Concord, Thoreau said, "is worth more to me than the entry of the allies into Paris....Only that traveling is good which reveals to me the value of home and enables me to enjoy it better."

Perhaps in all America, no other town so small has yet so large (and varied) a claim to fame. In 1635, the Puritans chose this place, set amid glacial ponds and wooded hills, as their first Massachusetts settlement away from the seacoast.

One hundred forty years later, the minutemen, forewarned by Paul Revere, faced the British militia on April 9, 1775. "The shot heard round the world" was fired at Concord's Old North Bridge, and thus the decision was made to fight for freedom.

The famous Minute-Man statue at Old North Bridge

came very near extinction in November, 1973. A tourist heard a ticking which he reported to a guard. A homemade bomb was discovered and removed minutes before it was scheduled to explode.

Concord's third reason for renown rests with its famous literary inhabitants of the nineteenth century. Ralph Waldo Emerson, Henry David Thoreau, Nathaniel Hawthorne, and Louisa May Alcott called it home.

What mysterious undercurrents work their magic to waken *place* to *purpose?* Salzburg, Austria, ("German Rome"), birthplace of Mozart, a renowned music center for centuries; Elizabethan London, with its flowering of the theatrical arts; and Jerusalem, an inspirational center for the three great monotheistic religions of Judaism, Christianity, and Islam come to mind.

There is about the town of Concord a quiet air of serenity steeped in the proud traditions of the past. It is a credit to the townspeople and the Chamber of Commerce, that this New England community has not become a tourist trap of crass commercialism. Indeed, the name Concord still befits it well in this October of 1973—a condition of agreement and harmony.

While eating breakfast at the counter of a small restaurant on Main Street, I interrupted the conversation of the waitress and a local librarian who was enjoying a toasted English muffin with her coffee. The lady behind the counter was speculating on her son's chances of being accepted at Harvard or Dartmouth. "You know the record Jimmy Bowen had, high grades, all kinds of activities, and he didn't get in. He was a leader too, didn't just join stuff in order to list a lot of credits."

"I know." The librarian sipped her coffee and twisted the corner of her mouth in resignation. "Sometimes I think even our top kids have the least chance. They seem to try and get a smattering of all types from across the country."

"Excuse me," I took advantage of a blank space in the conversation. "Would you please tell me how I can find the Emerson home and Walden Pond?"

"You tell her, Emma," the lady behind the counter tossed

my inquiry into her friend's lap.

"I expect you'd like to see the Old Manse as well as the other Emerson house." Directions were given with the added suggestion "Don't miss seeing the Alcott house. It's exactly as you read about it in *Little Women*. I think your best bet is to get a map at the drugstore on the corner."

We began our tour with the Old North Bridge and thereafter peeked through the windows of the Old Manse. It was closed for the season. The stately mansion was the home of Reverend William Emerson, grandfather of Ralph Waldo. From its windows, Reverend Emerson watched the battle of the patriots and the British militia.

In later years, the Old Manse was the first home of Nathaniel Hawthorne and his bride, Sophia Peabody. *Mosses from the Old Manse* describes their years in this house (1842-1845). They moved to Salem but returned in 1852 and bought a house known as "Wayside" on Lexington Road. It was formerly owned by the Alcotts. After Hawthorne's death, the house was purchased by publisher Daniel Lothrop. The literary ghost that hovers over the houses of Concord continued to occupy this one for Lothrop's wife, under the pen name Margaret Sidney, wrote the popular children's books, *Five Little Peppers.*

"The Trader's Shop," often mentioned by Thoreau, is open for business. On Lexington Road, old stone walls that divided the original 17th century land grants, still ramble across the landscape. In some of the old houses, the original timbers, hand-hewn by early settlers are visible.

Concord's mighty specters continue to weave a silent elusive web that tangles every today with famous yesterdays; not the least of which is Independence Day, 1845. On that day the rebel of Concord took up residence at Walden Pond, thereby forging his own Declaration of Independence.

Henry David Thoreau refused to vote, pay taxes, attend church, eat meat, pursue a career, or have much good to say about human beings in general or about their institutions in particular. "The church, the state, the school, the magazine, think they are liberal and free! It is the freedom of a prison-yard....I would like to suggest what a pack of fools and cowards we mankind are."

He favored simple living. "Most of the luxuries and so called comforts of life, are...positive hindrances to the elevation of mankind." (To those who sneer and say, "He lived on Emerson's land and ate at his mother's house twice a week," I counter, "And so?") Nor was 'doing-good' a virtue. "I have tried it fairly, and...am satisfied it does not agree with my constitution." He championed intuitive burrowing. "Direct your eye right inward, and you'll find a thousand regions in your mind yet undiscovered."

It's an approach I encouraged while visiting a high school English class. A young female student hesitated, before bravely sharing her misgivings. "I think Thoreau was insecure and lacked self confidence." A strange accusation to level at a man who chose "to brag lustily as a chanticleer...if only to wake my neighbors up."

"When he lectured at the Lyceum," she explained, "no one commented, but he was sure he'd made a favorable impression. How could he know that; wouldn't someone have said so? He was never comfortable with people. When I feel that way and afterward ask myself why, it's usually because I didn't like myself well enough. I lacked confidence."

If cockiness is a screen for lack of confidence, she may have a point. In one journal entry, Thoreau admitted he was not a successful lecturer and failed to get the attention of the audience. "I feel that the public demands an average man—average thoughts and manners—not originality, nor even absolute excellence." Chastising himself in a journal entry of March 12, 1854, he admits being goaded into making "reckless and sweeping expressions which I am wont to regret....I find I have used more harsh, extravagant, and cynical expressions concerning mankind and individuals than I intended....He asks for a paradox, an eccentric statement, and too often I give it to him."

Thoreau's eccentricities tend to engender more respect, or

at least more response, in the twentieth century than in the nineteenth. Perhaps because today the mass of men are *disallowed* the privilege of leading lives of *quiet* desperation. Quiet is allotted even less space in the space age than during the machine age, which was to have birthed a Utopia. Look at those deep-set, hooded eyes in his photograph and tell me he's not saying, 'I told you so'.

Walden, of course, is a distillation of accumulated journal entries. Interestingly, Joseph Wood Krutch points out that the famous passage about leading lives of quiet desperation is a condensation of this mess: "a stereotype but unconscious despair is concealed under what are called the amusements of mankind." It's obvious the man practiced what he preached, "Not that the story need be long, but it will take a long time to make it short."

Henry wrote two books in his lifetime and paid to have *A Week on the Concord and Merrimack Rivers* printed. After two years and about 220 sales, the remaining 706 books were dumped on his doorstep—before he had completed his installment payments to the printer. Undaunted, he recorded in his journal that very evening of October 28, 1853, "Indeed, I believe that this result is more inspiring and better for me than if a thousand had bought my wares. It affects my privacy less and leaves me freer."

That's enough to leave any rejected writer, if not freer, surely smiling and empathic.

Walden, published in 1854, fared somewhat better, but it took five years to sell 2,000 copies. If only Henry could know the ensuing impact of his words, which have been translated into nearly every major language of the world. He influenced Tolstoy, Gandhi, and early leaders of the British Labor Party...yet in his own time and territory, he was viewed by many as a village crank.

These thoughts and more played on my mind as we walked the shores of Walden Pond. I envisioned Thoreau in wide-brimmed hat and slouchy coat walking the forest listening to the music of the wild; crouching to observe a woodchuck or an army of ants; or foot-feeling his way along the old Indian path as he made his way home from the village in the black of night.

If I could choose but one day from a calendar of 365, for this visit, I could have selected none better. Only occasionally did we encounter tourists. A group of young folks—some wearing three-cornered Revolutionary hats, some drinking soda and eating sandwiches, still others calling to stragglers in their group—wandered past in groups of twos and threes. Now and then we encountered more serious visitors who wore quiet smiles, clutched books, and nodded in friendly greeting.

We came upon a young man working carefully and quietly, setting a camera on a tripod at the water's edge. Peering and testing, he moved this way and that, shifting his equipment about the edge of the cove. At this spot, we wandered inland and were surreptitiously rewarded with a cairn that marks the place where Thoreau's cabin once stood.

A young woman tossed another rock on the pile and remarked to her companion, "Do you think that's how all those stones got here? Maybe everyone's supposed to find a special stone and throw it with the others?"

I'm not convinced that a man who condemned "nations possessed with an insane ambition to perpetuate the memory of themselves by the amount of hammered stones they leave" would approve. "I love better to see stones in place," he said. Speaking of even larger hammered stones: "As for the Pyramids, there is nothing to wonder at in them so much as the fact that so many men could be found degraded enough to spend their lives constructing a tomb for some ambitious booby, whom it would have been wiser and manlier to have drowned in the Nile."

Blue sky, gold and russet birch and maple, verdant pine, browning grass and smooth gray stones were mirrored in the ageless green glass of Walden Pond. The bottom, readily visible was still "strewn with wrecks of the forest." I looked for the famous pickerel of Walden, but was disappointed. I listened for birdsong and was satisfied.

A replica of the house Thoreau built in the woods stands on the grounds of the Lyceum. "He was a real craftsman," the attendant reminded us. "He never referred to his home as a hut or shack, but always called it his house." It measured ten by fifteen feet and his careful records show it cost only $28.12 1/2 to build.

We visited Sleepy Hollow Cemetery at the close of day. We were alone in the graveyard among the pines, maples, and oaks. Needles, leaves, and acorns crackled underfoot. Ferreting out his resting place brought to mind his deathbed reply to a zealous relative who asked if he'd made his peace with God. "I am not aware," he said, "that we ever quarreled."

The first grave I found on Author's Ridge was Emerson's. A great quartz rock bore a copper plaque: "Born in Boston, May 25, 1803. Died in Concord, April 27, 1882." Hawthorne's grave, like Emerson's was within a chained area. Louisa May Alcott had a small arched marker in the Alcott family plot.

Henry David Thoreau's small stone, also within a family plot, said simply "Henry." He died of tuberculosis in 1862 at age forty-four. Lead pencil maker, school teacher, surveyor, grower of beans, and by his own definition, mystic, transcendentalist, and natural philosopher, he once asked, "With all your science can you tell how it is, and whence it is that light comes into the soul?"

It's a question I'd like to ask Thoreau, because it does seem that's what he was talking about in *Walden.* Don't you think?

***

A FARM IN NEBRASKA

Speaking of her visit to a friend's Midwest farm, May Sarton writes:

> ..."a farm once in her family, she has rescued from dilapidation. It has a wholesome, ancient sweetness about it....The village is called Fish-hook. What a feeling of frontier it still has!"

I was there last summer! More accurately, I traveled to a different farm seven miles south of Stockville, NE, (the county seat of *Frontier* County), where Sarton's every comment rings true. A wooden sign at the head of the long farm driveway reads: "Ambrose Shelley homestead—1872." Shelley is the great-great grandfather of the present owner.

The log cabin, which originally housed his family, stands in the county fairgrounds in Stockville. The present two-story, white clapboard farmhouse, a Sears Roebuck home, is almost a century old. This family farm, too, was rescued from dilapidation by a woman who was raised on the acreage. Cheryl Muilenburg and her husband, Todd, live in Long Beach, California. They spend two months each summer on their Nebraska farm and plan to move there following retirement.

The land is rolling and richly green, dotted with clumps of cedars. Cottonwoods line the banks of Medicine Creek which runs through their property. A windmill stands tall against a pale blue sky.

The 400 acres are worked by an area farmer who was, at the time of our visit, devastated by the loss of his corn crop after severe hailstorms. "May have to get me another job in Curtis," he said. His face forced a smile but it stopped short of his voice.

We were lucky guests because our granddaughter married into the family. For four days I was transported, with a little help from the creative imagination, not only to the 19th century

Nebraska frontier, but quite unwittingly to the small Wisconsin town where I grew up in the 1930's. I stand with Rene Dubos, "I do not live in the past, it is the past which is alive in me."

The countryside was black and quiet the night we arrived. A turn here, another there, a long stretch of straight gravel road ...still no signs of life or light. A pale moon did little to illuminate the landscape. Finally, we turned into a long driveway at the end of which a yard light on a high post splashed a pool of yellow into a sea of darkness. The family was in town at the county fair.

Our headlights shown on the lovely old home framed by ancient cottonwoods. A verandah (with gingerbread trim and rocking chairs and a porch swing), wrapped two sides of the house.

Ralph read my mind as we drank in the cool stillness from the porch swing. "Remind you of the porch swing in Marshall?" *It had followed my mother from the farmhouse where she grew up to the gray bungalow my father built. It was the setting for my parents' courting, and years later for my own.*

The leaves rustled in the soft wind and the moon hid behind the cottonwood branches. We were drenched in soothing quiet as we headed for bed around midnight.

Ours was the newly wallpapered downstairs bedroom. A flowered pink and green quilt matched the paper. The owners work hard at restoring and maintaining the property. This is not an ancient farmhouse redecorated "ala country 1997." When the house contents were placed on the auction block, Cheryl bought back the original furnishings including pots and pans, a framed picture of Grandpa and Old Mom on their sixty-fifth wedding anniversary, watercolors by her mother, an oak table, straight-back chairs, rockers, a sofa, Blue Willow dinnerware, *and* the player piano that stands in the parlor.

Cheryl grasped the lower edge of the piano keyboard, leaned back to brace herself and vigorously pumped the pedals. The coded music sheet unrolled and piano keys churned out "Let Me Call You Sweetheart" and "Sweet Adeline." We all bellowed, "Is there anyone finah in the state of Carolina...than my little Dinah-mite?"

Chores are unending—painting, planting, papering, baking, fence mending, and grass cutting. The owners are weighing the means to salvage the precariously listing weathered barn. Ralph laid sod and I hung out baskets of washing. *The washing machine stands on the enclosed back porch—as did our ancient wringer-style Maytag. We called our glassed-in porch the summer kitchen. Mother cooked out there on a kerosene stove in July and August.*

As shirts, sheets, and jeans billowed in the breeze, I recalled a recent item in *The Denver Post*. A woman objected to a ruling in her subdivision prohibiting outdoor clotheslines. "Are we so snooty," she asked, "that we're forced to forego the fresh smell of clothes dried in the open air?"

A small abandoned house stands some distance behind the Muilenburg place. We crept carefully through the crumbling rooms. Wrecked cars rest on their sides in order to fill a gap in the fencing. A sad tale, indeed a legend, prevails about the former owners who were drowned fighting floodwaters.

When we viewed the couples' graves in the local cemetery, *I was transported to our small-town graveyard remembering my grandmother's story—about the double grave that held a honeymoon couple who drove into a river in a dense fog and drowned. When the car was pulled from the river in Portage, the coroner called my dad—the name of his Chevy garage was printed on the cover of the spare tire. The newlyweds, too, became a legend; their story was passed from generation to generation in our town. Zona Gale wrote a short story, "Bridal Pond," based upon the fate of the young lovers.*

"Does the bell toll when someone dies?" I asked. *In our town it tolled the age of the departed. Grandma—whether weeding her garden, feeding her chickens, or baking kolaches—would fall to her knees and say a silent prayer. "Fifty-two," she counted, "must be Billy Skalitsky. He had a heart attack last week. I wonder who'll be next?" Village deaths came in threes!*

Cheryl and Todd showed us their lots beneath a linden tree. "There's room for our kids if they want to be buried here," Cheryl said. *How often my mother had said the same, the hint of a wish in her voice. But lives move on to different places.*

The town of Stockville seemed more dead than the burial ground. Neatly kept homes were interspersed with empty houses falling into disrepair. Junked cars and appliances, broken machinery, crumbled bird baths, and rusty bedsprings hid in the tall grass and tangled shrubs of abandoned yards.

Our last evening, a few neighbors came by for a supper of oven-fried chicken and peach cobbler. George, a local farmer, related, "Last month, a fella's car broke down in front of my place. I asked him did he know the bridge down the road was washed out? I give him my pickup to go find where another bridge was at so's he could get wherever it was he was headed for."

George's straw hat, stayed put all evening, but when he shoved it to the back of his head while contemplating his story, a band of milk-white skin contrasted sharply with his suntanned face...*just like the farmers who came into town to wedding dances and pumped the arms of their partners as they pranced around the old town hall. Fresh haircuts also revealed bands of white at the back of their necks.*

"His rig was pretty much of a wreck," George went on, "so I got to wonderin' would he bring back my truck? But he did, the very next day."

Now I understand full well that homesteaders' grit was tempered by back-breaking labor, natural disasters, and hardest of all, the early passing of loved ones. Cheryl's mother won't return even for a visit. "I remember the howling winds and the long, lonely winters," she says.

So tell me why bittersweet recollections of this quiet far-away place leave me wondering if a certain softness has left the face of the earth? The lament no doubt is timeless. Second childhood, I find, births a second innocence in which universality replaces naiveté. We know laughter and tears, each in a different way, yet also each the same. All stories are one story—deja vu experiences of pain and splendor shared by people of the earth, pilgrims seeking the blessed mystery of wholeness.

I write to find answers. In this instance, I only know I left the hurly-burly for four days and in some indecipherable way, a forsaken frontier town and a forgotten landscape fed my soul.

***

FIRST CLASS, AND WITH CHILDREN

In America there are two classes of travel—
first class, and with children.

...Robert Benchley

I wasn't sold on spending Christmas in the Caribbean and my misgivings were intensified when we found our seats in a crowded 727 were located just behind the bulkhead, that wall that separates first and second class passengers. It cramps my psyche when there's no room for visual stretching.

Ralph was stashing our baggage overhead when a voice next to the window piped, "Hello there, how are you today?"

Six little words and everything changed! Our seatmate was a bright lad of nine named David. He was small for his age and wiry. His deep blue eyes knew alertness, sharpened, no doubt, by his pale white face and faded blond hair. A few freckles flecked his nose and cheeks. His lips were thin—just right for smiling. I noticed his teeth were large. It takes a while for some kids to get synchronized, that is to grow up enough to catch up with their second teeth. I was such a kid myself, but I didn't feel mentioning it would make for immediate bonding. Instead, I asked the usual things—where he lived (Laramie), and what grade in school (fourth).

"I'm a teacher," I said.

"Really? What grade?"

"You might say I've tried them all."

His mother, he said, teaches Computer Science at the University of Wyoming.

The stewardess offered drinks and small packages of peanuts. I took Coke, David took Ginger Ale.

"Do you like math and computers? Seems most kids do. They scare me," I admitted. I'm a writer, but it took me a while to get used to a personal computer."

"You gonna write about us? You 'n' me?"

"I dunno. That depends."

"What did you ask me before?"

"If you liked math."

I knew I was sitting beside a wily sage when with blue eyes dancing and a smile playing around his mouth, he replied, "Don't all smart little boys like math?"

He told me he was on his way to a small town in Alabama where his grandmother lived. He was going to spend Christmas with his father. "My dad's gonna get married again—to Betty. She'll be there too."

"Do you like your new step-mom?" I asked, suddenly realizing I'd jumped the gun, but not backtracking to correct the mistake.

"Better than my mom," he quipped with a speed and straight-forwardness that scared me. I never got divorced and never intend to, but I have three kids and maybe I was imagining one of them shifting love and loyalty with that much ease at that young age.

"Don't be too sure too fast," I said. "It's probably easier to be popular when you don't have any real responsibility." I smiled and looked him in the eye. "I'll bet it's no picnic keeping you in line."

"Well, I know what you mean," he said. "I guess it's Chick that causes the problem."

"Chick?"

"The guy that my mom lives with. I mean, he lives with us."

"What does he do?"

"Nothin', except he watches a lot of TV and drinks a lot of beer." David puffed out his cheeks and tried to push out his stomach, but it didn't go very far. He placed his hands far out in front of his middle and touched fingertips.

"Fat, huh?"

"You said it. He doesn't like me too much. I don't even care except it makes trouble between me and my mom." He twisted sideways and looked out the window. It was a way of closing the subject and his downcast eyes told me he was a little sorry he'd said that much.

"You play cards?" I asked.

"Yea, some. I used to play Fish with my friend, Jimmy. I don't really know too many games."

The stewardess provided a deck of cards and I taught him to play "Crazy Eights."

"Where'd you learn this?" he wanted to know.

"My granddaughter taught me. It's fun, isn't it?"

"Yup, sure is." He slapped a king of clubs atop my king of hearts. He was kneeling on the floor in front of me and we had a lap table between us. Now you know we could never have done that in the cramped quarters behind us.

"My dad says I can have whatever I want for Christmas that costs $5. Did I tell you he's a painter?"

"Pictures?"

"Nope, houses. Maybe that's what I'll do when I grow up."

He played his last card, a three of diamonds. "You won," I said. "I think you deserve a prize." I dug into my purse, pulled out my billfold and handed him a dollar.

"Oh Boy!" He unbuttoned the small left-hand pocket of his plaid shirt, which had a plain blue yoke—western style. He folded the dollar over and over until it was the size of a postage stamp, then stuffed it in and rebuttoned the flap. "Now I can pick out something that costs *six* dollars!"

Lights flashed and the announcement was made to fasten seat belts for landing. We were approaching the Atlanta airport where we would transfer and David would meet his dad. The stewardess came by and asked him to wait in his seat until everyone left the plane. She would take him into the terminal along with other children who were traveling alone.

He asked me to get his package from the overhead baggage compartment. It was a present for his dad, and was carefully wrapped in Christmas paper. David zipped up his shiny blue jacket that had been on the floor and he pulled a stocking cap over his ears. It said "Dallas Cowboys." "They're my favorite team," he said. His face looked smaller, but his eyes loomed larger under the bulky cap. "Thanks for the dollar," he said once more.

Self confidence and openness notwithstanding, he looked so fragile and vulnerable standing there with one knee resting on the seat. From the aisle, I touched my finger to my lips and waved it in his direction. "Bye, David. Have a nice Christmas."

We were inching our way toward the door when he reached out one more time. "Hey, you know what?" he called. "My grandma'll love Crazy Eights."

"Oh, I know she will. Grandmas always do."

Who would think it could happen again on the same day—on our next plane to Tampa? Not so unusual, perhaps, when one realizes there were lots of kids traveling alone at holiday time. This time my seat partner was named Stephanie. And she, too, was nine. But she was much taller and more sophisticated than David. The hint of pink on her cheeks and lips, her dark lashes, as well as her demeanor, made her seem several years older. "I would have guessed pre-teen...maybe 12," I said.

"No, only nine," she said. And when she shook her head the thingamajigs she wore on each side of her face to hold back her long dark hair jiggled and bobbed—long plastic strands with beads on the ends. "I'm wearing a little makeup. That's probably why you thought I was older. My mother doesn't let me wear very much though."

She showed me a necklace and matching bracelet with a heart and a tiny diamond-like stone. "My mother gave it to me for Christmas. I got to open it early because I'm going to Tampa to be with my dad for Christmas. He lives with his mom on a farm. Maybe his ex-wife will be there. He's been divorced again since he and mom split up."

"You'll be seeing your grandma then?"

She nodded, "I don't know her all that well." A slight frown was followed by the admission, "I can't really remember what she looks like."

Stephanie didn't seem the type for Crazy Eights, so we settled for conversation.

"My mother's a secretary and she just got married...well, I mean, the second time, to a man who's older. He has two sons in high school in Illinois. They live with their mother and they came to visit last summer. We got along supremely well."

She showed me a picture of her mother that she carried in her wallet. "She's a lovely lady," I said. "No wonder you're so pretty." Stephanie's sweater was a soft pink, her skirt a muted pastel plaid; her tights matched her sweater.

Stephanie is her mother's only child. "I told Mom the other day that I don't think I want any kids. Maybe I won't even get married." She laughed when she imitated her mother. "'*What?*' my mom says, 'What? I *want* grandchildren.'"

She said her mother's life hadn't been too happy. "There was a big family. My mother was the youngest and she was only three or four when her mother left home and Mom never saw her again. She never got along with her dad and ran away from home when she was in high school."

She lifted her head and looked at me with soft brown eyes. I knew she was about to share something very important. "Do you know she always carries around this old picture of her mother. I mean, to this day she's still trying to

145

find her mother. It's really very pathetic. I'm pretty lucky. I have two dads and a mom and a step-mom. Well, an ex-step-mom," she corrected. I only met her a couple of times, but she was a very nice person. I guess I have quite a few grandparents." She smiled, too brightly it seemed—even for nine going on nineteen—and for just an instant I was reminded of a face I'd just seen in a magazine ad...for orange juice, I think.

The stewardess passed out trays. "No, thank you. I don't care for any lunch," she said. "I ate a late breakfast."

"But Stephanie, your mother asked if we were serving lunch. She said you hadn't eaten any breakfast."

"I'm not hungry."

"You're sure?"

The plastic strands wiggled as she bobbed her head. The stewardess handed the tray to the lady behind us.

***

NOTES FROM A MONASTERY

I have never encountered a richer expression
of contemplation-in-action than I have in the
Spiritual Life Institute, its founder Father
Willie McNamara, its monks and its
magazine. That they manifest so much
exuberance and sophistication at once, so
much depth and pure fun, is a miracle to me.

...Michael Murphy
Founder of the Esalen Institute
Big Sur, California

<u>Thursday, August 30</u>

After circuitous rambling, I found myself on the right path at last, traveling a remote, dusty, unpaved road marked now and again with a wooden cross and labeled Carmelite Way. The road rose, and in the distance the monastery bell tower and turrets "peaked" above a swell of land. The architecture of Nada Hermitage is described as a meeting of southwestern, medieval, ancient, and contemporary.

* * * * *

Quiet. I have heard the *word* all my life. Today I heard the *quiet*. I felt it. A silence that touched bone was not disturbed by the hot desert breeze that tempered the 94 degree temperature.

It was late afternoon when I arrived at Spiritual Life Institute in Crestone, Colorado. William McNamara O.C.D. founded this small Carmelite monastic community for both men and women (Nada Hermitage in Colorado and also Nova Nada in Nova Scotia) in 1960 via a mandate from the visionary Pope John XXIII. "We are Roman Catholic in origin" says their brochure, "universal in outreach, thinking globally and acting locally."

Men and women of all ages and occupations, of any or of no religious affiliation, are welcome retreatants. The monks prefer to let God do His work without their interference via screening. Retreatants may participate in monastic rhythms or establish their own patterns for solitude, silence, and Holy Leisure.

Initially, I chose to absorb the heat, the quiet, and the atmosphere, so I stood a while in the parking lot with the snow-capped Sango de Cristos mountains behind me rising abruptly to over 14,000 feet; and in front of me, to the west, the desert of the San Luis Valley with its harsh, abundant growth, tumbling toward the distant horizon. In the process, a great bowl of sky is upended.

Between the mountain peaks and the desert horizon, the monastery nestles at an altitude of 7,600 feet. Even the landscape reminds, the Nada is a place where contrasts dwell harmoniously. The turrets, towers, and peaked roofs are reminiscent of the jagged wall of mountains. The stucco, adobe-like walls seem to have sprung organically from the desert sand. And the massive handcrafted bridge, reminds one of an ancient drawbridge. Small wonder the monks have referred to the Chapel and the Agape as "Cair Paravel," C. S. Lewis's mythical castle in the land of Narnia.

The Agape (kitchen, library, lounge) and Sangre de Cristo Chapel are connected by a rugged wooden bridge. A big shaggy dog sprawling near the Agape door nudged a memory. Someone once told me every monastery has a dog. I was soon to learn this one is an honored member of the community, allowed to wander in and out of services in the chapel as he pleases. Father Will calls Saluki intrinsically authentic. "He will not be used."

There was not a human in sight as I walked down the bank and sat for a while on a bench in a covered alcove just outside the chapel, facing the desert to the west, absorbing the blessed stillness. (Little did I know at this point, that this monastery is not *all* quiet and contemplation.)

A zealous ceramic Elijah (the father of Carmel) hangs at the chapel entrance.

* * * * *

Individual hermitages house the monks and the retreatants. Well camouflaged, they are tucked into sandbanks, roofs alive with desert plants, hidden from one another, each with a private view of open desert.

Only the little stucco cottage east of mine, just up the hill on the way to chapel is clearly visible from my windows. Expecting a simple, barren hut, my guest house seems far too lovely and luxurious to be dubbed a hermitage. A terra cotta fireplace with full, round belly fits neatly into a corner facing the window wall. An open area fronts it and cushioned hearth benches placed at right angles edge the great firepot. An Indian rug, a cedar-paneled cathedral ceiling and a wall of built-ins—desk and book-filled shelves—spell added comfort and beauty. I write at a round table tucked into the windowed southeast corner.

North of the living room, a tiny modern kitchen. To the west a bedroom opens onto a small atrium. Not all hermitages are so fine. A couple built this one stipulating they could occupy it often. I suspect the robust young monks took pity on this aging female who just had a cast removed from her broken arm and thus assigned me the Juliana of Norwich Guest House.

* * * * *

What I do with my week is up to me. Contemplation, so necessary and so neglected, in our lives is defined as "loving awareness which begins with a long, loving look at the real and ends in the happy surprise of being in harmony with the universe, in the glory of God's presence, madly in love with all that is."

And all this, Father McNamara reminds us is more easily caught than taught. All of which says to me one must first be chronically infected with a "dis-ease" concerning a social, political, and domestic existence that suffers the lack of contemplative and loving awareness, in order to catch, then inadvertently pass along the germ.

From just such a person, many years ago, I caught a mild case of the bug. It changed my life and I still marvel at the wonder of it. He did not complete his studies for the priesthood, but he is a shaman all the same.

The chapel bell is ringing. It's 4:50 p.m. and vespers are at 5:00. Lauds will be at 6:00 a.m. Mass is celebrated on Wednesday, Friday, and Sunday. I see my neighbor up the hill walking to vespers. I shall do the same.

A tiny ant scurries across my table. I just killed a wasp buzzing on the inside of my window screen. A thought surfaced—I wondered if that was a bad way to begin a retreat. A Buddhist would have shooed him safely out an open door.

And so to chapel. Then I shall prepare the vegetable and rice stir-fry in my refrigerator which has been provided for the first supper. Thereafter, some reading, a step outside my door into the still, star-filled night—"and so to bed."

Friday, August 31

Today is son John and Margie's 22nd wedding anniversary. I remembered it as I awoke to the 5:45 chapel bell. I walked to 6:00 a.m. lauds in semi-darkness. The sun is slow in making its laborious way over the 14,000 foot peaks; even as I returned to my cottage at 7:45 it was just beginning to grow light. One is grateful for the morning coolness.

Betty is assigned to welcoming duties this week. She appeared at my door soon after lauds. In her 30's, she's prematurely gray (as I was) and she has a space between her front teeth (as I have). Formerly a nurse, she says she always knew it was not her real calling. After several retreats here at the Spiritual Life Institute in Crestone, she finally stayed. Betty wears the beige apron of the novitiate. Dark brown replaces the light, sleeveless over-garment after final vows. A two-year trial is followed by a five-year period before that comes to be.

* * * * *

I went for a long morning walk and explored the acreage to the north where eight new hermitages are being built. How well planned they are—burrowing into the sand dunes, each with a window wall, each oriented for privacy. From a distance, they are scarcely visible. The desert looks unoccupied.

Rambling roundabout, I scrambled down one sandy bank, and noticed interesting footprints in the sand. Are they mine, I wondered? Have I been here earlier? They looked too large and the pattern looked so complicated. I checked my sneakers—Sure enough...I didn't know my sole was so intricate! I laughed aloud at the thought, which was followed by a thought of my husband. Ralph would be proud of my play on words.

Well, it's what I've always preached in writing classes. Dig deeply. Reach for your soul and you'll be astounded at what you find. How often I've heard, "I have little formal education," or "Nothing has happened me," or sometimes a silly self-consciousness might take over, as with my dear young friend from Appalachia who refused to read aloud in class. "I cain't, cuz I talk funny. Ah'm a hillbilly. You read it for me." I did, and we were mesmerized as we listened to the song of a mountain bird just learning to fly. And fly she did, as she dug deeper and deeper exploring her own territory. She sold many stories and authored a book.

* * * * *

"All who enter here—No Fuss." So reads the sign over the door of the Agape. "Those words express the contemplative life," Brother Thomas explained. He said that, like Zacchaeus, he was a tax collector—an IRS man and a CPA. "CPAs help others, I guess. It's a good path, but I wanted to do more with my life."

Asked if the order to move to the Crestone Baca/Grande came because it has long been considered a sacred area, Thomas laughed. "What's sacred ground? We came because the land was given to us. We were in Sedona, Arizona. The city was moving out to meet us and we had no room to expand."

The general area comprises ancient Native American sites of worship, a San Luis Valley Tibetan project, Crestone Mountain Zen Center, Haidakhandi Ashram, Baptist and Episcopal churches, and the Spiritual Life Institute.

* * * * *

This afternoon I stamped brochures for mailing, then chopped veggies for Susan's gazpacho. At forty, she is one of the oldest monks. The women call themselves 'nunks.' Susan is a tall, vibrant, attractive young woman.

She told me Father William McNamara was a good friend of her physician father. He'd ride into Phoenix on his motorcycle and stay with her family.

"Mother had some problems with my joining the Carmelites," she admitted. A poem pasted in a library scrapbook captures a moving moment concerning Susie's father. While Susan sang at the chapel dedication, tears slide down her father's beaming face.

As we chopped tomatoes, peppers, and onions, Susan looked me in the eye and declared, "We *are* celibate." "I never doubted it," I said, taken somewhat aback by the comment. "People say, 'Yea, *sure* you are!' They aren't used to the idea of both men and women in a monastic order. We are celibate," she repeated.

Susan asked if I'd heard David Levin's story. It seems after Father McNamara met David, he recruited his help in planning a heist. Father Will's list of subscribers had been stolen by a bookstore owner. He was getting nowhere in requesting the list be returned. The conspirators cased the joint and set up a plan. David was to occupy the owner and meantime Father Will would telephone, at which time David was to surreptitiously grab the list from the files. Unfortunately, Father Will dialed the wrong number and had no second dime. Somehow, despite no phone call and no getaway car, David was able to recover the files. I'm not sure, nor did I ask, how this fiasco influenced David Levin to join the order, but I'm sure stranger things have happened. I suspect aiding and abetting such a unique clandestine operation could create a bond!

* * * * *

This evening we all ate together at one long table in the Agape kitchen. Gazpacho, French bread, and cookies were well received by all except Thomas. He chose to forego the cold, thick summer soup for leftovers he found in the refrigerator.

Never have I sat at a more boisterous, loving, fun-filled, philosophical, and joyous supper table. One rule prevails: One person may speak at a time. Brother Ross, in paint-spattered T-shirt and jeans, offered thanks "for the food, for the cooks who prepared the food, for the cleanup crew who swept the floors and would wash the dishes, for the workers who built hermitages, and for those who prayed for the cooks who prepared the food, for the cleanup crew who swept the floors, and for the workers who built the hermitages."

At the end of the meal, Father David Denny rushed out for his copy of a Shel Silverstein poem someone had sent him. Conversation moved to his sermon concerning a child's broken doll. Adults, he said, had failed to empathize. They could have suggested a Christian Requiem to ease the child's pain.

Now I was reminded there is the danger of wicked backlash in suggesting a ceremonial leave-taking. I shared a remembered Jim Bishop column in which a small boy mourned the loss of a pet turtle. Tommy was so inconsolable that Mom called Dad at the office and he rushed home at noon to find his young son devastated. In an effort to assuage the boy's pain, Dad got out his silver cigarette case offering it as a casket. A formal funeral was planned, a burial spot suggested, along with a proper marker. Tommy was told he could invite his friends to the ceremony. About that time, Tommy glanced toward the aquarium only to see the turtle scrambling onto a rock. A look of disbelief and letdown swept across the boy's face. "Let's kill him, Dad," he said.

I must remember to send Father David my copy of *Where the Sidewalk Ends.*

Saturday, September 1

After a one mile walk to the stables, I reported to the Agape for chores. Vacuuming, mopping floors, dusting furniture was followed by lunch in the kitchen. We ate leftovers. At the sound of an airplane overhead, two of the "nunks" leapt from the table and ran onto the deck where they waved to the pilot. Pilots are trained in a nearby airfield and we learned the waving is a regular ritual.

Allison and Jolene, two Denver nurses, are also on retreat. One talks too much and the other hardly at all. Talk went from Mother Tessa's impending trip to Holland, to abortion, to Barbara and George Bush, to Jim's (fellow-retreatant from California) square dance calling. He promised to bring his boom box and tapes to breakfast tomorrow after mass.

* * * * *

At 5:00 p.m. I met with Father David upstairs in the adobe cylinder that adjoins the chapel. Susan had suggested it when she learned I was not church-oriented although raised a Catholic (of sorts). These informal talks are their method of confession, she said. Wouldn't I like to do that? I had a few misgivings. "Bless me father, for I have sinned. My last confession was 25 years ago," did not seem a good beginning.

In looking back over my life, image consciousness reared its ugly head as my greatest sin. I know shamefully little about the Bible, but it is not by chance that "Pride goeth before destruction, and an haughty spirit before a fall" (Proverbs 16:18) is burned into my psyche.

We talked for an hour and when I left Father David asked "Will you go back to the church now?"

"I don't know," I said. "Perhaps not. This place is very different from the organized church."

Sunday, September 2

Maybe I was being overly sensitive (or was it pride rearing its ugly head?), but I felt David's sermon was directed toward me—certainly those of my ilk..."Free riders who only coast along reaping any benefits they can, but avoiding the hard work of being a Catholic"...or words to that effect.

After mass, the desert sun shone brightly on clusters of retreatants, monks, and folks from town. There was much hugging, chatter, and laughter. Small tots and infants were held and hugged and tossed on high. Was I the only one wondering if these celibates ever miss having babies of their own? I learned a few families moved here from Arizona, following the Carmelites who had become such an important part of their lives. Remarkable when you consider Crestone is remotely located and has less than 300 people. Even the Crestone-Baca brochure boasts on its cover, "We got plenty of nothin'." One of the monks told me that one young family who'd moved here, was in fact, having serious financial problems. Their business was not doing well.

Mother Tessa was here for breakfast and for mass (where she, too, gave a brief, but joyous, sermon), having come down from Nova Scotia. She leaves tomorrow for a conference in Amsterdam. She will be on a panel with artists, scientists, economists, and philosophers. There was some discussion of post-modernism, most of which sailed over my head. Tessa, so natural, vivacious, and young (in her thirties, perhaps), yet definitely a leader, asked questions of her fellow monks and the retreatants surrounding the huge table in the Agape library.

"What is real?" she asked. "What is common sense?"

One of the monks laughed and offered, "If one needs to ask the question, one probably wouldn't understand anyway." David interjects, "You know I don't think the Buddhist monks have common sense." I don't remember his exact words but he commented upon their need to leave this realm in favor of nothingness, or some sort of never-never land. I wish I had thought to ask, then why the "Nada" in Nada Hermitage and Nova Nada? I am remembering Thomas Merton expressed a deeper affinity with Buddhist monks than with his Trappist brothers.

Genesis tells us humans have dominion over the earth. The Tao Te Ching reminds those who would reshape the earth to their will, never succeed. I was again reminded of differences between east and west as the discussion moved to the senses. This order derives great joy in taking a long, loving look at the *real*, at nature. Hinduism regards sense experience (maya), as illusion. Both seek harmony, love, and peace...an end to alienation from the divine. The difference may be mainly in semantics. However, Huston Smith calls Christianity the most materialistic of all religions. Jesus came in the flesh. As Father Will reminds, "Matter matters to us...Western mysticism is notoriously earthy."

I like what May Sarton wrote: "If one looks long enough at anything, looks with absolute attention at a flower, a stone, the bark of a tree, grass, snow, a cloud, something like revelation takes place. Something is 'given,' and perhaps that something is always a reality *outside* the self. We are aware of God only when we cease to be aware of ourselves...in the sense of losing self in admiration and joy."

Sarton went on to say that laughter has the same effect in achieving detachment. Laughter, too, held a seat at this table. Frustrations were voiced concerning funding the fine bridge they had built from the Chapel to the Agape. Someone lamented that television evangelists are exceedingly rich. "All we need is money for a little old bridge."

At this point, Brother Thomas, in his Tennessee accent, announced a great fund-raising idea. "How about 'DUNK A MONK'?" He volunteered to sit in the cage, said he'd willingly fall in the drink. "I'd be a great draw as a former IRS man. People would have a chance to sock it to the government and religion. How could we lose?"

I was constantly reminded of the teaching staff at Mountain Open Alternative High School. The same wit, spontaneity, vigor, love of life, dedication...and *smarts*! However, I always felt a lack of reverence at Open High School.

Eric—a mischievous bearded elf with a disarming smile—wears the beige "apron" of the novitiate. And dear, happy little Kay, also wears the beige over-garment. Her long blond hair is tied back with a three-cornered kerchief. She told me they designed their own garb. Her straight white teeth protrude ever so slightly. She looks 16 and she has asked me to deliver a letter to the Potts family when I go home.

David Denny looking like a Christ, writing like a Christ might write, preaching like a Christ, leading his monks in their dance to heaven. And only 36 years old. Ross is a handsome hunk, to use the vernacular. Long, curly hair is bleached white by the sun. Before coming here, he was a beach bum, surfing the beaches of California.

Ceil is an artist, a fine writer, painter, and potter. She made the plates and mugs used in the monastery. It's disconcerting to hear such uproarious, outrageous laughter come out of such a regal beauty. Ceil's biblical reading at mass was from Jeremiah. "You duped me, Lord. They laugh at me." (I'm quoting as best I remember.) "Continue to dupe us, Oh Lord," began Ceil's blessing before breakfast.

Susan, of the heavenly voice, sang a fast, happy, vibrant song, "Carry the Light," at mass this morning. She belted the words from the heart and every face wore a smile. More than a smile—silent, joyful laughter.

* * * * *

After breakfast, Jim played his tapes and did the calling for square dancing on the deck. Some monks changed into shorts and T-shirts. Others whirled and flew and stomped in their brown robes, their long skirts and ready laughter riding on the hot desert wind.

Jim explained the call "stack the wood" means give a bear hug to your partner. A great cheer went up and a request for more "stack the wood." Ceil told me Father William had advised "You know I think we do way too much hugging," so they had been cooling it. This seemed a marvelous means to circumvent that recommendation.

The music and dancing and good fun were well timed. The following day the monks began two weeks of silence.

<u>Monday, September 3</u>

I am in my fourth day of my six day retreat and am wondering what the day will bring. Father Will McNamara, who was not here this week, prescribes "Holy Leisure"...a means of leaving room for the unexpected.

Today the monks begin their two weeks of silence. The blissful stillness reminds me how much I miss Ralph. I've had thoughts of scooting home, but surely he, too, is enjoying his solitude. It's good for everyone now and then.

Nevertheless, whether the sun beats down unmercifully, or the black clouds gather over the mountain tops, or the northeast winds whistle across the dunes, I am constantly reminded—Ralph would love this. Next time, I hope we can come together for a three-day retreat. *If* he wishes.

The sun is high above the eastern mountains and shines brightly on this page. My hand casts a shadow as I write. My lap is warm. I'm still in my striped jersey nightgown. No doubt another 90-plus degree day is on the way.

Last night I went for a walk at dusk and met my neighbor, Jim, coming back from a swim in the creek. He's a construction worker from Los Angeles and, of course, also a square dance caller. Late forties, I'd guess—a few years older than my kids.

As we chatted, he reversed direction and began to walk with me. Agnes and Joline, the nurses from Denver, left yesterday.

Jim tells me it may be several months before he can evaluate this retreat. Says he often takes his truck into the California mountains in the Big Sur country and sleeps in the back, so it's not that he doesn't like being direction-less and on his own, but he's used to retreats being more organized.

"Father Joe conducts wonderful retreats at a center on the Pacific shores," he tells me. "Usually about 50 people attend and each hour is carefully scheduled. "Father Joe can lead you into deep contemplative prayer better than anyone I've encountered. We laid on the floor in the church. He'd read in a soft voice and play strange music. The first time I was ready to leave after two or three days, but I stuck out the week and went back nine years in a row."

I tell Jim this is my first retreat.

"At my other retreats there was lots of writing," he says. He peeks over his glasses and looks into my eyes. "Writing is prayer, you know." He confesses he doesn't usually do much writing, "but, Gee, once I did five pages at a sitting."

* * * * *

Often, I listen to tapes I've taken out of the library...several by Father William McNamara on Christian Humanism and also Thomas Merton's "Life and Prayer: The Desert Source." Father Will has the deep, rolling (and rollicking) voice of an Irish story teller. Merton's voice seems rather high-pitched in comparison.

I shall buy several of Father Will's tapes. Love his out-spoken admonitions. There are two ways of taking God's name in vain, he says, profanely and piously. "Pretty poison," he says, "in our *nicest* people—that's what's killing the religious life." He stresses concentrating on *Being*, on openness, receptiveness, on living in the fresh, exciting, inventive realm of the imagination. In the manner of Thoreau, he advises, "Waste one day a week." He urges, "Work up to a whole week! Break out of old patterns. Lie on the grass. Climb a tree. Live, love, and be free. Begin now!"

He calls J. D. Salinger our greatest spiritual writer. Hallelujah! He says, "We need the *Upanishads* and the *Bhagavad Gita*." Hallelujah!

He also says, "Come in or go out, but don't hang around the edges or you will perish."

Tuesday, September 4

This is my last day at Nada Hermitage. The monks are into their two weeks of silence. Thomas plans a three day hike on the Colorado trail. I wonder if he'll relate his experiences after the ribbing he received following his last sojourn into the wild. His fellow monks dubbed him "St. Francis" when he told them of his canoe trip. It seems a deer followed along the shoreline for miles, slowing when the canoe slowed, now and again making eye contact with the creature in the canoe.

The same thing happened to me one day as I was making the return trip up our steep and long driveway after my morning walk. A big seven-point bull elk walked up beside me, looking back each time he got some distance ahead, waiting, then continuing beside me. I was frightened remembering I'd been told more people had been killed by elk and deer in Yellowstone Park than by bears. It was with a real sense of relief that I dashed into my front door as the elk wandered on up the hill. It was also with a feeling of guilt for living in Eden and having usurped their land.

I'm watching Jim wash his windows inside and out. He shakes rugs and places houseplants outside for sun and air. He could come down here next, for I'm not planning to wash these windows.

* * * * *

Despite the period of silence, Betty was assigned to come by to say good-bye. She brought along a cup of coffee and stayed for an hour.

She tells me three families (Kay's, David's, and Susan's), are coming to visit in October. It will be a happy time for the entire community.

"You said, so did Father Dave, that there are many aspects of monastic life that are far from idyllic...like what?" I asked.

"Like all the problems we had building the eight new hermitages. The first contractor ripped us off. Like all the hard physical labor of getting this place going. It's true that in this wild and windy desert, you do learn to know God. You also learn to know who you are and that can be very painful."

That kind of pain is not confined to a monastery. Only the cold, hard objectivity of recognition can precipitate change. Thereafter, inner direction takes the driver's seat. How much easier and more comfortable the more traveled path W. H. Auden describes: "We would rather be ruined than changed,/ We would rather die in our dread/ Than climb the cross of the moment/ And let our illusions die."

* * * * *

It's late afternoon and thunder belches in the mountains. Overall, the weather has been hot, but it's also been changeable. Sun streamed in the windows this morning. Now black clouds roll in from the northeast. The winds whistle across the dunes and hum around the corners of my hermitage. Reminds me of our Illinois farm. I had the same peaceful feeling tucked safely inside my farm kitchen with its twelve-inch walls as the winds howled and screeched and rain swept across the prairie, looking like billowing white sheets against the red barn.

It's 4:24 p.m. The mountain top is covered with snow as rain begins to fall. There go Jim's clean windows. He told me he took the window latches apart, cleaning out the sand, then oiling them.

* * * * *

Before going to bed, I took Kazantzakis's *The Last Temptation of Christ* from my stocked bookshelf and read far into the night. His *Report to Greco* is one of my favorite books. How thrilled I was to see his statue in Crete. What a wild and diligent pilgrim. A pious scream goes up from the populace over the filming of this book. I've not seen the film. Disciplined wild men and women seem to be the pilgrims of preference around here. Indeed their brochure dubs "God himself absolutely wild, untamed, and free." I think Kazantzakis would fit in well with the hermits of the desert. Father Will might well argue with gusto and Oh! wouldn't it be exhilarating to eavesdrop on the dialogue.

Wednesday, September 5

I must clean my hermitage, tuck my notes into my suitcase and be gone. Good-byes were said Sunday before silence began. My! what bear hugs.

Like my neighbor, Jim, I suspect evaluation of this experience will come much later. Pieces of conversation, images from my window (like seeing Susan walk into the desert at dusk, out-lined against the pink sky, bushes up to her knees and then slowly slipping from view as she descends behind a dune on her way to her hermitage), joyous quips, ready laughter, and square dance music will drift back at unexpected moments illuminating unrelated happenings. Poignancy and paradox will pepper my memories of monks who describe themselves as: "earthy and mystical; orthodox and subversive; critical and creative; catholic and ecumenical;

traditional and visionary; poetic, prophetic, and practical." A mix like that *will* be remembered.

As I write this, I realize I've said nothing about my solitary visits to chapel. The windows wielded silent impact. Sunlight streamed through brightly colored glass depicting not saints and angels, but the suffering brethren of our earth. In one window a Native American, a South Asian refugee and child, a black slave, a howling coyote and a tortured tree. In another a crippled man, a ghetto youth, an Auschwitz prisoner, a weary woman, and a suffering dog. These, too, bear the cross of Christ in our imperfect world.

I found myself thinking suffering itself, contrary to popular belief, is not ennobling, but redemption is. And what is redemption if not rebirth into the passionate realm of the spirit? The grace of God. The holy enigma of the Christ.

In my view, there is great wisdom and beauty and truth in what Albert Schweitzer, has to say in *The Quest of the Historical Jesus*:

> He comes to us as one unknown, without a name as of old, by the lakeside, He came to those men who knew him not. He speaks to us the same word: 'Follow thou me!' and sets us to the tasks which He has to fulfill for our time. He commands. And to those who obey Him, whether they be wise or simple, He will reveal Himself in the toils, the conflicts, the sufferings which they shall pass through in His fellowship, and as an ineffable mystery, they shall learn in their own experience who He is.

Interestingly enough, Schweitzer urges Christians to drop all reconstructed Christologies and follow instead the spiritual example of Jesus Himself.

Or does that take an Albert Schweitzer?

***

A DAWN TRIP IN THE HEARTLANDS

It's dark as midnight as Ralph and I leave the Wayside Motel at 5:30 a.m. We're relieved to vacate the tacky room with grimy carpeting and chintzy paneling. We drive across the highway to the Colonial Cafe, free breakfast coupons in hand. I ask the waitress if Oakley, Kansas, was Annie Oakley's home territory.

"Well, we claim her." The words roll out slow and easy just behind a matching smile.

Five men in overalls saunter in and seat themselves around a table near the front door. A sixth fellow enters by the side door and walks past our booth toward the table of men.

"Damn seagulls." I smile as I read the caption on his bright blue cap. White splotches splatter the top and the beak.

"They're a protected species," Ralph explains.

"Whattya up to, Billy?" a voice from the table asks.

"'Bout six-foot-two," Billy replies, pulling another chair toward the table.

Ralph slides out of the booth heading for the cash register. An antique cream separator stands beside the counter. I check the handcrafted items for sale while Ralph proffers our coupons. The men smile and nod as we leave the cafe.

Our headlights shine on a billboard that says, "Welcome to Bob Dole country." The sun begins to creep above the horizon and ultimately blinds us. Ralph reaches for his sunglasses tucked behind the visor.

Here and there I notice windmills outlined against the pink horizon and I am reminded of Willa Cather's great black plough silhouetted against "a circle of molten red.... Picture writing on the sun." Kansas, like Cather's Nebraska, is a flat plain given to spectacular risings and settings of the sun.

Beef cattle dot the beige expanse of faded grassland. Tumbleweeds roll across the highway, piling themselves against the fences. Huge rolls of hay are snow-frosted. Here and there oil wells are pumping away—like those toy birds, whose beaks, when dipped in water, start bobbing up and down, up and down.

Country music plays on the radio. Two women make a pitch for money, asking listeners to call in and pledge dollars to the local PBS radio station.

"It's such a beautiful sunrise," one says. "We should have a picture window that goes right down to the floor."

"Oh, my! we can't waste our money like that," the other interrupts. "Folks need to know we work on a very tight budget."

A highway sign says 65 miles to Salina and the weatherman is saying 24 degrees. High in the low 40's today. Then a male voice reminds, "Now you be sure and call Town and Country Chevy. And, yeah, I write my own stuff. You've got my name. You know who I am." His slow twang continues.

In my part of the world, automobile commercials are rattled off at the speed of an auctioneer's song, so they can crowd 100 words into ten seconds. This fellow takes his time. "I believe what I say," the Town and Country Chevy voice says. "You know that."

Thereafter, Paul Harvey reports—in that warm, trustworthy voice that seems so right in Kansas—that a fellow robbed three grain elevators. The first two went just fine, but the third time the culprit broke his ankle and issued a statement from jail. "There just ain't no use worryin'. Nuthin's gonna turn out all right anyway."

Now that's hard to believe as we travel an arrow-straight highway in Kansas. Often we can see for miles. We make guesses, then check the odometer to see who's best at estimating distance. A billboard says Brookville Inn. Ralph reads it aloud as "Brookfield Inn."

"That's Brookville. You said Brookfield. Don't tell me your eyes are going as well as your ears."

"No, I said Brookville. You're almost as deaf as I am," he says. "Sometimes I think you have the same problems as I do."

"You know you're absolutely right. Big of you to admit it." He laughs. "I like that," he says.

A sign advertises Prairie Dog Town. Another says, Salina, 29 miles. Then I see one that gives me pause.

"Did you see that sign?"

"Yeah." Ralph laughs. "Garden of Eden...it looked like a legitimate state road sign. Wonder what that's all about?"

I don't question it. As we pass Saline County line, it's early morning in America's heartland and all is right with the world. If we ever doubted it, a male voice sings a reassuring song just for us—tourists driving through. He will not be hurried. In a twangy, convincing tone, he croons:

"There's no place like Salina, not anywhere we know,
Some call it the good life, but we call it home.
Clean of mind and body, it's a place
where each can grow."

It was the winning entry, the announcer explains, in a song-writing contest sponsored by the National Bank of Salina, Kansas.

A sign reads: Abilene—28 miles.

And we have miles to go before we sleep.

***

THE NINETEENTH DAY OF SEPTEMBER

September looks warm and welcoming, but she keeps a cool steel scissors in her apron pocket. Now and again she snips a ribbon of wind. I shiver as I leave the house pulling my sweater tighter about me. The sunlight glazes our cut stone wall and darts through the flicking locust leaves. The green fronds move swiftly, like my mother's fingers on piano keys.

I have no planned destination so I head east and cut through the small park and playground. It's deserted now. The kids are back in school. The grass is long.

I dig my feet into the worn and dusty path and whirl myself about on the merry-go-round, much as I did half a century ago. I slide down the slide—after glancing quickly toward the windows of the houses nearby, but not really caring if I see faces peering back. I note the legs at the base of the slide are broken. That could be disastrous; I might be plopped in the mud. Risks turn minutes into moments, I decide. The downward sweep is extra steep because of the buckled lower legs. The swish is so exhilarating that I retrace my climb and risk another slide.

I climb the grassy bank to walk the path along the reservoir. Far ahead, outlined against the sky, I see two men cutting the grass. One leans toward his machine again and again jerking the rope to re-start the motor. I walk a great distance, and almost reach him before he finally gets it going. The men smile and wave. Their lips shape greetings I do not hear above the roar of the power mowers.

Farther on I sit on the rocky slope and wish for a pond more natural, but water soothes, even in a reservoir. A few fish jump and echoing rings explode around their vanishing point.

I've walked almost two miles before I swoop down the grassy bank and lose sight of a flock of ducks bobbing in the water. I head back toward the pathway through the park.

From the tall grass near the gate something suddenly flies in front of me and lands a few feet ahead. It's much too large for a grasshopper. Aha! a praying mantis. I kneel beside it. We are parallel and both positioned as in prayer. I laugh when the realization strikes me. It seems apropos as we study each other in fascination and wonder: strange, unique facets of creation and re-creation; two parts of that magical ongoing process.

The mantis has the look of a mechanical toy (a live body wouldn't bend the way his does). Even his movement seems mechanized as he turns his triangular head toward me. The long antennae shoot outward. In the upper corners of his three-sided face are two mammoth bright green eyes. In amazement, I note he has pupils just like mine! Then the tiny black pin dots sort of float to the top of the green circles. He looks cross-eyed and I tell him that.

As if insulted, he turns his head away looking straight ahead. I laugh and apologize, "I'm sorry if I hurt your feelings. Come on now, look around again at me." And he does!

His long delicate back legs, like jointed nylon thread with fringed ends for feet, rest lightly on the tops of blades of grass. Still he balances there, swaying with a strong and sudden wave of wind. He unfolds one front praying leg...or "hand."

The wings on his back are brown and glossy. They look like the thin tobacco leaves that wrap a cigar. I pick blades of grass and wave them in front of him, and when I almost touch him with a plucked dandelion leaf, he flies away wings flapping in the September sun. He sails into a roofed shelter house and I follow looking in the rafters and on the cement floor, but I've lost him for his shape disappeared when he left the sun and entered the shade of the building.

I take the homeward path. Three great lumps, and then a fourth, erupt from the asphalt walk. My first thought is moles, but moles couldn't crawl under macadam walkways. And there are no tunnels, just hills raised high with crumbling centers. I look into the craters hoping to meet the guilty culprits. I am not disappointed. Small seedlings are bursting through making mountains, buckling stone and tar that they may smile at the sky. They never stopped to consider this is

THE NINETEENTH DAY OF SEPTEMBER

September.   How brief their season in the sun but how contagious their celebration

How blind we become to the ongoing miracle of creation. Some days it takes a walk in the sun, a praying mantis, or an erupting seed to reawaken the wonder that is second nature to a child.

***

BEHIND THE WALLS OF AVILA

It was 9:30 on a cold night in February as my husband and I approached Avila, Spain, from the north, having driven from Salamanca, and having missed the new super highway. We later learned this roadway affords the best view of the walled medieval city and the snow-capped Gredos Sierra mountains behind the town. Serendipitous mishaps were to be the hallmark of our Avila adventure. The sudden sight of the massive lighted stone walls jumping from the darkness was unsettling. I sucked in my breath. Surely we'd taken an unlikely turn in the road, leading us back into the Middle Ages, or into a fictitious never-never land.

Ten feet thick, thirty-three feet high, with a rectangular perimeter of one and one-half miles, the stone barricades have nine gateways and are reinforced with eighty-eight cylindrical turrets. Although construction began in 1090, soon after the town was reclaimed from the Moors, the walls are intact, so unlike the crumbling remnants that pepper the hilltops of Spain.

"The walls accentuate the city's closed-in-upon-itself austerity.... the sense of gravity and sobriety is almost tangible," states the Berlitz travel guide. Most travel books paint a dour picture of this city of churches, birthplace and home of Saint Teresa, mystic and diligent reformer of the Carmelite order of nuns. "Avila looks wild and slightly sinister in the middle of a windswept plateau littered with giant primeval-looking boulders....Avila today is well preserved, but with a sad, austere, and desolate atmosphere," says Fodor's book on Spain. "Few towns this size are so disturbingly quiet after dark."

A welcome change, we felt, from boisterous Madrid. Madrilènes never sleep. Troubadours strummed guitars and sang lustily beneath our hotel window while vehicles swarmed Madrid's streets—all night long. We slept well in Avila's Parador Raimundo de Borgona...after a gracious young couple escorted us through a labyrinth of winding passageways to the front door.

I had serious misgivings about this trip. We don't speak Spanish and we had no guide to marshal us about. Two elderly innocents abroad, dashing about in a tiny red Citroen, Baedeker firmly in hand. In Avila, as elsewhere, we were rescued.

We stopped to ask directions of a strolling couple. The young woman spoke only Spanish. Her companion said he'd not spoken English in nine years. He shrugged helplessly— there was simply no way to map the circuitous route we must take. "It's on the other side of the city." Suddenly, his face brightened, "We'll take you there!"

They folded themselves into the tiny back seat and directed us, via halting English and flailing arms, through a bewildering maze of narrow cobblestone streets with sharp turns and steep inclines, until the restored palace which was our parador, loomed before us.

No, no, they would not allow us to drive them anywhere, nor would they accept payment. "We're just out walking," they said. They smiled, waved, and were enveloped by the night.

The next morning we set forth to explore the city of Teresa Sanchez de Cepeda y Ahumanda...Santa Teresa de Jesus. Born in 1515 to an affluent Avila family, she became a Carmelite nun at eighteen and by age forty began reforming her order, which she felt had become lazy and dissolute. Teresa founded seventeen convents, preached throughout Spain, and wrote extensively. Among her writings are letters to her spiritual advisor, Saint John of the Cross, who also lived in Avila.

We trudged the narrow, cobblestone streets that now and again opened into plazas. Steep, twisting passageways rose and fell among shops and palaces, churches and monasteries. Sweet shops asked high prices for Saint Teresa's yemas, the rich egg-yolk candies she distributed to the poor. Enormous stork nests balanced on skinny convent chimneys. The lanky birds paraded atop stone walls, unfolding their wings, making clacking noises.   Avila offers a feast for fanciers of Romanesque art and architecture.   Churches abound, within and without the walls.   The 12th century cathedral is itself embedded in the walls, thus becoming a part of the defense system.   The San Juan Church where Saint Teresa was baptized stands in the center of the city.   The   Basilica   of   Saint Vincent, located outside the walls is near the main entrance and the oldest gate.   It was founded in 1307 on the site where Saint Vincent and his sisters were martyred around 304.

Other churches include San Andres, San Segundo, San Pedro, and the Monastery of Saint Thomas.   The latter was founded by Ferdinand and Isabella in 1482, and once housed the tomb of Grand Inquisitor Tomas de Torquemada, which was destroyed by 19th century revolutionaries.   A simple slab now marks his burial site in the sacristy.

It is, of course, Saint Teresa, patron saint of Spain, who gives renown to Avila.   In the 17th century, the Convent of Santa Teresa was founded on the site of her birthplace.   A small museum contains artifacts, relics, and her beautifully handwritten manuscripts.

Just north of the walled city is the Convento de la Encarnacion, where Saint Teresa spent her first twenty-two years as a nun before beginning her reforms.   The museum houses a reconstruction of Teresa's tiny cell.   Her letters and personal effects are displayed upstairs.   The guidebook also mentioned an "interesting drawing of the crucifixion by Saint John of the Cross," and his small chair, indicating he was a man of slight physical stature.

It was 4:30 in the afternoon when we arrived at la Encarnacion.   The sun, still warm and bright, was sliding to meet the land.   Long gray shadows were falling on the forbidding walls of Avila to the south.

To our dismay, the door to the museum was locked, although a sign said it should be open until 6:00 p.m.   A young man in black emerged from heavy wooden double doors in a stone wall edging the courtyard.   He spoke to five women clustered outside the main entrance, then continued his liquid

Spanish lingo to four men who were rushing about, sputtering in Spanish, frantically trying doors that were locked. The men paced about in utter frustration but finally they climbed into their tiny black car. One fellow was not about to give up until the occupants in the car called angrily and motioned him into the door they held open. They wheeled from the curb and sped away.

After awkward attempts to make ourselves understood, we discovered the young man who'd been offering help spoke English. Roberto was a Catholic missionary from Puerto Rico. These Carmelites, he told us, live via the strict austerity of Saint Teresa.

Roberto attends mass in the church each morning. "The sisters put heaters in the chapel for us, but have none themselves, and it's sometimes *very* cold. We hear them sing at mass, but can never see them. Their voices are so beautiful."

He told us he had just put in a request for their prayers concerning the success of his impending mission. "I always come and ask for their prayers." Then his eyes smiled and caught my own as if seeking to reinforce his conviction: "They sound so happy. I believe they are very close to God." His teeth were straight and white, his eyes almost black and very merry.

We talked at length and finally he suggested, "Come with me, you may talk to one of the sisters." Ignoring my feeble protests, he swept his arm forward. "Come along." He led us through the heavy double doors into an enclosed stone hallway. It was like emerging from the warmth and light of day into a cool, darkened theater. We groped and felt our way with small, careful footsteps that echoed in the stillness. Another door opened into a tiny, dimly lit room with stone walls and floors. There was no artificial light, but a few shafts of sunlight slid through narrow slits in the walls and made bright patches on the floor.

Roberto motioned toward the button on the wall next to "the turn." He whispered, "Ring the bell," and he was gone.

"Would you like me to leave too?" my husband asked.

Feeling very unsure of myself, I nodded yes, and pushed the button to summon I knew not who.

A voice responded, in Spanish. "Oh, dear, can anyone speak English?" I asked.

Immediately, she shifted to English. I explained I was from the United States and had hoped to visit the museum. About now, I was feeling pretty foolish. (Why did I do this? What great reason do I have for ringing the bell in a cloistered convent?)

The lively voice behind the wooden turn explained that she, too, was from the United States. What a shock. (My Goodness! she sounds so young. Well, why not? Are all nuns old?)

Why didn't I ask where in the United States? I wish I had. Each time I would begin a timid and apologetic farewell, she would ask another question. "Where are you from?" "Have you seen the Cathedral...or visited the Convent Saint Teresa founded in Avila?" "Have you seen much of Spain?" "What are your impressions?" "Do you like it?" "Are you traveling alone?" Her conversation was punctuated with a bright and lilting laugh. She seemed to welcome, indeed relish, small talk concerning the world outside her walls of stone.

She suggested I ring the bell at the museum door. "If the caretaker is there, she may let you inside." (This came to naught.) She asked if I knew of the Carmelite nuns in Littleton, Colorado, since I lived so near. Did I know Sister Bernadette? No. (Why, I wonder, would she think I might know a cloistered nun?)

Suddenly, with happy surprise in her voice, "Would you take a letter to the sisters in Littleton?"

"Of course, I'd be happy to do that."

"Oh, good, good!" she said. "Now don't go away. I will be right back." After a few minutes, she placed two envelopes on the turn, one unsealed, one sealed. "One for you and your husband," she said. "One for the sisters in Littleton."

Perhaps it wasn't all that unusual. I do know it was an engulfing and unexpected happiness, the kind that characterized Avila. Making my way through the heavy wooden doors, I stepped back into the sunlight, shielding my eyes, feeling warm, filled with delight, and struck with the wonder of a child,

When I delivered the letter to another wooden "turn" in Littleton, I asked the nun if she knew where in the U.S. the sister in Avila had lived. She didn't know. Sister Bernadette had not answered the bell, but the nun to whom I spoke laughed incredulously, "Can you *imagine that?* A letter from the other side of the world!" She sounded old.

She said, yes, they too, live under the rigid and austere rules in effect at the Avila convent.

I told the Littleton nun that I was going to read all the works of Saint Teresa I could get my hands on. Somerset Maugham called her autobiography one of the greatest ever written.

"You're welcome in our chapel and library any time. You might find material of interest," she said. "It's usually open, but unfortunately, today it's locked for cleaning."

Deja vu! I remember Avila.

***

THE WALK TO VISIT MOTHER

Each day I walk to mother's house, and so the walk is familiar but rarely pleasant.

She used to live in a small gray bungalow Dad built when they were newly married. The house perched comfortably among box elders and a stately pine. A slightly listing picket fence of faded white placed a loving arm along the south lot line. Mother wanted it constructed so that cars entering the repair shop at the back of Dad's Chevy garage wouldn't run onto the lawn.

After Dad died, following fifty-three years of marriage, mother left her own small and quiet town for another nearer us. A year later, my husband's job change necessitated moving three hundred miles to another state. When we moved, so did my octogenarian mother and mother-in-law.

Mother's apartment is one and one-half miles from our home. Leaving stillness, space, and certitude for unfamiliar, busy urbanity has meant unpleasant change for all concerned.

In my daily trek, I postpone walking along the busy highway and hug the golf course as far as I am able. Synthetic nature is better, I guess, than no nature.

Rambling roses edge the fairways. Clasping the thorny hedge: plastic bags, tin cans, beer bottles, foil wrappers, bent boxes, paper plates and crumpled newspapers. An old inner tube, inflated, dangles from atop a twisted shrub. A torn jacket lies sodden in the mud. Last Monday I found a dandy aluminum mixing bowl.

On today's journey, my face is licked by winds. I encounter three robins, one crow, one mourning dove; two dogs running free, one tied and barking. I meet one person— unisex—in slacks and hooded tweed jacket. "It" nods, smiles, and hurries on its way.

Reluctantly, as I reach the hamburger joint, I turn and head toward the thoroughfare. It's a U.S. highway. Traffic roars unceasingly. From inside my house, I can hear it through

176

the day and through the night.

I meet the driver of a semi-truck, a young girl with long blond hair. My liberated, married, but maiden-named daughter would say, "And so?" So it just looked a little odd, that's all. Such an enormous machine maneuvered by such a fragile-looking creature.

A semi I saw yesterday had what looked like a pretty girl seated near the driver. A raised hand coyly covered her smile. The driver waved as he zoomed past. I noticed then that the beautiful girl was a cardboard figure. I wonder, does a paper doll to call your own, alleviate loneliness?

For quite a stretch there is no sidewalk. I duck under a viaduct. Large stones poke at my feet through the soles of my boots. Where do all the trucks come from and where are they going? They rumble overhead and roll under the raised highway. The swelling sounds and pungent smells are tightened, concentrated, and funneled through the under-passage. I, too, fumble through the mire of noise, blurred machines, and rancid air.

I check mother's mailbox in the hall before rapping "Shave and a haircut—two bits." It takes Mama a while to answer the door. Creeping from the davenport, she seems half-awake, sans glasses, teeth, most of her hair, and the bounce and buoyancy that once marked her step. Her knees are swollen, her broken wrist, though mended, twists painfully to one side. I smell Ben Gay ointment.

Whatever the time, she's had no food that day. "I'm just not hungry, really." By the time I leave, we've had a small ham sandwich, a cookie, and a cup of green tea. With mouth and eye appendages attached, she has joined the land of the living one more time. However, her refrain remains the same, "If only I could die. I want to be with Dad." Tears well behind her glasses.

She's had no interests, ever, except perpetual and extreme worrying about her loved ones. Just last week, a few minutes after I left, she walked out her front door peering down the street to check on my progress. I had stopped in the store and she was terrified when she couldn't spot my red jacket. She asked her neighbor to drive her toward my house.

With little to fill her aging hours, her anxiety has grown. She looks into my eyes and almost whispers, "I wish," she sighs, and then repeats, "I wish...I could have peace of mind."

"Mama, did you ever?"

"No, never," she replies.

The pain in her eyes will haunt me for hours. She refuses to live with me, as does my mother-in-law, so afraid she'll be a burden.

Grabbing her navy blue coat and little knitted cap that ties under her chin, she walks part way with me when I leave. She cuts across the super-market parking lot and suggests I cross the street quickly while the light is red. We wave good-bye.

From the motel, I look back and she's nearing the store. We wave to one another one more time. Her tiny figure blurs through watery eyes.

***

THE NUMINOUS

REBA

And the light shineth in darkness,
and the darkness did not comprehend it.

John 1,5

A friend from Ohio just sent me Reba Carter's obituary. It says she died at age 99. It's enough to make me question the indomitable tenacity for life that seems imbedded in the human species—that which is usually marked for passing from generation to generation, but which in Reba seemed cemented to her bulky frame. From all indications, she felt destined to remain on this earth to the bitter end...to keep things going when the parts squeaked or seemed to be wearing thin, to poke and prod, to rouse the lazy and the old, to put the apathetic to shame. So convincing was her determination, that I am more than a little doubtful she has really died. I am tempted to telephone, to hear it first hand, but in remembering Reba, I wonder what that would prove.

Instead, I sit in the October dusk with the clipping in my lap. In the newspaper picture, her face is shaded by a broad-brimmed black hat. Her unusual hats were a kind of trademark; they were often large. The write-up describes her as the founder of the city's symphony orchestra, a distinguished piano teacher and patron of the arts. Reba was all those things and more: wife, then widow of a state senator; mother, grandmother, great-grandmother; grand matriarch and fairy godmother of the town. Rumor said she was the generous and anonymous million dollar donor for the proposed Center for the Performing Arts.

One of her famous former students came from New York one cold, snowy day in January and performed in the Great Memorial Hall downtown. He dedicated an original composition to Reba, said she was responsible for his success: "She positively *willed* it!" She was spotlighted and asked to stand.   The pianist, in white tie and tails, bowed toward her from the stage and the filled hall reverberated with clapping and cries of "BRAVO!"

When I lived in her town, Reba was in her mid-90's and she walked with two canes, heaving her considerable weight from one side to the other as she stumbled forward— unsteadily, but surely, nonetheless, refusing any offers of help. "I can manage better alone." She'd wave one of her canes in a manner less menacing than definitive.   She never wore glasses and could read fine print without them.   Her large straight teeth were her own.   Reba did, however, suffer from severe palsy. Her head, as well as her hands, shook and even her deep voice had a quaver.   It was something she chose to belittle, if not ignore, as if refusing to succumb to its humiliations would deny it power over her person.

But if she were to keep active socially, there were certain concessions she had to make.   In the dining room of the Argonne Hotel (where she lived), and at Shawnee Country Club (of which she was a charter member), her place was always set with heavy silverware bearing thick bamboo handles—the better for grasping.   She ate from a large, flat bowl rather than a dinner plate and a bent glass straw wobbled around in her glass of milk.

Tim Blakely still runs the old Argonne Hotel his father built at the turn of the century.   It's the tallest building in the heart of town and celebrities stayed there when the Opera House stood on Market Street, where Kresge's five and dime is now.   A model of the Opera House is on display in the Historical Museum.   Reba remembered it well.   She told stories about Madam Schumann-Heink and Caruso and the town's dignitaries in top hats and velvet gowns.   "It was an exciting time to be alive.   All the glamour of Hollywood without the chintzy glitz."

Those days disappeared, and with them the heyday of the Argonne Hotel.   Tim made efficiency apartments out of several of the upstairs rooms.   A creaky ancient elevator carries the old folks up and down.

Reba moved to the sixth floor after her pillared mansion on Carter Boulevard (named for Senator Carter) was sold. From there she could keep a careful eye on Market Street and Vine and she had a clear view of the library, Gregg's Department Store, and the center square with its new fountain and gazebo.

We were fairly new in town the Wednesday noon that Mother and I walked into the faded elegance of the Crystal Dining Room of the Argonne Hotel. There were red carpets, crystal chandeliers, and dusty velvet drapes tied back to reveal intricately patterned lace curtains. Tim Blakely himself was ushering us into the room when Reba Carter waved him toward her table. She was presiding at a long table where 14 persons were seated. A couple of empty chairs remained and she directed us to take them. Whether she mistook us for invited guests, or chose to extend a welcome to newcomers, I was never sure. She asked our names and thereafter proceeded to behave as if she'd always known us. Thus, quite unwittingly, we stumbled into "Wednesday at the Argonne."

That was but one more cultural institution begun by Reba. She noticed too many of her peers spent their afternoons glued to TV sets watching soap operas. When she took the elevator to the lobby, things were no better. She noted Fred Hall, bald and eighty-eight, sleeping in a tattered, overstuffed chair. Mamie Darcy, once an elementary school teacher, played solitaire under the lighted lamp on a little corner table. The room was dark, even though it was midday. The ceilings were high, the draperies heavy. Reba would swing her cane and tap the foot of a snoozing old man or woman, then try to engage either in conversation.

All in all, she saw need for immediate action. "Disgusting! Why vegetate?" she'd complain. "I never could see the sense in it!" And so her creation known as "Wednesday at the Argonne" was duly inaugurated.

Some said she also instigated it to help Tim's finances. A few local businessmen stopped in for lunch and one Tuesday each month the Rotary Club ate there, but usually only the old people who lived upstairs occupied the dining room at noontime.

Reba called her good friend, a lady insurance agent, to help organize bimonthly programs which were open to the public. No fee was paid to those making presentations, but local participants rallied to the cause, inviting their own guests to insure a good turnout and willingly contributing time and talent.

The young artist-in-residence from the local branch of the state university showed his paintings and read Shel Silverstein's poems. To the latter, Reba Carter responded spontaneously: "Bravo!" she cried, clapping, and leaping to her feet with uncommon grace after a captivating and capricious poem about a boy who'd lost his head, then couldn't find it because his eyes were in it. Thinking it a rock, he stopped to rest and sat upon it.

"Read it again," she said. "It's perfectly delightful. Too many of us forget what our heads are for. I've seen several that were attached and could still be mistaken for rocks. Don't you agree, young man?"

Her own head, attached and still in working order, nevertheless bobbed about, quite out of control. Like a cruel joke, it kept time to her laughter. The poem was read once more; the illustration held on high.

The museum director showed slides of historic buildings and the oldest homes in town. A missionary from India, on a hometown visit, shared stories and slides and saris. Musicians from the Symphony Orchestra, many of whom had taken piano lessons from Reba, comprised duets, trios, and quartets; playing violins, flutes, and cellos. Travelogues were presented by vacationers returned from exotic locations.

Reba Carter asked me to present a program and a few days after the presentation, she called and invited me, and also my mother, to join her for lunch at the Shawnee Country Club. She sounded offended at my offer to drive. "My old Cadillac doesn't get enough exercise," she said. This despite her trek to the hotel garage each morning to start the engine and let it run a few minutes. "It mustn't give up. There's a lot of good life left in it."

She told me when John was alive she did all the driving. "He'd sleep, but he kidded me—said he always woke up to see a policeman at my car window—writing out a ticket, don't you see?"

Reba never outgrew the speeding habit. She had to drive to the opposite side of town to pick us up...first me, and then my mother. We sailed to the far north side as if jet-propelled. A light turning amber was her signal to push the gas pedal to the floor. We burned rubber. As we careened around a corner, she glanced backward waving her arm in that general direction. "I grew up in that big green house with the huge front porch." It was a blur behind us. "Horrible color. My father always kept it painted white."

Mother's frail white hand grabbed my arm as she evoked her maker. "God help us!" she cried. Her tiny frame whipped next to mine, like a peanut finger-snapped from a table top.

"I've been driving for well over 70 years. Never had a serious accident. A bump here, a scratch there. No lives lost." Reba laughed. She was attempting to pacify my mother. "Comes time to renew my license, I go over to Elida. It's much easier to spin around that little town. I always ask for the same young fellow to run me through my paces. Name's Charlie Simms. He's a lad of about 50. Last time I did miss one stop sign. 'Let's try that one more time,' says I. You know he let me whiz around the block once more. You can be sure I didn't miss it the next time."

Hobbling into the luxurious foyer of the country club, Reba marveled at my 86 year old mother. "Just look at her—perking along without a cane."

And Mother, wide-eyed and overwhelmed, was saying, "My, I'm glad we moved to Ohio—I'd never have known what the inside of a country club looked like." She peeked into the cloak room but decided to keep her coat. "I don't see anyone in charge. A body could walk off with any wrap he took a mind to." Hers was from the Goodwill, but it was cashmere and had a real mink collar. She could well have afforded to buy it in the finest store, but there was no greater thrill than finding second-hand bargains.

Mama leaned forward for a closer look at the big oil paintings with the little lights attached to the top of the frames. "Saints be praised! How elegant can they get? Now do you think we'll know how to behave?"

When Mother had difficulty reading the menu, Reba was visibly alarmed. "Take off your glasses, dear. Let me have a look." Mama did as she was bade, but unused to seeing the world firsthand, sans spectacles, she squeezed her tired eyes open and closed, as if to focus her vision. Reba's nose almost bumped Mother's as she tilted her head this way, then that, peering into my mother's eyes. Reluctantly admitting she couldn't make a diagnosis, she settled for reading the menu choices aloud to Mother.

A bent old dowager crept to our table. "And how's Charlie?" Reba Carter asked her friend.

"Why he died last April."

"He *did*?" She was incredulous. "What on earth of?"

"It's called old age, Reba. He was 92," the little lady answered with a chuckle. She patted Reba's shoulder before moving on to her own table. It was an explanation Reba brushed aside—by design or otherwise, it seemed beyond her understanding.

Her own husband, John, died at eighty-five. Reba blamed it on his lack of exercise. As a state senator and a lawyer, she felt he sat at a desk too much. "Although I will say his mind was always busy. But he plain forgot about his body."

Reba never neglected her own exercise. She walked to the hotel garage each day to exercise her "Caddy." On her way back, she made an extra trip down the hall and back. She did the same when she returned from lunch and dinner. One day she lay on the floor to try a workout with Jack Lelaine on the television. Trouble was she couldn't get up again. She managed to maneuver herself toward the telephone, pulled it to the floor and called Tim Blakely to come and rescue her. Tim's wife told me, "Tim was scared to death. Thought she'd fallen or had a stroke. Honest to God, I think she forgets she'll never see 90 again." Milly Blakely laughed and gave Reba credit, "What a woman!"

I was thinking about that as I sat across the table from my hostess at the country club. The image of Reba floundering on the floor like a beached whale was funny-sad, and it ill-befitted her present dignity. Her black velvet-trimmed hat had a generous brim which swept away from her face on the left side. It complemented her gray crepe dress which was likewise trimmed with black velvet.

My mother was telling Reba she had also been a piano teacher in her younger years. Reba's eyes registered a delighted empathy and she leaned forward to reveal a secret. "You see this?" From beneath her dress, Reba pulled forth a gold medal on a chain. It had a small diamond in the center and the engraving said she'd won "First Prize" in a competition sponsored by the Chicago Symphony Orchestra.

"It's a long story," she said. There was a kind of sweet anguish in her voice. "I was sixteen and could have followed a career as a concert pianist. But I met John a few years later and knew my path should take that turn. No regrets." Still, I wondered just a mite why she wore the tiny medal near her heart for all those years.

Before we left, she insisted the chef come out into the dining room, even though she was told he was extremely busy. She complimented him and he bowed with his hands folded beneath his apron. Then Reba advised our young waitress on how to improve her service. The girl, following the chef's example, was equally obsequious. I found it embarrassing to witness the exhibition.

When my husband accepted a new job in Colorado which was to begin in January, I went to the Argonne to say goodbye to Reba. She was sitting in the lobby wearing her heavy coat and scarf. Her hair was stuffed under a ridiculous brown knitted cap that had a beak in the front. Wisps of white hair stuck out at the back of her neck. Perhaps she'd been out to the hotel garage or next door to pick up sweets at the bakery. She was not her stylish self, but she offered neither excuse nor explanation.

"I hate to see you go—you know that," she said.

"Maybe you can come to Colorado to see us."

She shifted her body in the chair and laughed. "I rather doubt that." I knew that each winter she flew alone to Florida to see her daughter and I also knew I had become very close to her.

"Lots of paths cross," she said, "and then part, and that's the end of that. It doesn't always mean a lot. With us, it's special. We both know it." She patted my hand. "My dear, I wish you well. It was probably meant to be—the light is all around us, always pointing the way. We have only to open our hearts to see the splendor." She said something about St. John. It was her favorite book of the Bible. "Oh, that John," her eyes crinkled. "He was a poet!"

We talked of many things that day. She told me lately she was now and then leaving her body and looking down at herself. "Now mind you, I don't tell that to just anyone. A good many would call me dotty. To tell the truth, it surprised me the first time it happened. Well, of course, I meditate and pray, but I didn't expect *that*, I tell you." While she talked, she was glancing across the room to the lobby desk where Tim was sorting the residents' mail and tucking letters into boxes. Her eyes shifted back to me. "The experience is teaching me a lot about myself."

I couldn't keep that conversation going. I hardly knew what to say. She had a parting warning about our impending move. "Every time one door closes, other doors open. That's very true, you know. I've noticed it in the patterns of my life. But you have to be awake to see them open."

Her eyes were faded and blue and watery, and my eyes fell on her black oxfords and heavy legs when I leaned over to kiss her goodbye. One cane slipped to the floor and I propped it up next to her chair.

I wrote her several times, but she never wrote back. I'm sure her palsied hands would not allow it. Occasionally she would call, like the time my mother fell and broke her hip. "Why she's not even 90!" The voice shook, but the message was strong and clear. "Don't *allow* her to give up." Mother did give up and she died three days later. Once more Reba couldn't understand it, although she called and said she figured it must have happened.

"My dear, I entered your consciousness that very afternoon," she said. "Had me baffled. I didn't think such a thing was possible. It was a new one on me, but that's the only way I can explain it. I entered your consciousness and you were so very sad. Your husband was near and one of your daughters. It was very real—nothing at all like a dream."

Then she wanted to know if new doors had opened in our Colorado location. When she didn't receive a quick, straightforward answer, she said she knew they would. "But you must be aware," she warned.

I'm staring at her picture and I try to see her eyes, but they're shaded by the hat. No matter, for they could only gaze lifelessly from a photograph. Reba wasn't really into looking anyway. She favored seeing.

I reach behind me to turn off the lamp. The obituary and the evening darkness fall softly into my lap as I listen and open myself to all that is. The Chinook hums through the canyon and a cool chill settles into the hollows as the sun slips behind Doubleheader Mountain.

***

HALLOWE'EN MEANS HOLY

October 31, 1983

I'm teaching at an alternative high school—like many of its kind, a step-child of the district. The roof leaks, the furniture is hand-me-down, the classrooms are grim and foreboding.

My feelings, too, are bleak as I reassess priorities. I am confused and baffled by the unorthodox goings-on...no grades, no rules nor regulations, no consequences. I am more comfortable with the mores of another age.

Nevertheless, this hallowed day I will remember.

Two veterans of the Vietnam conflict have come to show us the movie they made. The recording studio is crowded—a pleasant surprise. Too often it's embarrassing how few students show up at special functions.

Students are sitting on the floor and on tattered sofas and chairs. A white-faced clown with 'starry eyes' and a wide crimson smile sits cross-legged on a wobbly table. The polka-dot suit has ruffles at the neck, cuffs, and ankles. A white scalp-cap is fringed with orange hair.

John has oiled his blond hair until it looks black. His sleeveless black T-shirt says "Stray Cats." He wears one golden earring. A rock band member wears her usual black leather vest with laced front exposing too much of her bosom. The regular punks are joined today by masqueraders with painted faces and hair that is shaved, dyed, frazzled, or spiked. When Brenda enters made up as a prominently pregnant nun, I feel a vague discomfiture. As I sidle behind the piano, my jacket rubs against the chalkboard and I read the message I've blurred: "Let it be known that I am insane, and therefore null and void according to the guidelines of society."

The two young veterans step forward wearing jeans, plaid shirts and hiking boots. One has wavy brown hair that touches his collar and a luxuriant beard. The other fellow is clean-shaven, with short red hair and clear blue eyes. He must have worn freckles as a boy and their disappearance seems his single reluctant concession to adulthood. His face wears the open look of an innocent child. He is called Rusty.

Their documentary, "How Far from Home," focuses on the adjustments of vets returning from Vietnam. The film-makers point out the same things have been happening in our society that happened to the fighting men of this war: "Our culture has faced the same crisis, metamorphosed in much the same way as has the veteran of Vietnam." No one interrupts to ask exactly what they mean. I find myself remembering an earlier war, which in our age of innocence, we found easier to justify.

No doubt about it, something exciting and wondrous is happening to human consciousness in our time. It's hard now to imagine anyone regarding war as a noble kind of glory. Terrifying technological leaps may, of necessity, give birth to a corresponding quantum leap in mind and spirit. Ernest Renan noted in 1863, "The most beautiful things in the world are done in a state of fever; every great creation involves a breach of equilibrium; a violent state of being which draws it forth."

The lights dim. The film rolls. The audience watches as one, until even that separation evaporates and witnesses become emotional participants in what they see.

There are scenes at the dedication of the Vietnam War Memorial in Washington, D.C. Not content to let the stark monument speak its eloquence alone, families prop flags, photographs, and flowers in front of the names etched on the shiny black granite—in order of dying. Land and sky, men who lived and men who died, are mirrored in the monolith—until one cannot separate real from unreal, the living from the dead, man from reflected image, mind from spirit. The intellect draws lines, the imagination denies boundaries.

A veteran in the film (it happens to be Rusty) sobs on another's shoulder. Overcome, he gestures toward the monument, "Why?" Men huddle, hugging each other; weeping, staring. A finger is placed on a name. Mutilated men, sans legs or arms, sit in wheelchairs or hobble on crutches. Returned warriors who were scorned, or worse, ignored.

The film eavesdrops on cafe conversations. "They brought us home too fast. Tuesday I was killing gooks. Saturday I was in Yale Bowl watching a football game. One man, thrice married, confesses he fears he's lost the capacity to feel. "I'll make it," vows another; preening in a new suit he bought in Penney's basement. "No doubt in my mind."

The lights go on. It's time for questions and comments, but it takes a while before watchers can talk about what they've witnessed. Stillness blankets the room. Each is an insider now. You don't banter about the secrets of men's souls.

A teacher named Susie raises her hand. "My twin brother was in Vietnam for eleven months. He was a marine." Her voice breaks when she says he never talks of the experience. "I called him after seeing *The Deerslayer* just to say, "Hey, I'm glad you're alive." John, made up as a greaser, is shaking. "We're the next ones in line. That scares the shit out of me." Eric, leader of the school's Nuclear Awareness Group (NAG) speculates on the horror of another war.

"What do you feel toward those who refused to fight?" The two men agree they harbor no animosity. "If men went to prison or to Canada, they did what they felt was right at the time. So did we."

The clown speaks with a soft and halting voice. It's Judi, the Biology teacher: She says something about her husband, I can't hear it all. "Maybe this is good," she says. "It's making me deal with feelings I've kept hidden for so long."

This single image, more than all others, hit the tuning fork of my mind. A "grinning clown" sharing serious introspection...a parody epitomizing the dual nature of mankind. Like a haunting Midsummer Night's Dream, I am witnessing a play within a play within a play. What, if not life is the stage? Who, if not we are the players?

The bearded filmmaker agrees with Judi. "Yes, in our film we are dealing with feelings. I spent two years alone in

192

Alaska, thinking things over, coming to know who I am. We're changed persons. We think we understand pain. We feel our experience has helped us to reach out to others, to touch people."

Arnie, our principal, steps forward. In lieu of jeans, he wears a dark business suit with shirt and tie...his "Halloween costume," he announces. "This is far more than you could hope to get from a class in social studies," he says. He recalls teaching a class with an ex-marine. "He came to me mid-term. We had to quit. He was getting flashbacks of the Vietnam war."

Indeed this is not a formal class in a manicured classroom with varnished desks, neatly in rows—fluorescent lights gleaming on blank faces. Rather it is crusaders, born of the blasphemy that is war; reaching out to the young, the hope of the world. Among the most obstinate truths of human existence is that indomitable spirit which will not be stilled by a Golgotha, an Auschwitz, or a Vietnam.

That today's setting is sadly grim and shabby only intensifies the impact. E.B.White once described watching circus riders perform in the practice ring of a semi-darkened barn. "The richness of the scene was in its plainness, its natural condition. All would be lost, he felt, under the bright lights of the big top with horse and rider bedecked in gold. For then, "a performer need only reflect the electric candle power that is directed upon him; but in the dark and dirty old training rings...whatever light is generated...must come from original sources—from internal fires...from the exuberance and gravity of youth. It is the difference between planetary light and the combustion of stars."

I have been confused by the chaos of Mountain Open High School. The frustration and hassle of dealing with it has seemed ridiculous at my stage of life. But I am reminded today that we may become complacent when our personal lives fall into place and remain unruffled. Perhaps we need a circus of sorts to awaken us to the comical and complex wonder of the world. From chaos, order; from darkness, new and splendorous visions are born.

Never before has what happens here made as much sense to me as on "All Hallows Eve," nor has it ever made less. Life's memorable moments were never meant to be defined in rational terms.

***

REFLECTIONS OF A FENCE PAINTER

When I was a young girl and cared about the boys, painting our white picket fence led to my first date to prom. "He" came by...six foot two, blond, a basketball hero, and he asked, did I need some help? From my perch upon the ground I looked up and I swear he wore a halo in the sun. Another brush was found, a can for paint, and the whole world shown in the noonday glow.

A quarter century down the road, 1,000 feet of faded horizontal boards framed our Midwest farm. It was the first time I'd lived in the country. I made fence painting last through the sunny days of spring, summer, and early fall, absorbing the sights, sounds, and smells of the flat farmland I came to love.

The rewards were not so glistening and explosive as when I was sixteen, yet in a sense, they were more spectacular. It's a matter of perspective.

My dog sprawled beside me, and we listened to a foolish rooster crow in mid-afternoon and watched fat geese waddle in the yard. A woodpecker I dubbed Don Quixote made a dreadful racket tapping on a metal fin of the windmill. Growing things bowed before the winds that swept across the prairie.

Our neighbor, George, waved each day from his tractor, the drone of his machine surging and fading as he traveled to and fro, cultivating long rows of corn.

I recall my concern when bristles of my brush reached into crevices where boards were nailed to the post and loosened paperlike cocoons, I hoped I was destroying some dreadful pest and not denying a beautiful butterfly his day in the sun. In looking back, I believe I was breaking free from my own cocoon.

When you think about it, there really is no earthly time but the present—the past is gone, and the future is pure conjecture. A task like fence painting kind of rolls it all together, removes the boundaries, lets you float free as you remember yesterday, visualize tomorrow, and relish today. Times like that are precious few.

Those years on the farm came when I needed them. They followed a difficult and painful period. And that fence seemed placed there to help me put things in order, to discover new priorities, to see through and beyond the fences we build in our mind.

Now we've moved to a mountain house in Colorado, with faded deck floors and railings. This summer is another painting time. "Don't you get bored?" my husband asks. *Bored?* Well, I know what he means, lots of menial tasks are boring. But applying pigment to fences, deck floors, or railings—now there's a noble occupation. And what better way to get to know the territory?

Midwest hummingbirds weren't musical. The metallic clatter of tiny hummingbird wings on their way to the feeder is eerie—like sleigh bells emitting a supersonic jingle. And Colorado grasshoppers have very noisy motors. Maybe it's the extra energy expended at high altitudes? I listen to the raucous squawks of the Stellar Jay, the magpie, and the crow. An occasional shrill whistle I cannot identify provides pleasant counter-melody. Rocky Mountain squirrels—black ones with long, pointed ears—provide steady background chatter. These creatures talk to one another, I swear. Even about me, I suspect, although I've not decoded their conversation.

Heavy spring run-off from the mountains has filled Turkey Creek and given it, too, a lively song to sing. A bee buzzes too near and hovers too long. I remain very still. It makes its way to the flowers.

I must get a book on mountain flowers. Far below me on crusty ground, covered with moss-rock outcroppings, fallen pine cones, and brown needles, a profusion of wildflowers grows. No manicured yards here—instead purple bells, clusters of yellow-gold, blossoms with broad white petals, and tiny blue ones. I feel a little ashamed for not knowing the birds and flowers by name, then wonder why appreciation of a gem

196

of nature should hang on naming. After all, it *was* before we stamped it with a label so that doesn't change anything, does it? Something there is within us that demands a naming.

Often I begin my work early when the day is new and cool and quiet. A sliver of moon still hangs in the west. One morning, still on my knees, I looked up over the mountain and there was a huge red and yellow balloon. I let out a silent whoop of joy. You can't look at a balloon without feeling good, and wishing you were in it.

Just one more serendipitous perk of painting. I was thinking about all that when I painted the posts of the railing today and I decided to write it down.

***

GERTRUDE M. PUELICHER

A letter always seems to me like immortality
because it is the mind alone without
corporeal friend...there seems a spectral
power in thought that walks alone.

...Emily Dickinson

Gertrude Puelicher and I corresponded regularly for 22 years. Many times we talked of visits to her guest house in Three Lakes, Wisconsin, but we never actually met until September 26, 1992, five months before she made "the transition"—which came to pass ten days before her 99th birthday on February 4, 1993. Our meeting did not occur quite as she had imagined it in a letter of February 26, 1984:

You will be coming when it is warm. I'll be waiting for you in my swing. When your car comes up our birch-lined drive, I'll be smiling. Here she comes, my dear Catherine dear. She is really here. You will step out of the car and I'll walk to meet you, and we'll look into each other's heart, we'll look deep—and be glad.

Instead, eight years later, there she sat, poised and beautifully groomed in an over-stuffed chair near a wall of windows, wearing a lovely paisley dress with matching earrings and necklace. She wore no glasses, her short white hair was perfectly coifed. In contrast, I wore slacks, sweatshirt, and windblown hair. I leaned toward her and couldn't speak. "It's been 22 years," she said. I nodded, my throat strangled with emotion. With a single glance she read my mind...namely my amazement at meeting such a keen-witted, sharp-eyed, self-contained lady.

"But of course, I'm *fine*—what in the world did you expect?" It was almost a reprimand. Without waiting for a flustered reply, she went on, "Oh, it's my voice. My voice has gone raspy." Now and again we talked on the telephone and I had noticed the aristocratic voice had gone raspy, undoubtedly deluding me to at last visualize her (at 98) as getting along in years.

When she wrote that she was retiring from writing "God's Corner" in *Exclusively Yours* magazine, she said, "Forty years is long enough for any single endeavor... something new and exciting will come along." She scoffed at folks taking Psalm 90, verse 10, too literally ('The days of our years are three score years and ten'). "They start thinking they're old at sixty."

When asked to give a talk at a "Pioneer Days" celebration, Gertrude declined. "Pioneer Days indeed! How old do they think I am!!!"

On this sunny September afternoon a stuffed cat curled comfortably on her lap...where Smokey used to nestle. She grieved when her beloved Siamese cat died. Once she'd sent a snapshot, "The funny little black spot on my lap is Smokey's black face. He is a Russian blue, smoky colored body, blue eyes, with one crossed, and a black tail and face. He is an enchanting cat, demanding, aristocratic, and very affectionate where I am concerned." What is it they say about pets resembling their masters?

A friend had sent her the stuffed animal she held—to rest on her lap while watching football games. "At first I didn't want it to take Smokey's place, but Snoozer is a comfort now," she explained, stroking the soft fur. "Some folks might think I've gone batty."

We talked of many things. She feared Bush wouldn't get reelected and admitted she was losing patience with him herself, as well as with all the candidates. "Catherine, you like Perot because you want action," she said. Then turning to my husband, "But you know, Ralph, we can't let those college boys run things." The voters did not agree.

Conversation grew hushed when a deer entered the

clearing surrounding the house and walked to the feeder. She spoke of the bears and foxes and of the eagles nesting in the trees near the lake. "I love the animals," she said. As in 'God's Corner,' the comings and goings of her animal friends were often reported in her letters.

Joe, who has lived with the Puelichers since he was a teenager, came by and posed with us for photographs. When we left, Cindy, Gertrude's caretaker, guided us along the wooded private road past Lake Julia, back to the highway.

The letter following our meeting said, "At last—finally—here we were. What fun it is now to see you as I write." Of Ralph, she said, "I shall always love him for patting Snoozer on the head as he said good-bye. No wonder you love that man, Catherine. He has a rare type of gentleness. So few men these days are gentle. It's all 'huff' and 'puff.' I thought of your dear Ralph as that conventional lawyer type (he is an engineer) who gaze around a room and look bored to death. He is just the opposite...as interested in the friendship you and I have founded as though he had a hand in it." Then came the announcement that she was flying us to northern Wisconsin in 1994 to attend her 100th birthday celebration in Three Lakes.

It seems doubtful that any celebration could outweigh that of her ninetieth birthday. Her letter had called it a wonderful sea of love on which she floated. "The symphony beamed a concert live from the stage in Milwaukee up to me— a children's concert of 1,200 children. It began with beautiful speeches. O Catherine, such lovely things they said. I dissolved in tears and Joe brought me tons of tissues and a glass of sherry. The last speaker was my nephew, Jack Puelicher, who told me I had been his second mother.... A concert by satellite—that was really something!"

In looking back, our single personal visit seems less real and tangible than 22 years of letters. Our epistles were chronicles of our inner lives. And still...how does one explain a pervading spirit that pierced your being to become a part of your soul? I am sure I am not alone in that feeling. Gertrude's letters, like her columns, were rooted in the heart and were therefore universal and timeless. She lived in the rich, full awareness of the moment, seeing the world in a grain of sand, heaven in a wildflower, and eternity in an hour.

Since being invited to share my memories of Gertrude, the song "Maria" from *The Sound of Music* keeps playing through my mind. "How do you solve a problem like Maria? How do you catch a cloud and pin it down?...How do you keep a wave upon the sand? Oh, how do you solve a problem like Maria? How do you hold a moonbeam in your hand?"

While Gertrude herself could hardly be regarded as a problem, writing about her *is*! Larger than life, she was yet completely approachable. Open and non-judgmental, she was yet in firm possession of unshakable personal spiritual truths, values, and morals. Small wonder that young and old and in-between came to her with their problems.

A fifteen-year-old at odds with her parents was contemplating abortion. A frustrated mother wanted Gertrude to pull strings to further her son's career. An angry follow-up call from the son wished his mother would mind her own business. Shortly, he too became a confidant. A proud grandfather sent his grandson's essay on Blake. Would Gertrude please comment? A wealthy young entrepreneur was considering chucking it all to go into the ministry. What did she think? "I'm not God, Catherine! I know in my heart folks only want someone to *listen*. Each must work things out with God."

Especially moving was Gertrude's account of a young woman who'd given birth to a brain-damaged baby girl and who had asked if she might come and visit and bring her child. "She put that baby on my lap, and do you know, Catherine, for one whole second I didn't see the blank stare and the seizures that went on constantly—I saw only God's perfect creation. It was a wonderful moment. After she left, I sat alone for a number of hours, thinking. It was so clear to me that if we could always look at the world around us—all the people with whom we are in contact—through spiritual eyes, seeing them as the created of God—with God only able to create that which is perfect—if we could eliminate mental concepts, what a different world this would be."

When a middle-aged lady professor came weeping and lamenting over unrequited love, and then left in tears, thanking Gertrude for helping her, Joe lost patience and scolded, "What in the hell was the matter with that woman? She came crying, she did nothing but cry while here, and she left crying. For God's sake, forget it. You ought to know you can't help *everyone!*"

While her divine light was blinding, she was yet fully human. I knew she was "to the manor born," but didn't really grasp the reality of that until visiting her 500 acre private paradise. One might surmise she was accustomed to having things done exactly as she desired by those in her employ—for if not, the message was undoubtedly made clear, namely there are always others who will oblige. Here was a tough-minded, strong-willed, no-nonsense woman, but those traits were cushioned in grace. Her heart went out to the world and every creature in it. She was LOVE personified.

Our correspondence began in the early 1970s when I began submitting pieces to *Exclusively Yours*. As a good many Wisconsin writers know, one basked in her glowing rejections and only later realized this was not, after all, an acceptance.

When I moved to Ohio, our letters continued and grew ever more frequent. Her every letter began the same way, "Dear Catherine dear," and ended with words that enveloped me in a comforting blanket of love.

January 1, 1991, she suggested a mutual New Year's resolution. "It seems to me we should be able to correspond twice a month, or at least, once. We have so much to share with one another—we both think all kinds of thoughts that really differ from the 'acquaintance' type of conversation and I am convinced that I am losing very much when I don't hear from you or when we fail to exchange ideas."

In truth, I believe it was the communicating via "God's Corner" that she missed, for the next paragraph went on to say she was being inundated with long distance telephone calls and letters she was trying to answer, "because people have been taken aback by my no longer writing God's Corner."

She was weighing considerations concerning publishing a new hard cover edition of *God's Corner.* The first volume, she felt was not as all-inclusive as she wished. The original publisher "chose out of some 100 samples what I call the 'comforting' ones. He stayed clear of the ones like 'Are You Thinking What You Are Thinking?' For two years I asked that question; at first readers thought I was being humorous."

The written word, unfortunately, is often interpreted in different ways. A prominent Methodist clergyman sent her Lenten blessings and what I'm sure he regarded as a compliment. He and his wife, he reported, continued to profit from God's Corner—"from reading your cogent outlook on life and your timely and winsome point of view." Gertrude cried out, "Catherine, tell me I'm not winsome."

Perhaps 'winsome' in the sense of 'engaging,' but certainly not 'sweet.' Her life was a vigilant spiritual quest, an individualized journey that led her to firm convictions that were rooted in Self and the teachings of "The Nazarene."

Her own certitude may well explain why she was so widely read and loved. I happen to be one who is acutely embarrassed, by noisy public proselytizing. For me, spiritual matters are quiet and deeply personal; the richest lodes are mined in solitude. I suspect others may feel the same. I believe her authenticity touched the tuning fork in the deepest consciousness of her reader; it echoed what we know in the marrow of our bones.

On April 16, 1988, she filled two legal size sheets of yellow lined paper with elegant tiny script.

I'm sure that God is pure Being and therefore I must also be just pure Being. I'm made in the image and likeness of God, am I not? I know that God constitutes individual being; He fulfills Himself in me. As the Creative Principle of the universe, He can only be Infinite

203

Consciousness; therefore, I must be that consciousness individualized. "I and my Father are one" and I can never be separated from Him...Only God Is!

She went on to describe sitting in her 'electric' chair while the rest of the household went on. "I dig away at the Inner Self because before I make the transition, I want to have daily contact with that Self. It is the only way I write God's Corner. 'Father, what would you have me write about for this one?' Often when I cannot get the right word, I say, 'Father, I need a better word here.' It always comes because Infinite Wisdom and Divine Love *are* the invisible Presence and Power—one advises me, one enfolds me."

Three firm beliefs she named as beyond dissuasion: "1. God *is!* 2. We experience what we hold in consciousness. 3. God constitutes individual being. If you read God's Corner in the light of those three statements, you'll see what I mean."

When I mentioned that she never spelled out those findings in her column, she wrote back, "You seem to feel I rather 'lay back' in God's Corner...that I don't come right out and say what I think from the religious angles. Catherine dear, if I said any more about my views, rest assured the readership would drop. I receive as many if not more letters from men than from women and that can be only because I am not 'sermonizing.'"

A Catholic priest, a Christian Scientist, and a Protestant minister were each convinced she belonged to his particular denomination. She once shared a complimentary letter she'd received from the president of Notre Dame University. Often persons would telephone to inquire her church affiliation, and just as often be horrified to learn she preferred to dig up her beliefs from within herself. "But what is your *authority*?" was often the next question, after which she said the conversation usually ended. "There is a loneliness in much of my thinking," she said. "I would like to have known Emerson. He would have understood." More than once she reminded, "You are the same in having to find your own path. It comes out in everything you write."

She confided it was not easy to reach her own peaceful meditation methods. It took more than twenty years. "But when I worked out my own totally unorthodox fashion, I found there was spiritual fruitage.... Only twice in all these years, have I heard the still, small voice, but many times I have felt guidance and Divine love."

An amaryllis I had sent quite unwittingly became a focus of meditation. "The vase was on a small marble table a few feet from my chair, and every time I looked up, I was looking directly into the heart of the flower facing me. Out of that has come a most remarkable experience: a meditation so beautiful that it is constantly with me." She reported that sometimes she digs too hard to reach the invisible. "In this instance, however, I can close my eyes, settle back, and instantly I am back with the beauty of this amaryllis and the depth of its origin. I have this feeling that I am looking through it, way beyond it, to what I am trying to find. I felt you ought to know: it has made of your gift a wonderfully strengthening of our friendship, were that possible."

In February, 1980, she wrote, "I've done my own thinking....I have long been convinced that God constitutes individual being because God has to express Itself some way. So what is God? For me, the answer lies in consciousness. It removes the idea of a Santa Claus God, who holds or withholds—no more petitioning or pleading for this or that— right now I am all that I was intended to be. I am *God being* (not the noun—you know what I mean, Catherine). I am consciousness being and it is there that I find my peace." She was sending me two books, she said, *The Mystical I* and *Consciousness Is What I am.* "I am staying with consciousness as the basis for what I am determined to understand and it truly brings fruitage. Look what happened when you and I met in consciousness!?"

No surprise when she proclaims she is not a follower, but absolutely must figure things out for herself. "I want to be able to be a part of what is going on. The 'I' of me is the same 'I' of you and of everyone else in the world— Iranians, Russians—and if we hold to that we shall wake them up some day to their identity. Then wars will be a thing of the past."

Letter after letter reiterated her personal certainties. "The great comfort I have is that I *know,* I really know, that nothing can separate me from the presence of God. And to me, God is consciousness....Since God must be Divine Consciousness and I and my Father are one, then I am that God consciousness individualized and I cannot ever be separated from it. I hold to that constantly. The affirmation and denial business is not for me.... When the whole world seems tumbling around me, when people seem to have lost all conception of something greater than humanhood, then I just retreat into myself, and let whatever thought comes forth be my guideline. 'There is a spirit in man and the inspiration of the Almighty giveth them understanding.' I cling to that spirit."

Gertrude knew I was deeply concerned about my son's involvement in Desert Storm. Constantly, she reminded me that God is pure being and in the Divine Presence there can only be harmony and wholeness. "So far as the war is concerned," she wrote, "I have spent hours every night trying to find an answer to man's inhumanity to man.... For my own peace of mind I have chipped away all sides, top and bottom, much as Michelangelo chipped away until he found, as he said, the famous statue of David, and I have found comfort in just two words—God is. I have made up my mind not to criticize, judge, or condemn. Nothing is my business except that *God is.*"

She offered comfort when my husband had prostate cancer surgery. "'The Lord will perfect that which concerns me.' Hold to that and rest in it."

When she felt I was off track, I was reprimanded. My teaching stint at an alternative high school, she regarded as sheer nonsense. She softened a bit after I sent a poignant story written by a 16-year-old student. It was published in *Crosscurrents,* a fine literary magazine. Gertrude said it left her in tears.

Nevertheless, she concluded her letter advising, "Frankly, I can't see you continuing. In this attempt to save one sheep of the 99 (never my intention), aren't we overdoing? The whole thing reminds me of Alice in Wonderland and the bad Queen. Everything went backwards." She was also reminded of a 14-year-old lad who was going to Haiti to work with the poor and diseased.... His parents must be crazy—to what are we coming? "I presume one of these days you will write that you and your experimentalists are moving to Africa to change the genes of wild animals."

When I left the school after two years, which was my intention all along, Gertrude was delighted. "I've seen this type of so-called education before, and it certainly is a misnomer."

A letter admonished, "For the love of Pete, stop living life so intensely. Give life a chance to live for you. As I review your letters mentally, I have come to the conclusion you are on a treadmill of 'doing.' I think it's time you stopped. Why not relax for a month and take time to sort out priorities?"

Nevertheless, a one-week retreat to a monastery was not her idea of sensibly taking time out. "Why are you, of all people, going on a retreat?" This was followed by a long list of reasons why it was a foolish course of action. "I read the retreat brochure you sent me," she said, "and I simply cannot imagine you profiting from a week spent with only yourself when you could accomplish as much on your own mountaintop."

After years of corresponding, I finally asked about her early life, realizing she'd rarely written about the past. I did know how much her nephew, Jack, meant to her, just as she knew my granddaughter, Nicole (who was born the year we began writing each other in earnest), was a very special person in my life. Other than that, now and then, she might vividly describe a remembered incident that had bearing on something I had reported.

For instance, when I was angered and astonished by a vicious personal attack made in class by a teacher of a continuing education course, she shared a story about a teacher at Milwaukee Downer College who seemed to take great glee in mispronouncing the name Puelicher. Enough was enough. One day a shy young student stood tall and refused to answer the roll until her name was pronounced correctly. "It never happened again," she said.

Another letter piqued her memory..."You certainly have started me on a trend of thought long shut away." She recalled her term as national president of the National Federation of Press Women. A small group gave her a difficult time and "did some devilish things.... But you know, Catherine, I had a ringleader in tears the night I made my final speech. It was in Montana. I developed the theme of those who had been of greatest help to me. I started with friends from whom I got loyalty, right or wrong; impersonal friends, etc. And I ended up thanking 'dear enemies' because they had forced me to see good where none was and to hold no resentment. I'd completely forgotten this until your letter came; now I remember the stunned silence, the furtive glances, and the ring leader and her cohorts in tears."

In response to my direct request for remembrances of things past, I received her shortest letter ever. She was concerned about Joe's carotid artery operation, so that may have accounted in part for the brief listing of a few highlights in a remarkable, exemplary life: Milwaukee Downer College, teaching positions ("I insisted upon getting my own job although my banker father was President of the Milwaukee School Board"), travel, radio and television work, and wartime assignments. "I was on all kinds of commissions and committees in Milwaukee. My greatest loves have been the Milwaukee Symphony and Junior Achievement. That's enough, dear heart. Fill in the spaces with travel and all the things one does. There have been awards. They still come. I tell Joe and Jack they can have a big bonfire some day—I am grateful, of course, but Catherine dear, I get more happiness out of feeding the deer and writing God's Corner. The December column brought a flood of comments."

A quick closure informed me, "I would not have done this for anyone but you—it's all behind me. I rarely think about it. I try to live wisely and with God in the present."

Gertrude's biblical quotations in her column might well lead one to believe she knew the book by heart. Perhaps so, but she also read widely and voraciously. There was scarcely a letter that didn't offer comment on her current reading. She would recommend a book, then suggest, "If you don't have access, I'll send it to you." Then the usual, "I am withholding comment on this until you have read it." I usually promised to pick it up at the library, but I found I couldn't keep up with her. She kept my mailman busy. I have one long bookshelf filled with volumes she sent beginning with *Your God Is Too Small* and ending with several books on Consciousness.

Ralph and I were advised to pick up Peggy Noonan's book describing her experiences as Reagan's speech writer. "And do get Kennan's *Memories* and Pozner's *Illusions.* A friend sent me Tom Clancy's latest, but I don't care about that type of so-called literature." Neither did she care for *The Firm,* although she read the entire book aloud to Joe.

"Last week someone sent me four of Danielle Steele's novels. Ye Gods! What a gift. The explicit sex was terrible. I was horrified and disgusted." Her lady caretaker warned, "If you think that's bad, you'd better not see today's movies." The letter closed, "Why ruin your day with such a lousy letter?! I may mail this. I may not."

Andrew Greeley's work, she felt, might upset a few Catholics, but of Joseph F. Girzone she said, "I enjoyed the simplicity of the Joshua books. However, this latest novel which I am sending was too Pollyannish for me."

From Beirut to Jerusalem, by Thomas L. Friedman, was fascinating reading, but "his vivid descriptions of the horrible things the various so-called religious sects do to each other are difficult to read about, especially if one suffers from an imagination like mine." The book, like the Bill Moyers/Joseph Campbell interviews, was heavy to hold.

Ireland's best seller, *To School Through the Fields,* by

Alice Taylor, "was a delightful, absolutely charming little book worth a dozen of those over-500-page-books, so lofty in spirit and so heavy to hold." She preferred it to Gertrude Ehrlich's *Solace of Open Spaces*, which I sent. Ehrlich's descriptions, she felt, while brilliantly done, were mental concepts in contrast to Taylor's simple, comfortable descriptions of spiritual reality.

"I found it fascinating that *The New Yorker* called John Baskin's *New Burlington* a social history," she said, "because it is not a mental concept, rather it possesses spiritual reality."

I was sure Annie Dillard would strike a home run, but unlike me, Gertrude was not overwhelmed. She did, however, love an essay collection I sent, *For the Love of God*. Her favorite was written by William McNamara, OCD, "the monk that looked after you." (She was referring to my retreat.) She expressed disappointment in Mother Teresa's essay. "The book came at a most propitious moment. I had just laid aside Segal's *The Call of Faith*...really a powerful novel."

Consciousness was ever the primary area of concentration and she frequently recommended books on the subject. Three letters urged the reading of Elaine Pagels' *Gnostic Gospels*. A fourth letter said she was reserving comment until I'd read it. In other words, Get with it, Catherine!

Reading, watching sports events, listening to music, and observing her animal friends in the Wisconsin northwoods were favored activities. One letter described creeping to the living room at 3:30 a.m., watching the deer at the feeder. Deer hunting season was a time of anxiety. "We put corn and alfalfa out four times a day. Ted says the deer are congregating in the meadow because they know they are safe. The ten-point buck hasn't been here for two nights and we're worried that the hunters may have shot him. I hope not. He is such a magnificent specimen of God in expression."

No surprise when she wrote, "Our meadow is to me what Walden Pond was to Thoreau. I'm learning from it."

My life was blessed and enriched by Gertrude Puelicher.

Strangely enough, I think she, too, placed great value on our friendship.

In November, 1983, she wrote a Thanksgiving letter. "Let's persuade Ralph to go to California on a regular basis twice a month. That is when your letters are such a reality of you that as I read them I can reach out and touch you. It is quite wonderful to have an invisible friend who is a reality. Did you ever stop to think, Catherine dear, that our relationship is one entirely of the spirit?" She concluded, "And believe it or not, on the fringe of it is that enchanting granddaughter, Nicole."

Once she referred to our friendship as "not the teacup kind...nor a solid, matter-of-fact kind. It is Baccarat crystal— beautifully fragile, full of sunlight glinting against crystal— striking a spark, lighting up the whole piece, sending glimpses of thoughts that otherwise lie hidden in fear of being misinterpreted.... You know what, Catherine? There is a mystique in our friendship and I just love it."

In looking back over those treasured epistles filled with kindness, stability, holiness, and an unconditional love I ill-deserved, I blush in remembering several of my brash letters. Once she wrote back the day my letter arrived, worried because it didn't sound like me. "Are you all right? I almost called."

In a way, I blame Gertrude for my own nonsense. There was delicious unrestraint in knowing I could be my ridiculous, serious, contemplative, foolish, contradictory self and still be cherished. There were no masks, ever, to jeopardize our intimacy.

Here was a lady so filled with peace and purpose that she refused to succumb to creaking bones or failing mind. Her wisdom was bursting with a Love that was the motivating force, the essence, the be-all and end-all of Gertrude Puelicher. There will never be another like her. For me, she will always BE.

***

AFTERWORD

We were in Portugal when Gertrude Puelicher died. On Thursday morning, February 11, 1993, at 4:00 a.m. I awakened and thought about our wonderfully close friendship and how unusual it was. The idea brushed across my mind—I wonder if this means she has died.

As we were touring the area in our little red Citroen later in the morning, I told Ralph about waking and thinking of Gertrude. He was very quiet and then he said, "I was half-awake at 4:00 a.m.; I looked at the clock and sort of drifted off. I was levitating (I assume he meant he *thought* he was levitating). You and Gertrude, meantime were communicating via ESP." Now Ralph is a hard-core realist, a mechanical engineer. He looked at me and in all seriousness asked, "What were you two talking about?"

I could scarcely believe my ears. I laughed, "Oh, Ralph it wasn't anything like that. I was just thinking about her." I did admit that the thought had occurred—does this mean she has passed on?

"She was here," he said.

I telephoned Three Lakes after our return and Joe said she had "made the transition" on February 4. I told Ralph we weren't as psychic as we thought. "You'll never convince me," he said. "It took her a week to find us." He insists it was a very real experience, unlike any other he'd ever had.

One year later, in February, 1994, while we were in New Zealand, I lost the book *Consciousness is What I Am*, which Gertrude had sent and which I had taken along. Upon leaving the train, I noticed the book was gone from the side pocket of my traveling bag.

For months after returning home, I made every effort to secure a copy of the book. Library searches failed, as did a trip to the Unity book center in Denver and numerous inquiries made via used bookstores. I left my name on countless lists. I had not said one word about this to Ralph...either because I was too ashamed at having lost it, or it was too hurtful in view of my carelessness. It was gnawing at my innards.

One morning at breakfast Ralph announced, "I had a dream about Gertrude last night. She said, "Tell Catherine not to worry about the book. Does that make any sense to you?"

But I didn't give up, the book was found in a library in Iowa.

***

DAYS FOR DANCING

When you do dance, I wish you
A wave o' the sea, that you might ever do
Nothing but that; move still, still so,
And own no other function

William Shakespeare
The Winter's Tale

Tuesday was cricket-crisp and sapphire blue. I didn't dance barefooted across my lawn, but I did ride my bicycle nine and one-half miles. Feet whirling 'round, I left the ground. Flying, wind at my back, wind at my face, it was all the same; a rightness prevailed. I was Zorba leaping his life story on the Grecian shore; Blake celebrating Eternity's sunrise. One moment was all moments.

To everything there is a rhythm and a reason. Too often the chaos and tragedy of existence blind us to the universal order. Too few are the golden days when the spirit transcends despair, lifting us to a peaceful reality that surpasses finite understanding. Tuesday was a day for dancing. I moved to the music and smiled.

Havelock Ellis calls dancing "the loftiest, the most moving, the most beautiful of the arts, because it is no mere translation or abstraction from life; it is life itself." It weds spirit to flesh, sacred to secular, religion to art.

It is the Bantu who asks, "What do you dance?" Not "What is your name?" or "Where do you dwell?" but "What do you dance?" for what a man dances embodies his tribe, his social customs and his religion; all that he is.

Ancient cultures did not separate dance from religion. Western Christianity, however, frowned on bodies swaying, melodious chanting, and feet slapping the earth. Only the

Shakers used the dance drama as a part of communal worship.

The American Indian danced to announce birth or death, to prepare for war, to celebrate victory, to summon good spirits and frighten evil ones, to worship and to pray. The Omaha had but one word for dancing and for love. It seems fitting. Every special relationship knows moments of perfect attunement... like the autumn day we journeyed to Beaver Dam, you and I. Without speaking, without even touching, except in our minds, we danced in harmony. We knew communion with an 'October'd' earth.

Dancing days came more often when we lived on the farm. Violent storms lashed across our prairie. Maples, cedars, and elms strained earthward, bowing before the onslaught of wind and rain and hail.

But more than fury, I loved the country quiet and the squeaky windmill that sliced it into slender strands. There were days in all seasons when I walked to the woods. In autumn, the trees caught fire. In winter, I followed bird and animal tracks in the snow, listened to the cold stillness of January, and watched my breath take shape in silver. In spring, birdsong sparked the meadow. And in summer, I sat on the forest carpet of brown pine needles, my back resting against a trunk. Even when there was no visible movement, I could feel that great tree bend and sway with the wind. I could hear it moan softly. Eternal lessons were shared with me. A squirrel scurried between the trees, a cardinal whistled from a tall pine.

Before man, the dance was. Yet it didn't take him long to improvise on tempo, to alter rhythms to suit his needs, to attempt a control over mystical cycles.

Amid the earthswarm, there are too few days for dancing. Machines and traffic and noise expand economies, but drown the ferocious quiet of the natural world.

Listening to that quiet requires special time and care. Artificial has become our daily bread. One can't rush through a sanctuary of the forest or of the soul. If you would touch the quiet, you must move softly among those silences that slip between leaf and branch and sky, and then slide into the spirit. Welded to earth, the spirit yearns to fly.

To every being there is an allotted time we've labeled life. And within each being there is an innate longing for the timeless. How good the day when time and timeless couple in the dance and the soul moves to the mystic rhythm of the unseen piper until it becomes the music.

***

CREATIVITY:
RECOURSE IN TROUBLED TIMES?

God guard me from those
Thoughts men think
In the mind alone
He that sings a lasting song
Thinks in a marrow bone.

...William Butler Yeats

Unlike Yeats, we cannot all sing a lasting song; but that should not preclude our thinking, at least occasionally, in a marrow bone. It is this kind of thinking that characterizes creative endeavor. True creativity is "you-ness." It involves digging deeply for the simple and the true; it is discovering the music and the miracle that we each find in our own subconscious.

Several renowned writers, artists, sociologists, and scientists are telling us that human salvation in today's technological age lies in the realm of creativity

Rene Dubos, Pulitzer Prize winning microbiologist, says one of the reasons for emotional impoverishment in countries where industry and technology have taken over is the loss of identification with the natural world. In our transient society, the nuclear family replaces the old extended family of agrarian society. Despite population explosions, man has lost his link with man. Loneliness and alienation characterize our computerized culture.

If we are to discover our true natures, reach out to others and rescue our own humanity, we had best begin to reach inside ourselves to get in touch with our feelings, instincts, and intuitions. "Only when one is connected to one's own core," says Anne Morrow Lindbergh, "is one connected to others." She observes that woman can best find herself by losing herself in some creative activity of her own."

In 1972, Buckminster Fuller wrote the book, *Intuition* in poetic form. The cover blurb states, "Only by using our whole minds, our intuition as well as our reason, will we be able to fulfill our unique role in the universe."

Far more radical is this quote from within the book:

> If humanity is going to survive
> It will be only because it commits itself
> Unselfishly, courageously, and exclusively
> To its most longingfully creative inclinations.
> Visionary conceptions
> And intuitively formulated objectifications
> ...constitute humanity's
> Last and highest order of survival recourse.

That sounds like rather high-falutin' language, but please keep in mind the expressions "visionary conceptions" and "intuitively formulated objectifications," particularly as they tie in with other writers', scientists', and artists' definitions of creativity.

Freud viewed artistic creativity as originating in the unconscious depths, an expression of emotional impulses. He called the artist an unsatisfied man who turns away from reality. Yet he also dubbed creative beings valuable allies. "They are apt to know a whole host of things between heaven and earth of which our philosophy has not let us dream. In their knowledge of the mind, they are far in advance of us everyday people; for they draw upon sources which we have not yet opened up for science." In numerous writings, Freud conceded that psychoanalysis was unable to explain creativity.

Not until the close of the nineteenth century were any systematic attempts made to investigate the matter scientifically. Anthony Storr, in *Dynamics of Creation*, notes that an artist does not turn to creative activity because he possesses a particular skill. He defines creativity as a kind of defense mechanism against anxiety or despair.

Arthur Koestler, scientist and novelist, author of *The Act*

218

of Creation, similarly describes creativity as an actualization of surplus potentials—capacities which are untapped or dormant under ordinary conditions, but which reveal themselves when conditions are abnormal or exceptional.

Critics of all time have echoed the cry of Goethe: "No great work ever has, or ever will be produced by a man who has not known pain. I am tempted to ask, can anyone who is able to love, go through earthly existence without knowing pain? It is in the falling that we are given wings."

Koestler devotes a full chapter to the archetype he deemed of special significance to the act of creation: the "Night Journey." Some overwhelming, catastrophic experience plunges a being downward and backward to the tragic plane. There man travels alone, as did Orpheus and Odysseus in the underworld, as did the prophets in the desert, as did Jonah in the belly of the whale. After a fall through the manhole, life is never the same. The shattering pain leads to a kind of fresh perceiving, the like of which is usually possessed solely by the child.

Silvano Arieti says much the same in *Creativity* when he describes the creative person as one who has known a profound experience that changed him and his appreciation of the world. He agrees that creativity is an attribute of everyone, but he hastens to point out that not all possess the quality at the level of a Shakespeare or a Newton.

Jacob Bronowski holds that creation is finding order in what was disorderly. Not only is creative activity normal to all living things, but also he maintains that phenomena analogous to creative originality operate throughout the organic hierarchy on all levels.

All of the above propose similar intriguing theories concerning the conscious and unconscious processes underlying scientific discovery, artistic originality, and comic inspiration. *All* creative activities, they profess, follow a common basic pattern.

The most widely accepted pattern theory which has been applied to every field of creativity was advanced by Wallas in

1926. It has four stages: 1. Preparation, 2. Incubation, 3. Illumination, and 4. Verification.

During the preparatory stage, the problem is fully investigated. The entire being is saturated with the subject. Incubation may range from a few minutes to months or years. Work at the conscious level ceases, often in frustration. Thinking is set aside in favor of what Koestler calls underground games. In primitive levels of the unconscious, liquid, free-flowing ideation takes place. Verbal logic, common sense, and reasoning are non-existent. Contradiction is at home here. Unrelated matrices yield surprising Eurekas. "The discoveries of science and works of art," says Bronowski, "are explorations in finding pattern; finding order in explosions of hidden likenesses."

The unlikely marriages of cabbages and kings which may be unexpectedly thrust into the lap of the conscious must pass the stage of verification. The conscious mind decides whether to accept or reject the illumination. It was Nietzsche who said, "Every extension of knowledge arises from making conscious the unconscious."

The novelist, E.M. Forster, describes the creative task according to the steps just outlined...data gathering followed by mental mulling. Then he adds, "As we work, something often comes to us that is normally beyond our reach.... When the process is over, when the picture or lyric or novel is complete, the artist looking back will wonder how on earth he did it. And indeed he did not do it on earth."

Forster is not alone in his metaphysical assumption. Creative geniuses in all fields confess that any wisdom they possess comes not only from plumbing the mother lode of the unconscious, but often from an inexplicable awesome force emanating from quite beyond their conscious volition.

In the fifth century B.C., the Greek tragedian, Aeschylus, wrote, "And even in our sleep, pain, which we cannot forget, falls drop by drop upon the heart until, in our own despair, against our will, comes wisdom through the awful grace of God."

Walt Whitman said his poems came from outside himself. "I just let her come until the fountain is dry."

Solzenitsyn writes: "Atop the ridge of earthly fame I look back in wonder at the path which I alone could never have found, a wondrous path through despair...from which I could transmit to mankind a reflection of Your rays. And as much as I must still reflect, you will give me. But as much as I cannot take up, you will have already assigned to others."

Paula Randall, research biochemist, sculptress, published author and poet, says her images come finally from God, a name she uses for ultimate energy and power. "I feel any art is reactivated imagery...stored and indexed in the unconscious from whence we may recall it dressed up as self-expression." She asks, "Does one need proof of God?" then answers, "Does one light a torch to see the sun?"

In his voluminous work, Koestler states, "Large chunks of irrationality are imbedded in the creative process, not only in art, but in the exact sciences as well."

Kekule urged the regression and retreat which prepares the forward leap: "Let us dream, gentlemen!" One night in 1865, his vision of a whirling serpent biting its tail led to his theory of molecular constitution. Poincaire's account of Fuschian functions reads like a fantasy. He acknowledged the role of the unconscious as incontestable in mathematical invention. The renowned physicist, Faraday, a visionary lacking mathematical education or gift, arrived at his theorems by a kind of intuition.

Edison was shockingly ignorant of science. "The key to successful methods comes right out of the air... A real new thing like an idea or a beautiful melody is pulled out of space."

Einstein had an absolute and adamant faith in his own insight and intuition and a distinct distrust of his senses. "I value my gift of fantasy far more than my gift of intellect." His discoveries were made almost entirely by thought alone, unsupported, at first, by experiment or mathematics.

In 1945, replying to a questionnaire of Jacques Hadamard, Einstein explained his working methods:

> The words of the language...do not seem to play any role in my mechanics of thought. The combinatory play of images seems to be the essential feature in productive thought...some visual, some of muscular type. Conventional words or signs have to be sought for laboriously only in the secondary stage; when the mentioned associative play is sufficiently established and can be reproduced at will.

Hadamard summed up the results of his inquiry in this way:

> Practically all American mathematicians describe phenomena I've also noticed in my own case. They not only avoid the use of mental words, but avoid mental use of algebraic or any other precise signs. They use, as I do, vague images—mental pictures which may also be kinetic or auditive.

Could it be that mathematical discoveries were born out of the airy nothings Shakespeare described in *A Midsummer Night's Dream*?

> And as imagination bodies forth
> The forms of things unknown, the poet's pen
> Turns them to shapes and gives to airy nothing
> A habitation and a name.

Was Wordsworth describing the same process when he said, "Often we have to get away from speech in order to think clearly?" Was Emerson alluding to the same phenomenon in noting, "No wonder a writer is rare. It requires one inspiration or transmutation of Nature into thought to yield him the truth, quite another inspiration to write it"?

Thus far I have talked about professional investigations into the creative process and what geniuses have had to say about their own creative experience. What about ordinary folk like you and me? Of what importance is the creative process to us? I like David Williamson's observation in *Unity* magazine:

We need mind and spirit-stretching exercise to help people develop their humanity instead of becoming insensitive and mechanical in a push-button, computer-run society.

Alex Noble, writing in *The Christian Science Monitor*, views poetry as "vision intuition." "Why poetry? Why life? Why communication? Why awareness? Why growth? Why sharing? Why love?" The inward journey into our "intuitive poet selves," she regards as "the only way to go from here, the only way up and out."

Creative activity is an instinctive recourse in time of pain. On a lesser level of intensity, it helps us deal with the personal problems we encounter in day to day living. It is a terrific way to combat boredom, a fresh and invigorating change of pace. The dividends are amazingly rewarding.

I don't believe anyone could write seriously and diligently for a two or three year period without becoming a very different person than he or she was at the outset. Writing is introspective. It involves delving into subconscious areas we keep "safely" hidden. It's a lonely endeavor. That's one of the reasons conducting writing classes has been such a joy. The endeavor has introduced me to some of the finest people I've ever come to know. I'm convinced this is true because we were all open and honest with one another, sharing sincere feelings concerning what it means to be human. We knew moments of communion that shed light upon our lives.

"You must not become a mere peddler of words," says teacher Kate Swift taking a firm hold of George Willard's shoulders in Sherwood Anderson's *Winesburg, Ohio.* "The thing to learn is to know what people are thinking, not what they say."

When people *say* what they *think,* the heart listens.

A note attached to a final assignment by a middle-aged practical nurse best explains the magic. She sold two pieces written in class; more importantly, she had this to say: "Listening to my fellow writers pour out their ideas and feelings has made me realize what gems we humans really are. It has given me greater depth of insight into all the people I come into contact with daily. I want to promote more understanding, love, and happiness. How about that?"

How about that indeed? Those are the exciting things creative activity can accomplish for you and for me, for anyone willing to pursue the inner path. In my opinion, creativity can never be fully explained in rational or scientific terms. Joyce Carol Oates calls it "one of the most mysterious of all human endeavors."

Reason alone is unreasonable. We had best give thought and form to subjectivity, to our visions and intuitions, and stop ignoring the realm of the spirit. It may be our last recourse!

***

ON INTIMACY

Which of us has known his brother?
Which of us has looked into his father's heart?
Which of us has not remained forever prison-pent?
Which of us is not forever a stranger and alone?

Thomas Wolfe thus epitomized the piteous lamentation of humankind. Naked and alone, from the darkness of our mother's womb have we come into the incommunicable prison of this earth.

Thenceforth, until death, our innate longing for intimate communication directs each lonely and perpetual pilgrimage, each search for wholeness, each quest for God.

How filled with joy the search, how perilous and painful the journey that unfolds layer upon layer of hidden being. Like the ripe red berry beneath the green and thorny branches, the pearl of great price lies deeply hidden, silent and unrevealed.

What clumsy tools are words. Thoughts stumble over knock-kneed words, are painfully born, dreadfully deformed. Such unexpected transformations from verbal expression to a listening heart! With their innumerable shades of meaning, their endless gamut of interpretation, words are naught but groping gestures through the glass. Often eyes say more than words. Eyes look out, in, beyond, and through. Like touching, they can comfort, wound, or terrorize. Mysterious pools of wonder, eyes.

Those deep intuitive pits of perception, those bristling setae of sensitivity which serve us best in "seeing" life, are yet frustrations to the soul. We haven't crept far enough from the wet womb of darkness (or have we crept too far?) to effectively plumb those depths of consciousness.

Intimacy is experienced rarely. There are few along the way with whom we share our inner selves. With those few, there is neither the desire nor the time for silly manipulatory games. Masks are left behind. Visions, dreams, fantasies, sufferings, hopes, deep and beautiful truths, sparkling fragments of quietude are too precious to scatter indiscriminately. Souls are entered worshipfully, secrets are revealed and received with reverence.

There must be fertile ground for such sharing. The weeds of fear and insincerity are not rooted there. How can one be free if he/she fears being discovered? Superficiality and guilt cast long gray shadows. Openness and acceptance need prevail. Defense-less and vulnerable, pain and love deserve tender rapport.

Honesty begets honesty. Almost too great an order for any human being, for we all have hidden corners which are veiled, not only from others, but even more dangerously from ourselves. How good it is to be our absurd, ridiculous, romantic, contradictory, angry selves and still be cherished.

If, on this arid earth, we happen upon an oasis of *real* communication...we share a precious gift, we experience awe. We travel an excruciating, yet exciting, path of discovery with initial curves of reticence, rough detours of misunderstanding, still corners of reflection, long lanes of puzzlement, and finally free open vistas leading to glorious revelations and insights. A beautifully supportive relationship results...with its own delicate complexities and complications. For inevitably, the fiber of the soul is tugged now this way, now that, depending upon the sounds and silences, the comforts and stresses, the solitude or the company, the feelings which descend and flee.

There is a strange attunement when flashing beacons of the soul intercept and illuminate one another. Intimacy is a relaxation in the startling wonder that is truth; an exultation that is yet a comfortable affinity; an empathy that is all the more precious because it is sadly mercurial.

Through intimacy we transcend the world and touch the spirit. It is an epiphanic experience. The wonder of it awakens wisdom. Intuitively, we know there exists a greater dimension to our lives than those sensory perceptions which curtain the eyes of the soul. Such a sharing is Love—God's own image in humankind.

***

CONUNDRUMS

SOMEONE'S LAUGHING, LORD

Forgive, O Lord, my little jokes on Thee
And I'll forgive Thy great big one on me.

...Robert Frost

Humor is a funny thing...an uncanny mixture of sadness and of joy. A cat can purr, a bird can sing, a flower can bloom, and a capricious little dachshund I once knew could curl his lip and 'smile' on cue. But only humans can laugh (or cry), for as William Hazlitt pointed out, only we can see the difference between what is and what ought to be. Making a joke of life's absurdities makes them bearable. "And if I laugh," says Byron, "'tis that I may not weep."

E. B. White warns that attempts to define and describe humor can be futile and disheartening. Max Eastman agrees when he declares that once you analyze laughter, it evaporates. Voltaire concurs in noting laughter is a sign of joy..."anyone who pushes his curiosity further in the matter is a fool."

Facial muscles flex, lips move upward and outward, explosive sounds may be emitted from the throat, eyes suddenly change expression...and this unique phenomenon we term laughter. It can cheer, encourage, entice, crush, thwart, amuse, shock, embarrass, or even warp one's fellow man.

It's a universal means of communication, but as with language, the message intended is not always the message received. "Laughing with" may be misinterpreted as "laughing at."

John Mason Brown differentiated between merriment, "a kindly, spontaneous accompaniment to the body comfortable," and wit, which he dubbed "laughter of the mind."

Wit can be caustic. Oscar Wilde, Alexander Woollcott, Groucho Marx, and Don Rickels often showed small concern for personal feelings. Conversely, a certain kindness characterizes the wit of Ogden Nash, Bill Cosby, and George Burns. When he was referred to as a great wit, George Bernard Shaw protested. "I only tell the truth," he said. "People are so shocked at hearing the truth that they laugh in embarrassment and call it wit."

Satire and irony have ever been a means to criticize institutions and senseless foibles. Jonathan Winters, a humorist who makes no secret of his frequent trips to psychiatric wards, says his paintings "make statements about things that concern me—war, animal preservation, the fate of America's Indians, religion, death, life..." Doris Day is an activist for animal rights, so consider the statement Winters makes in a painting titled, "Two Birds Watching Doris Day's Cat and Dog Drown." Walt Kelly (Pogo), Jim Davis (Garfield), and Gary Larson (The Far Side) are also incisive spokesmen who use humor to champion animal rights.

Despite the laughter they evoked, it is doubtful if Mark Twain, James Thurber, and W. C. Fields really thought life was so funny. Irony and pathos filled their lives and their work.

On a television news magazine show, Dave Barry was quick to admit that his father was an alcoholic, his mother took her own life, and his sister was committed to a mental hospital. Yet he shrugged off those written accounts that trace his humor to tragedy. It seems to be a universal tendency to respond to life's horrors with black and sick jokes, he said. Whenever serial killers make headlines, or victims are mutilated, or disaster strikes an area, or a political leader is in hot water, shocking punch lines are quick to find their way into private parties, late night talk shows, and incisive cartoons.

Will Rogers was one of those rare humorists able to poke holes in political leaders and ridicule the contradictions in our system, while yet creeping into hearts to become the conscience and common sense of America. His kind of laughter is the guardian of liberty.

While freedom *is* a right to laughter (dictators quickly curtail it), I recall reading an essay saying we nevertheless expect our statesmen to be sententious in public. That writer felt Adlai Stevenson's wit was a liability inasmuch as the ordinary person felt an uncomfortable inferiority in recognizing the man's sharpness of mind.

Churchill was an exception—a witty statesman who dared indulge in irony and eloquence without reaping harm. John F. Kennedy's style and grace were comfortably enhanced by his talent for twisting his wit upon himself.

A more folksy humor finds greater popularity with the masses. Lincoln (a manic depressive) was a great story teller. He vexed his cabinet members with his hefty store of comical tales. Lyndon Johnson and Ronald Reagan were similarly accused.

Humor is often poignant; like poetry it touches bone. Roz Chast's *New Yorker* cartoons have been described by her editor as "little pages from her very private diary." The comic strip "Cathy" likewise permits a secret peek into the female psyche.

Often I've wanted to drop *New Yorker* cartoons into letters. But one dares not risk sharing the right cartoon with the right person—not even with your daughter—even though humor is relative. For instance, a matron surveying her daughter resplendent in white gown and veil, confides to a friend, "We wanted her first wedding to be a special time to remember."

Ziggie and Charlie Brown seem safest for sharing— witness their popularity in greeting cards. Who hasn't felt put upon, or seen oneself as the fall guy, the perpetual loser in the game of life? Those little fellows possess an innocence that makes them harmless, certainly more gentle than the caricatured couple seated at a breakfast table.

The woman, hands on her chin, asks her husband who is reading the paper, "Maynard, what would you do if I suddenly went cuckoo?" I must have a sadistic streak—I'd love to send that in a letter to my dear friend, Jennie, with a quip of my own. Something like, "Haven't you considered this a viable option?" She has an insufferable fool for a husband and she's smart enough to know it, yet loyal enough to go along with his absurdities, his carryings-on; holding things together, trying to give some semblance of normalcy to the relationship.

I know a sponge who's been living for years on government grants. His annual maneuvers for renewals are uncannily creative. I would relish shipping him the sketch of a fellow standing amid his tasteless display of flamingos, fawns, and spurting fountains—wondering if his national endowment for the arts would be renewed.

Humor is a little like TNT. My mother has, through the years, lent an ear to her neighbor's grief and far-fetched tales concerning a drunken husband. In a cartoon, the drunk staggers in the door to be met by an angry wife with arms akimbo. His stammering explanation went like this: "You'll never believe this. It has plot, conflict, drama, suspense, climax, and sub-plot." When the conflict and drama include beatings and broken furniture, drunkenness seems a sorry subject for the cartoonist's pen and quite unfit for sharing with a victim.

Poets and philosophers have ever pondered the paradox and saving grace of humor. Malamud has a Yiddish actor in his play "Suppose a Wedding" exclaim, "Leid macht auch lachen" (Suffering also makes for laughter).

W. H. Auden observes, "We oscillate between wishing we were unreflective animals and wishing we were disembodied spirits, for in either case we should not be problematic to ourselves. The Carnival solution of this ambiguity is to laugh, for laughter is simultaneously a protest and an acceptance." He felt laughter sat very close to prayer.

The philosopher, Soren Kierkegaard, with characteristic profundity, also sees irony and humor as closely related to worship. He divides the thinking man's life into three periods, the aesthetic, the ethical, and the religious. Irony (which turns on the artist's personality) is the boundary between the aesthetic and the ethical, and humor is the boundary between the ethical and the religious. The humorist, says Kierkegaard, is familiar with suffering and pain. Humor, he regards as the last stage of existential inwardness before faith.

Small wonder that touching the funny bone triggers a mysterious admixture of ache and tickle. Methinks I feel the sharpest twinge of all when I wonder which cartoons my friends would never dare to share with me.

Perhaps life's cruelest joke, He did not that "giftie gie us to see oursels as others see us."

***

WHHHHOOOOOOMMMMPH!

On the mountain there is freedom!
The world is perfect everywhere
Save where man comes with his torment.

...Schiller, "The Bride of Messina,"1803

Whhhhoooooommmmph! I stole my title from a headline over a color photograph on the front page of *The Denver Post.* "A giant explosion lifts 17,000 cubic yards of rock into the air along U.S. 285 at Parmalee Gulch Road," the caption explained. It took thirty seconds and 15,000 pounds of explosive to blast away a mountainside that was a million years in the making. Traffic, it said, was held up for a mere thirty minutes for the blast and subsequent cleanup. How quickly we make molehills of mountains! This happened one week before Earth Day!

I drive through Turkey Creek Canyon on my way to Denver. They're widening eleven miles of highway and putting in underpasses and overpasses. The work will take two years.

Whenever I am stopped in a line of cars for the blasting of rock and the felling of trees, I close my ears to the thunder of dynamite and the whine of the chain saw. I wince and turn away as stately pines topple and slide down the mountain—"senior citizen" pines that were sixty years and more in the growing.

Natural rock outcroppings, at the snap of a finger, are turned to rubble. Monstrous metal jaws voraciously scoop up earth, rocks, and pine trees, then spew the waste into enormous trucks that wait in rows. The debris crashes into metal truck beds and is hauled away to fill a green valley just up the road.

"They" will shrug and explain that widening the scenic mountain road is expedient. More vehicles can reach their destinations in less time. "They" will say straightening curves will save lives. A double highway facilitating one-way traffic means less accidents. And that is true.

Let's hope "they" are also planning ahead to reduce the subsequent increase in pollution which, in turn, is destined to intensify the brown cloud that hangs over Denver.

How fruitless to wring one's hands in despair. How about hard answers? I wish I knew. My husband blames over-population. He laughs and facetiously suggests, "Get rid of the people." Maybe that's no joke. T. C. McLuhan is responsible for a phrase that sticks like glue in my mind: "...in the destruction of nature will follow the destruction of ourselves."

In a *Denver Post* article, a retiring professor of Environ-mental Ethics reminded when we harm nature we harm ourselves, for the planet can cure itself of the human cancer.

I remember the lamentation of a Wintu woman observing white men mining gold in California. "When we dig roots or build houses, we make little holes. When we burn grass for grasshoppers, we don't ruin things. We shake down acorns and pinenuts. We don't chop down trees. We use dead wood. But the white people plow up the ground, pull down the trees, kill everything. The tree says, 'Don't. I am sore.' But they chop it down and cut it up.... The White people blast rocks and scatter them on the ground. The rock says, 'Don't. You are hurting me.'.... How can the spirit of the earth like the White man?... Everywhere the White man has touched it, it is sore."

Sadly enough, I also realize once the widened highway is operating—as my good neighbor suggests—I will forget. Today I hear Aldo Leopold plead, "Help us to think like a mountain." WHHHHOOOOOOMMMMPH! It's an old familiar requiem called Progress. Music to work by, while a beautiful stretch of wooded canyon is wiped forever from the face of the earth.

***

SEEDS OF DISCONTENT
KEEP CROPPING UP

Nowhere is paradox more alive for me than in the making of a garden—or lately, in not making a garden. When I was a kid growing up in Wisconsin, our backyard vegetable garden was as perennial as the grass. Each spring tiny verdant rows hemstitched the rich, black earth. Each summer and fall we harvested peas, potatoes, beans, corn, tomatoes, squash, onions, lettuce, spinach, and cauliflower.

I'm a nature lover, but I never did experience the mystical joy that is said to accompany gardening. "He who makes a garden," says Douglas Mallock, "works hand in hand with God." And Rudyard Kipling reminds, "Oh, Adam was a gardener and God who made him sees that half a proper gardener's work is done upon his knees." Before gardeners, the garden was. According to the Book of Genesis, the Lord God planted a garden eastward in Eden not too many hours after the light shown upon the world. Newly created man was placed in the pleasure paradise to care for the herbs and grasses and especially for the tree of life and the tree of knowledge.

Although the spiritual charisma of gardening passed me by, in keeping with my childhood roots, each Midwest spring, I planted my own garden. I promoted the process for one reason: I love fresh vegetables. And so I bought seeds and seedlings, hoes and hoses, a wheelbarrow and a Rototiller. I nurtured the compost pile. I strung strings for perfect rows, stretched chicken wire to deter rabbits, sprayed and dusted leaves to reduce the aphid population, and pounded metal thingamajigs in the soil to keep tomato plants up and love apples off the ground.

However, since moving to the mountains of Colorado, I haven't had a garden. The temperatures are too erratic, the terrain too rocky, the wild critters too abundant. It's not worth the struggle. Then too, things I read seem to be reinforcing my decision—like the piece Kurt Vonnegut wrote for an automobile ad describing life in 2088. "If people think nature is their friend," Vonnegut says, "they sure don't need an enemy." I'm thinking about the elk eating the bark off our aspens and the blossoms off my geraniums, the severe winds that uprooted huge trees, and the hail that tore up our shingles and broke glass in the solar room.

As if that weren't enough to dash my leftover dreams of an idyllic vegetable garden, a few days later, I saw the menacing headline, "Many Foods Full of Carcinogens." A scientist named Ames, chairman of the biochemistry department at the University of California, pointed out that apples contain formaldehyde, a potent carcinogen (Do you suppose Eve suspected?). Broccoli contains a substance that's chemically similar to dioxin. And hey, watch out for peanut butter: it's filled with a fungus that can cause cancer.

According to Ames, carcinogens in plants evolved as a normal defense mechanism. You see plants don't have teeth or claws. They can't even run away. So they developed toxins to fight off predators. What better reason not to plant a garden? In today's world, who needs an arsenal in the backyard?

Historically, there seem to be two approaches to nature—you either confront it or accept it. More and more, I find, I'm leaning toward acceptance.

Our Western-world gardening methods confront with vengeful ferocity. We battle bugs with pesticides, change the chemical content of the soil, alter the contour of the land, fell trees that block our path—in short, impose our will upon the Earth. Our gardens are acts of conquest.

Native Americans, on the other hand, treated the land with deference and saw no virtue in imposing their will upon the natural environment. Similarly, Japanese gardeners believe that through respect and acceptance of nature, man learns self-respect. They work with Mother Nature's ingrained tendencies, using pruning and placement to unveil the lines of a tree or a stone. Like artists, Japanese gardeners idealize by making us see what's real in a way that is deeper than reality.

Consider Oriental symbolic dry gardens wherein sand

rep-resents water and stone represents mountains. The simpler the expression, the deeper the content. Contemplation of the garden aims for spiritual awakening through intuition. The world is presented in microcosm. Such gardens are regarded as an aesthetic necessity to feed man's love of nature.

My own love of nature is presently fed by my life in the mountains of Colorado. I have no need for small rocks to represent mountains, nor for raked sand to suggest water. A mountain overlooks my deck. A creek runs past my door.

This landscape dictates its own destiny, sprouting pine trees, rock outcroppings, and prolific wildflowers with an abandon I envy. These minor miracles happen, and I witness. I watch. Lilies of the field—they and I—each doing what comes naturally, each allowing the other to be.

So I'm *usually* benignly content to settle for corn, beans, and tomatoes purchased from the back of a pickup truck parked on U.S. 285. It seems a relatively small price to pay for my natural pleasure garden.

Nevertheless, now and then guilt rears its ugly head. Inasmuch as the vegetables are not labeled "organic," am I still aiding and abetting the ferocious gardening methods of the Western world? Letting someone else take the rap, so to speak? I hope the "entrepreneur gardeners" are not tearing up Colorado's scenic wonders and polluting the atmosphere with insecticides. And which fruits are friends, which vegetables are really waging war against us?

Contemplation doesn't always spell contentment.

***

CAN WE EVER KNOW OURSELVES?

O wad some Pow'r the giftie gie us
To see oursels as others see us!
It wad frae monie a blunder free us,
An' foolish notion.

...from "To A Louse," by Robert Burns

I've known me longer than anybody. Can't get away from myself even when I want to. The same is true of you. Isn't it odd then that we have such difficulty in seeing ourselves as we are? Maybe the riddle has roots in what Joan Didion calls finding a narrative line. Do we tell ourselves stories in order to live? And why...when Truth alone will set us free?

This was brought home to me when Jo, my poet friend, told me that she became exceedingly nervous when her sister-in-law arrived unexpectedly and picked up a notebook of her poems.

"She never paid the slightest attention to my published work," Jo said, "yet here she was reaching for my latest scratchings. One day I had gotten so sick of her bragging that I got my frustrations out by writing a graphic, derogatory poem about this know-it-all woman. The references were so explicit I was sure she'd recognize herself. I tried my best to focus her attention elsewhere, but she would not put the book aside.

"To my amazement, of the 40 poems, the one I feared she would find, turned out to be her favorite. 'Don't we all know over-bearing people like that?' she said. 'That's a gem. I'd like a copy.' I guess I shouldn't have been so dumbfounded. I suspect none of us see ourselves as others see us. Maybe that's good. We'd probably die of shock."

The leap to objectivity is painful. Before change, there must be recognition and that can mean suffering and humiliation. Carl Jung commiserated with people on their successes and congratulated them on their failures because from the latter comes growth and learning if we let it happen. He also recommended we pay close attention to traits in others that we find irritating. Chances are, we're looking at a mirror.

Following interminable suffering and pain, a friend past fifty, confided to me in deep sincerity...more than sincerity, a sense of wonder, "Why did I wait so long to *act* the way I *feel?*" The same friend has a favorite observation he has voiced often through the years. "You are what you think you are." Do we think we have images to maintain? Do we convince ourselves we must always be cheerful, or tolerant, or kind, or successful—that we must be a fine host or hostess, an efficient organizer, an example of careful self control, a respected figure in the community, or a perfect parent? Why? So we will be liked? Respected? Admired? So we can like ourselves?

Too often, acting impulsively or spontaneously is too dangerous. Masks keep us insulated, safe, and blind. They protect us from ridicule, guard us from being found out, insulate us against risk. God forbid that our fears and foibles show through the facade. God forbid that we should reflect and think, and give sudden birth to ideas, insights, or revelations.

Standards are legitimate only when validated from within. Integrity is discovering our own nature and, insofar as we are able, being absolutely true to what we find. Masks alienate. They put distance between our social selves and our real selves; consequently between ourselves and others.

Humankind has the capacity to develop a vision that sees beyond the vitreous humor of the eye, beyond the blindness of the senses. However, we constantly fight it by separating ourselves from all that is. Perhaps natural enough for a finite creature possessing consciousness. We cannot grasp the essence of infinity, but we have an awareness that it is.

When you think about it, it's ridiculous for humans to build delusions of grandeur. Who needs it? Like it or not, we are far greater than we can possibly imagine—likewise, far smaller—as an inseparable part of a magnificent whole.

Makes you wonder how to categorize the et ceteras of life. N.C. Wyeth, Andrew's father and only teacher, was an excellent painting instructor. He would point to a certain fold in the cloth he'd draped for a still-life. Then he would caution his students with something like, "Notice that fold. That's as important as the motion of the planets or the position of the sun in holding our universe together."

Now that's elevating an et cetera. Unless, of course you happen to believe all things in the universe are connected to one another. His father's philosophy may explain Andrew Wyeth's work—a serious statement concerning the mystery in what we mistakenly dub realism.

You have to step back a bit for a larger view before life becomes a Sunday in the park, before it resembles a Seurat painting made up of tiny detached strokes of shimmering color. And then it becomes difficult to decide which dots are the most important and which ones are the et ceteras.

You could say our significance reaches cosmic proportions. When we know this through *experience*, there is hope for a loss of self-consciousness in favor of an honest openness that is real. Great prophets have ever told us that in finding self, we lose it.

I recall reading that an open person floating or hanging in a web, can become a guru. I don't know if this is true, but it reminds me of Henry James's description of experience: ..."an immense sensibility, a kind of huge spider-web of the finest silken threads suspended in the chamber of consciousness, and catching every air-borne particle in its tissue." I have known a few acutely sensitive and aware individuals. One whom I came to know intimately changed my life without trying or meaning to. Al-though he abandoned his studies for the priesthood, he was a shaman nonetheless.

We must dig deeply when we mine for Truth. It often hides in those myths and metaphors that speak the language of the heart and move beyond the "facts" of history. In his book, *C.G. Jung and Herman Hesse,* Miguel Serrano relates an interesting conversation in which Ochwiay Biano (Mountain Lake), a Pueblo chief, tells Jung he is perplexed by the eternal restlessness of the whites. He felt they were crazy since they maintained they thought with their heads, whereas it is well known only crazy people do that. An astounded Jung asked the Indian how he thought. "With my heart, naturally," Ochwiay replied.

Jung noted that is also the way the ancient Greeks thought. And modern white man? "Only with their tongues," Jung maintained. Placing his hand on his neck, he said, "They think only with words...words today have replaced the Logos."

We have lost touch with the frightening, primitive, inexplicable experiencing of the Logos...that which silences the endless cackle of men.

Why are we so fearful of self-knowledge? What are we really afraid of? A fleeting glimpse of the awesomeness we've labeled God?

***

AN ENCHANTED COTTAGE

I can see her now, standing in the rain, one hand holding an umbrella, the other waving goodbye as our bus passed Ivy Cottage. Bringing bits and pieces into focus is like clearing patches of mist from a foggy window...the better to visualize a memory. At the time, you see, I didn't write it down. Someone has said a dull pencil stub will ever surpass memory.

We were on a two-week tour of New Zealand, and had chosen an overnight home-stay with a farm family. Rather than a farm, Ivy Cottage turned out to be a charming five-room house on a small lot. Hidden from the road by tall trees, isolated from the busy-ness of the world by luxuriant hedges, entangled in vines, like a boulder or a fallen tree, the cottage was an organic part of a fragrant garden in full bloom...in February.

The sky had opened. Rain was spilling down when Brian Leckie, our host, met our tour bus in Dunedin and picked up three of our tour group (an English lady named Tessa, my husband, Ralph, and me) and drove us to Waihola, a town of 250 population located 40 kilometers to the south.

Arrangements were made whereby the bus driver would pick us up in Waihola the following morning...the town was located on the bus route of State Highway 1. (No super-highways in New Zealand.)

Brian, thinking we might be disappointed by a small town bed and breakfast rather than a real farm, drove extra kilometers to show us an Agricultural Research Center, a lamb slaughter-house, a Holstein dairy farm, a deer farm, and a unique veterinary clinic. In each instance, we pulled into the drive and were given vital statistics about the special state-of-the-art work being done there. Windshield wipers flapped while Tessa and I, seated in back, wiped away circles of moisture from side windows as we looked and listened. Brian parked on the bank of the Taieri River. "Gold was discovered here a century ago," he said.

Most intriguing of all was the house he called home. "Welcome to Ivy Cottage," he announced, driving into his secluded haven—the place his Scottish grandfather had built when he came to New Zealand in the mid 1800's.

Motioning to a small guest house which he called 'the shed', Brian said, "You'll be staying there."

Can't be right, methinks. I was sure I'd misunderstood when I peeked through the glass in the door and saw a 1936 Austin roadster, the car his son had driven to school, he explained later. The sight of that little auto hit a tuning fork in my brain. My first car, the one I learned to drive in 1934, was a lavender Austin. My father had driven it home from Madison. It was a gift for my *tenth* birthday—much to my mother's horror.

Inside, a strip of carpeting led us, via a circuitous path, to a charming bedroom with bay window, a loft, and small bath.

In the main cottage, we met Robin Leckie, our hostess— what a rare gift is a face that radiates goodwill making you feel you've encountered a friend. Such mischief in her smile. Such fun in the way she said "Yay-ess," and then repeated "Yay-ess" again, agreeing wholeheartedly with a remark I'd made. Her blue eyes danced; her short and straight gray hair hugged her head like a cap.

Brian, a hale and husky gentleman, had full lips and thick brows. He was soft-spoken and a lazy smile played across his heavy features. A retired engineer (like my husband), his children had him pegged. "They say, 'Just give Dad a level and a measuring stick for checking this and that and he'll be happy for all of his years,'" Robin explained with a laugh. There was between the couple an abiding comfort that knew no camouflage.

While we were enjoying drinks and pre-dinner

conversation in a sitting room, their son Richard, his little daughter, and a young German woman stopped by. The young folks wore shorts and Richard wore a loose-fitting, sleeveless tunic that resembled a gunny sack with a hole for a head cut in the top. Even the beige color was about right, but the fabric was richly soft and fuzzy. He wore sandals and his luxuriant dark hair curled over his ears. He lacked only a staff and slingshot, for I was reminded of biblical drawings of young David when he slew the giant.

I mistook the attractive German woman for Richard's wife, mother of the small girl, whereupon Robin, who was seated beside me on the sofa, shielded her mouth with her hand, and whispered, "It's not his wife. I'll explain later. When my friends declare their families are so perfect—no problems—I don't even believe them. Not in this crazy age!" And then, in wistful tones, "He's such a gentle boy."

"Who does Richard remind you of?" I asked Ralph, "especially when he smiles?" His teeth were large and straight and white.

"Tim," my husband replied. "Uncanny, isn't it? Spittin' image." He could have been a twin to our son-in-law.

After the young folks left, I pointed to the vines that crept inside through the window frames and crawled up the wall, making their way to the ceiling. "Reminds me of my childhood. Vines that covered our house came creeping inside my upstairs bedroom exactly like that. I've never seen the like anywhere else before or since."

Brian chuckled. "So it makes you feel right at home."

"It does," I admitted. The buffet with heavy, carved legs was similar to the one we had in the dining room when I was a child. I walked toward it to have a closer look and examined a piece of framed needlework hanging above it. Robin explained she had made a sampler with the birthdates of their six children.

I began to read: Philip, April 4, 1951. "Our son, John, has the same birthday," I noted with excitement, "except he was born in 1946." The next entry: Susan, September 16, 1954. It was our daughter Beth's day and year of birth!

The table sat next to the windows facing the lake. The backyard garden exploded with color. Roses were white, pink, and red. Magenta blooms stood on slender stalks; blue and yellow blossoms hugged the ground. Violets tumbled over rocks, clusters of tiny white stars shot from green pockets. Lush green shrubs, twisting vines, and a grass carpet gave the display weight and substance, pinning it to reality.

Beyond the garden, black swans swam on Lake Waihola while we ate chicken breasts stuffed with apricots and carrots with a ginger-orange sauce. A dessert of homegrown black currants and raspberries topped the meal.

We talked of the British royals, of New Zealand sheep and sheep dogs and birds, and of ancestors—theirs and ours.

Breakfast saw the five of us seated at the same table enjoying a special cereal mix, apricots, juice, eggs, bacon, and (always in New Zealand!) broiled tomatoes.

It was *still* raining and the swans were still 'a-swimming' on Lake Waihola when Brian held an umbrella and hurried us into his automobile. We drove into the center of town where a tavern serves meals and has a beer garden, and where the general store provides postal services. We stopped in front of the local garage, parking to the far left of the gas pumps. "My father owned and operated the Chevrolet garage and a gas station in our small Wisconsin town for over fifty years," I said. "And my Aunt Mary was the local postmistress. I guess the right word is postmaster, but everyone called her the postmistress."

We listened to what had become the Waihola refrain—windshield wipers slapping forward and back. Tessa and I swished moisture from the windows and peering through the messy swirls, we awaited the bus from Dunedin.

"There it is!" Hurried goodbyes as we rushed from car to coach. When we passed Ivy Cottage, there was Robin standing at the roadside holding a yellow umbrella, waving in the rain.

At the time, I suspected I'd been privy to a memorable highlight in the pristine, yesterday land that is New Zealand.

I know it now. I received a note from Robin with the recipes I'd forgotten in our mad scramble to the car in the morning rain...recipes for cheese sticks, bran muesli, ginger marmalade—and, most importantly, a memory that gives me pause.

***

A MATTER OF INTEGRITY

In the summer of 1923, before I was born, Elwyn Brooks White was writing in his journal "A man must have something to cling to. Without that he is as a pea vine sprawling in search of a trellis."

Forty years later, he quoted the entry in an essay and scoffed at his early writing style, which he dubbed "a stomach-twisting blend of the *Bible*, Carl Sandburg, H.L. Mencken, and a few other writers including Franklin Pierce Adams imitating Samuel Pepys."

Looking back, he regarded his dismissal from *The Times* as inevitable. "As a newspaper reporter, I was almost useless, and it came as no surprise when one more trellis collapsed on me."

Nevertheless, his inner response was one of relief when he found himself rootless and adrift rather than firmly planted in the city newsroom. In what must have been a mood of righteous joy, one month later in that summer of 1923, he pasted in the same journal a Morley sonnet which advised, "so put your trust in poets."

It was a pinch of pain and a pleasurable pinch of empathy that I came upon that bit of reading. The response is deep when you identify physically, mentally, and emotionally with a given experience.

It happened not too long ago and I learned a great deal from it. With only minor trepidation, I innocently consented to fill in temporarily as Public Information Coordinator at our local branch of the State University.

For a few months, I went in three days each week, at which time I was the liaison between the campus and the media. I compiled the bi-weekly faculty bulletin and processed schedules for visiting tour groups. Remembering the experience sets my molars to grinding and makes my breathing grow uneasy.

The Arts Council called to say I'd neglected a few dates, hours, and room numbers on the list I'd sent to be included in their calendar of events. To a real journalist, those all-important four Ws constitute unconscious behavior. A true reporter would be more apt to neglect brushing his teeth than to forget a what, when, why, or where.

I noticed my news story on new enrollment figures had been revamped and revised by the time it hit the local newspaper. I realized then why a note had suggested sending the piece to the President's office before release. One does not mention any drops in totals, I learned. Increases are emphasized. It's not dishonesty, but deft maneuvering of statistics that can make a minus appear a plus. A simple basic principle of public relations had passed me by: You accent the positive...and whenever possible, *e*-liminate the negative.

There was the day the Professor of Music asked me to write about the Renaissance Christmas Festival. I was pleased with the natural rhythmic way in which imagery had enriched my description. When she sat opposite my desk and slashed her pencil through a line, I winced, "You've ruined my alliteration." She gave me a withering look.

Not every experience was unpleasant. Dr. Leslie Fiedler visited our campus and talked about his latest book. I drove him to his television and radio appointments and we had a chance to chat over coffee. Would he mind if I wrote a story about him? I sold the profile to a New York magazine.

However, in general it went against my nature to go probing into professors' offices seeking newsworthy tidbits about conferences they'd chaired or their most recent academic publications. For me, roaming about for stories had different connotations. I wanted to write about the humor, poignancy, and irony of conversations overheard in elevators, about the graffiti scribbled on bathroom walls, even the way October sunlight bounced off the elm leaves outside my window.

There were metaphors and truths and humorous paradoxes in the poetry that was life being lived on campus. These were the things I wished to record; the timeless universal things one could write about *honestly.*

And so at home I wrote essays about my aging mother and short stories about my old hometown. In my writing classes I pleaded with students to dig deeply. "No need to bare your soul, but anything you *choose* to write about merits complete honesty."

It was with mutual relief, I'm sure, that the Office of Public Relations and I said Good-bye. A young woman left her post at the newspaper office to become the new and efficient Director of Communications.

I rejoiced at being free to choose writing subjects about which I could be sincere and enthusiastic. I was being true to my nature. It was a matter of integrity.

I've always enjoyed exploring interesting places and have kept somewhat sketchy records of trips and vacations. The getting there is usually less than pleasureful. Jet travel is dehumanizing. Hotels are filled with noisy people. However, I love experiencing the feel and flavor of quiet hideaways.

And so I began revisiting my notebooks. What joy reliving that long week of summer at Kitty Hawk. It was our first stay on an ocean shore and we learned the sandy peninsula, known as the North Carolina Outer Banks, abounds with legend and history.

We were there in late May before the summer hordes descended. Our secluded cabin of weather-beaten shingles wind whipped to gray and beige, faded into the treeless dunes of Nags Head. The house stood some distance from other cottages that perched near the sea on stilts, like a cluster of herons.

We examined seaweed and crustacea and fish that had been washed ashore and compared their shapes with illustrations in our sea-encyclopedia. We sat on the windy deck, binoculars in hand, spying dolphins hemstitching the waves and kids sailing long-tailed kites. We examined clumps of faded grass and watched the sand crabs scurry sideways. We were observers of sand and sea shells; of boats falling off the far edge of the world and barnacles clinging to ocean piers. We watched ungainly gulls gain sudden grace with wingspread and a lift of wind.

Like Thoreau, we threw away whole days for a single expansion of air. Poetic truth, the wisdom that will not be fenced by time, became our daily breath.

Delighted were we to be some distance from motels and entertainment centers—roller rinks, bowling alleys, and sand hills alive with rented gliders. Our beach house was ideally located on a rare fragment of unspoiled shoreline where commercialism had not reared its ugly head.

That reminds me, one day soon I must write a travel piece about our sequestered stay on the Baja peninsula. Might bring a right tidy sum. What's more, if I'm able to sell it, it would mean I could deduct at least part of our vacation expenses. Of course, the trick would be to find a purist editor, who puts his trust in a writer, who puts her trust in poets.

These days that's probably impossible. Seems the only thing people are interested in is the almighty dollar.

***

OUR STRANJ LANGWAJ, OR THERE'S SOMETHING FISHY ABOUT PHONETICS

In a scathing report delivered to the American people, The National Commission on Excellence in Education stated: "A tide of mediocrity has devastated public education." Not only students, but also teachers (in states where examinations are required for certification) did poorly on standardized tests in spelling and language.

While I'm not suggesting we shift *all* the blame on our strange English language, it does seem the originators could have given more thought to consistency, phonetics, and simple common sense. Surely they must have foreseen a few problems.

We seem to have created contradictory complexities. For instance, can you fathom why break doesn't sound like freak? Why do we pronounce sew so unlike few? Wouldn't you think in making a verse, that you could rhyme horse with worse, instead of hearse with purse?

Sometimes 'oe' is o as in foe; other times it's oo as in shoe. Sometimes 'ow' is pronounced like ou in ouch—as in cow. Often it's a long o as in low. But in bow, it can be either depending upon context. Don't look for rules or reasons, and don't expect rules to be spelled like tools.

For added perplexity, how about hose and dose and lose? Or consider the hunter who does not shoot does. Comb and tomb and bomb you'd think might sound somewhat the same. If say rhymes with pay, why not said with paid?

Looking at the letters, you'd think you could match good with food and blood, rather than with could and would. And why not mould, which incidentally, is also mold?

If heard is spelled like beard, why does it sound like bird? Why should dead be said like bed, when it looks so much like bead, which goes right well with deed?

Here's another to ask your mother—why doesn't moth

rhyme with both? Add "er" and another puzzle perplexes...mother sounds slightly different than bother. Explain to me, if you please, why meat and great and threat rhyme respectively with suite and straight and debt? Rhyme and rime can mean different things, but the second spelling makes more sense to me. Seems more rooted in logicality.

Makes you question the worth of those crazy dictionaries for bad spellers. The idea is you look up your own "sensible phonetic" version, and Voila! thereby unveil the correct spelling in the process.

No doubt about it, there's something mighty fishy about phonetics. George Bernard Shaw came up with this unusual spelling for an everyday word: GHOTI. Stumped? Gh as in enough, o as in women, ti as in nation spells FISH. Simple! Just use your hed and you, too, can be a perfect speller.

***

I MARRIED AN ENGINEER

Recently a woman complained to Ann Landers about her engineer husband, then asked, "Are engineers really different?" Landers printed letters written in reply to the initial complaint. The majority of those who responded felt engineers were indeed "different" and also "cut from the same cloth."

While a good many regarded them as fine husbands and family men, most admitted, engineers could be exasperating. As a group they were described as highly intelligent perfectionists with little patience. "He expects our kids to behave like robots," one wife complained. One man felt his wife, an engineer, was insufferable and vowed next time he'd marry a bimbo.

Being married to an engineer, whose father was an engineer, and whose brother and two brothers-in-law are engineers, and whose son (who is also my son) is an engineer, gives me reason, perhaps even credibility, to comment.

I am reminded of a poem by Carl Sandburg. The first line goes like this: "Arithmetic is where numbers fly like pigeons in and out of your head." Poems I like. Arithmetic I hate.

So how do you think I feel being a poem-lover in a family of precision tick-tock minded arithmetic-lovers? Given departure and arrival times, they can tell you (quick as a wink) how fast an airplane travels from Dubuque to San Diego with a stopover in Oklahoma City, compared to a bus, traveling on land.

They can tell you how much fuel each uses per mile, when each will reach a certain spot, and how many nickels you save on one or the other when you figure in meals and overnight stops.

Brain-twisters are their cup of tea. Tea, too, gets mathematically analyzed. My husband decided it's more economical to buy it loose rather than bagged. Ralph looks at the tiny print on the box and figures out (while you snap a finger), how many cups we'll get from the package—thereby saving three cents each time. And we save six cents per cup compared to coffee—when you consider how many cups we get from a pound—finely ground.

I'm married to a mind that looks at a bare spot on the lawn and calculates (just like that) how many ounces of grass seed we need to cover it. He'll spout the square feet of wallpaper needed for two walls of a room and a hallway (in nothing flat).

My kids are the same: My son, the engineer; my daughter, the business manager; my daughter, the veterinarian. They can do puzzles—Whoosh! Minds like steel traps. "Give it to Mom," they sneer, after solving some complex conundrum (in a snap).

Pffft! So what? Who cares? There's more to life than figuring gas mileage, calculating gains and losses, comparing penny savings per ounce, and carefully filing every doggoned charge-card slip.

At least so I keep telling my husband, the engineer. My daughter-in-law understands. One day in frustration she complained to my son, "OOOHH, you're *just* like your father!"

"Thank you," he said.

Reminds me of the day I was at my wits end when I couldn't remember if I'd made a long distance call in question. Telephone bill in hand, Ralph suggested, "You really ought to mark calls on the calendar."

Tearing my hair, I shrieked, "How did we *ever* get together?"

He looked at me with that little crooked grin I love and offered patient explanation, "You're just a fool for luck, Hon."

***

LINEAR VISION

"Katie, are you busy? Come here a minute!" I was sure my engineer husband needed help on a project. He was doing something with an electrical socket in the living room.

But there Ralph stood, pointing toward the beamed ceiling. "Look at that," he directed, tilting his head in an awkward position. Try as I might, I saw nothing unusual or noteworthy.

He steered me toward the sunbeams streaming in the west windows, then maneuvered my position and pointed up once more. "There, now can you see it?"

One single strand of spider web spanned one end of the living room. A few silken threads branched off from the edge of the corner wall and then a single one sailed across twelve feet of open space before latching onto a macramé plant hanger.

I looked up web construction in my encyclopedia, but I couldn't really find a satisfactory explanation. Seems there are trap door spiders who build silk-lined tubes as well as funnel-weaving spiders and web spiders. The most elaborate orb webs that you see covered with dew in the early morning are constructed by several families. Such an intricate web can be completed in about an hour, usually before daybreak.

Initially, a spider releases a silk thread which is carried by the wind. If it does not attach to an object, the spider pulls it back and feeds upon it. When it does fasten itself to a twig or leaf, that thread gets reinforced as a bridge and the hub is established from its center. A spiral web results. But this was not a spiral web and there is little wind in my living room.

The bolas spider, I learned, releases a single thread with a sticky droplet at the end, holds it with one leg and swings it into space.

I don't know if our variety was bolas or the common house spider, but I get quite a picture in my mind imagining that fellow winding up and swinging the old discus. But twelve feet? Come on!

The episode sent Ralph looking up accounts of Roebling and the steel suspension construction of the Brooklyn Bridge.

As for me, I was recalling that yesterday's newspaper mentioned an elementary school teacher was taking his class to the Cape Kennedy Space Center to witness the launching of a shuttle. A worthy crusade, an awesome mission. I only hope the kids, in being hustled so far, don't become shortsighted. No doubt about it, man has made spectacular advances. Nevertheless, he needs a carrier for his ventures into space. Even birds require wings.

How in the world did that spider span an entire room and leave his own jet stream as evidence? Chances are it's not a matter of brains—although I did read drugging spiders adversely affected their web-spinning efforts. All the same, it makes you pause and wonder—exactly who are the smart guys in the scheme of things?

Author note: The shuttle launching referred to in the essay ended in a disastrous explosion which killed all aboard, including a young mother who was an elementary school teacher. The irony of the piece was thus intensified and its editorial appeal was lessened significantly.

***

TENDING THE EMPTINESS

I'm tending the Gallery Shop at the Art Center. It's hot in this room. Steam pipes hiss. Fluorescent lamps hum...a billion bees, no less.

Mary leaves. Pat leaves. I'm alone, surrounded by art objects of wood, fabric, clay, glass, and stone, as well as paintings done in watercolor, oil, and acrylic. Macramé hangings and collages hug the walls, mobiles dangle from the ceiling, photographs are displayed on folding screens, stoneware pots rest on shelves and pedestals.

Cars and trucks roar past. Occasionally a car pulls in or out of the parking spaces right outside the big front windows, but no one looks this way. It requires careful attention to maneuver safely through city traffic.

Nancy Gavin stops by for her free watercolor. She's one of the Art Council's first fifty members this year.

A young mother with a babe in arms fingers the handmade wooden toys. She pushes forward, then back, the little train that comes apart. Would she like help?

"No, thank you, we're only looking. We just came from the doctor's office." She's addressing me, but her eyes never leave the infant. With her free arm, she wiggles a bird mobile to amuse her child, then heads for the door.

"Thank you for stopping."

She smiles, nods, and the door chimes crackle the warm.

A woman asks for handmade notepaper, finds none, but browses a while.

A man wearing a gray tattered coat, a vacant stare, and a half-grown beard, shuffles in from the street. (The thought crosses my mind, could I exit quickly from the rear if necessary?) "Do ya need an artist's model?" he asks. "I can give ya references."

"References?" I manage to squelch a smile.

He says he has posed for art classes at the university.

"I'm just a volunteer," I explain. "Stop by tomorrow

when the director is here."

Four interruptions punctuate four silent hours.

I pick up a book of poems written by a local poet and published by a university press. It sells for $5. The poet looks at me from the back cover. She's young and beautiful. Paging through the chapbook, I am magically transported into an old woman's lonely existence. I read about death and revelation and joy; I peek inside a mother's heart at birthing time. She looks too young to possess such wisdom. She must have given Pain careful attention when it came to call.

One poem is titled, "Tending The Emptiness." Three em-blazoned words take on sudden and personal meaning in this high-ceilinged room with white walls, humming lights, hissing heat pipes, door chimes, and a telephone that buzzes once in a while.

It occurs to me, not only do people need Art to enrich their lives and help them 'see'; Art needs people. Art may take on a life of its own, but of what value *life* without communication—without a perceiving mind, a seeing eye, a listening heart?

I envision the potter at his wheel breathing life into clay, the weaver at her loom turning color and texture into textile hymns, the poet in the dim light of a snow-filled dawn recalling the birth of her girl-child, Abigail Anne.

There is silent exultation in creating, an activity which very often is not a matter of personal choice. Life's major decisions are often not made in the mind. Once you've plugged into the deepest rhythms of life (even accidentally), into that generative energy which is a part of us and apart from us, compulsion and intuition become directive forces. Artists find themselves sculpting, painting, composing music, or writing poems, with recompense farthest from the mind, as toil continues doggedly in solitude during secret, stolen hours.

Once in awhile, if one is lucky, in the penurious, precious quiet time after the mundane tasks of daily life are completed, joy erupts from knowing the work is "good"—a resultant elation from hoping its birth communicates the creator's vision.

At least, that's often been my experience while alone and writing. Now, sitting at the other end of the line, I realize how hollow the loneliness of the tending time—the waiting for shoppers with shekels they're spending across town at the mall. Perhaps they're playing video games, selecting synthetic baubles, buying food, clothes, stoves, or televisions—even medicine for the baby. Natural enough. Life has its priorities. Nevertheless, Art, too, is a sustainer—of sacred proportion.

Alone in this room with vaulted ceilings, I am reminded of an essay in which Lewis Lapham laments the lagging of the human imagination. He scolds us for becoming literal-minded, short-sighted people who demand earthquakes and explosions to make visible the reality we cannot otherwise see. We fail, he says, to see the heroic in the commonplace, which is as much a part of our daily lives as eating toast for breakfast or waiting in line for a bus.

Is even tending the emptiness, if not heroic, at least worthwhile, if in quiet desperation, one shapes of it a simple examined moment pulled from time?

***

SUNSET

ON JOINING THE COMMUNITY
OF WISE WOMEN

As a closing exercise of a recent weekend retreat, we were given a papier-mâché mold of a face. "Be free. Work silently, opening yourself to God and let the mask reveal who you are," the facilitator advised. A table overflowed with feathers and beads, scissors and glue, sequins, paints, crayons, magic markers, ribbons, and yarn. "Nature music" provided a soothing backdrop of singing birds and falling water.

It just wasn't working for me. A few facial lines of green, flowers for eyes, purple polka dots falling down the left cheek, a feather hat with flowers atop curly hair. The open mouth revealed the space between my teeth.

"Ridiculous," I murmured. My frustration intensified as I glanced at the masterpieces taking form around me. I whispered to my neighbor, "If God is speaking to me, I'm in deep trouble. This poor thing is a joke!"

"Put them on this table," our leader advised, "and let's gather 'round so each may comment upon her mask."

"Do we *have* to?" I groaned.

Suddenly I was reminded of what I'd written minutes before. (Perhaps there *was* after all a message in my mask!) We had been asked to reflect upon, then write about: (1) "What it means for me personally to join the community of wise women? What roles and new beliefs will I embrace?" (2) "Write a simple prayer or commitment for whatever you desire as you take this step. (Do not be afraid—you are already precious in God's eyes.)"

Rather than comment verbally, I chose to read my written reflections as I showed my mask:

I don't know that I like the categorization implied in the phrase "join the community of wise women." I don't know that I believe there is such a group "set apart" from others. Matter of fact, I think humans could learn a lot from other species if they paid attention.

Only humans find it difficult to tap into their own music. An acorn "doin' what comes natcherly" becomes an oak tree, a tadpole becomes a frog, and from a caterpillar—a butterfly. But humans suffer, toil, ache with remorse and guilt, chastise and correct, even murder their own kind. However, they also know compassion for one another, create and appreciate beauty, and they *love*, listen, and pray.

All this because they ate from the tree of knowledge. Consciousness dawned!

The Grand Inquisitor in *The Brothers Karamazov* insisted he was only correcting God's mistake in bequeathing free will to humankind. Humans, he felt were ill-equipped to handle that awesome responsibility. They only need "some means of uniting all in one unanimous and harmonious ant-heap," he said. They need to be told, corrected, led, and shown the way.

Who should lead? The same divine wisdom lies deep inside everyone. The nonsensical inconsistencies of being human dwell there too. We are each the fool—something we might do well to remember.

I will admit one of my finest spiritual teachers was a wise female, namely my mongrel terrier, Duchess. Is it silly to say a *dog* brought out the best in me? To Duchess, I had no faults. She had a remarkable way of making me feel good and loved and needed. She was 'lost' when I was gone and she ran in crazy circles when I returned. How few folks know the art of living. Duchess knew it well. There was no hidden reality behind the outward show. Hers was a hardy soul at peace with itself and its fellow man.

I taught writing for nigh on a quarter century. In every class I urged, "Dig deeply. Write honestly." When men and women did that, the self shown through for all to see. It freed others who were initially afraid to dig and reluctant to share. I'm talking about the self that God knows, the one that tugs a string attached to every heart.

Therefore, my prayer, my commitment would be: Help me to remember WHO I AM and to live accordingly.

***

AN OLD WIVES' TALE

Pilgrims are persons in motion—passing through
territories not their own—seeking something we
might call completion, or perhaps the word clarity
will do as well, a goal to which only the spirit's
compass points the way.

Richard R. Niebuhr
"Pilgrims and Pioneers"

Pilgrims will ever pioneer the wilderness, exploring frontiers not simply of the earth and the heavens, but of the human mind and soul as well. Recently I embarked on just such a journey at a South Georgia College Elderhostel, which offered a course in *The Canterbury Tales*. The pilgrimage, quite unexpectedly, led me home.

First let me explain that upon occasion I may forget my social security number or my anniversary—but *never* the first few lines of the Prologue to the Canterbury Tales:

> When that Aprille with his schowres soote
> The droghte of Marche hath perced to the roote
> And bathed every veyne in swich licour
> Of which vertu engendred is the flour....

...Geoffrey Chaucer (1340? -1400)

Memorized at age 15, the words came splashing into my life over half a century later.

It would seem that in the spring of the year after a long hard winter, a pilgrimage appeals as much to folks in the 20th as in the 14th century. Our destination was an Elderhostel on Jekyll Island, Georgia; not nearly as impressive a journey as the one made in the late 1300s from the outskirts of London to the shrine of St. Thomas Becket at Canterbury. The latter was the sort of holiday which earned church approval and impressed one's neighbors. Chaucer had his travelers tell stories to "shorten the way" along the sixty-mile, four-day trip.

Nevill Coghill, translator of the Penquin Classic version of *The Canterbury Tales,* says, "In all literature there is nothing that touches or resembles the *Prologue.* It is the concise portrait of an entire nation, high and low, old and young, male and female, lay and clerical, learned and ignorant, rogue and righteous, land and sea, town and country.... They are the perennial progeny of men and women. Sharply individual, together they make a party."

And make a party we did that spring of 1994. Nine and forty of us came together from all parts of our nation to study Chaucer at a hostelry on Jekyll Island off the coast of Georgia.

We traveled with friends we'd known since college. Our classes: "Human Nature in Chaucer's Canterbury Pilgrims," "Big Bands Swing Again," and "History of Coastal Georgia."

The Big Bands class was the drawing card. In their youth, my husband and my college roommate's husband played in the University of Wisconsin band—tenor sax and drums respectively. And once upon a day, when their sacroiliacs allowed it, they were jitterbugs extraordinaire. My husband and others I chanced to overhear, were sure they'd not cotton to Chaucer, but thanks to an excellent teacher, it turned out to be a popular offering. No class-cutting all week despite a golf course adjacent to the inn.

Kathleen Lundahl, a retired educator, proved an excellent instructor. By way of introduction to her subject, she bounced from podium to blackboard sketching diagrams, pulling facts from her well-stocked mind, in short, making the history of the English language not simply palatable, but fascinating.

By the time we got to the *Prologue,* she was on fire with her subject, drawing parallels between the diverse travelers in our group and Chaucer's party trekking to Canterbury.

We dissected the idiosyncrasies and hypocrisies of the nine and twenty who gathered that first night in Southwark just outside of London at the Tabard hostelry.

There was the Knight who'd done nobly in his sovereign's wars—both Christian and heathen. He'd fought in Prussia, Russia, Granada, and Anatolia—and always killed his man. Distinguished and wise, he was modest as a maid...and gentle.

The Nun was all sentiment and tender heart, weeping if she saw a mouse bleeding, speaking daintily in French, ever mindful "to counterfeit a courtly kind of grace."

The Monk was fat and liked to eat. The Friar encouraged penance-giving, for it meant a decent living. He knew the taverns well and barmaids too. In short, he was a good and crafty beggar.

The Franklin loved a morning sop of cake and wine and lived for pleasure, while the Summoner had carbuncles and narrow eyes. He was lecherous as a sparrow with scabby brows and thin beard. Children were afraid when he appeared. He took bribes of food, money, wine, and favors of concubines.

How little folks change in 600 years! Then as now, a good man or woman was hard to find. Not the Merchant, the Franklin, nor the Friar; not the Summoner, the Holy Nun, nor the Haberdasher. Only the Country Parson and the Plowman were holy-minded

Our fellow traveler was a farmer and so that correlation was made in class. In this instance, no one knew as well as we, how very accurate was the comparison—another plowman who was wise and honest, good and true.

It was, however, when the master-teacher got to the lusty, five-times-married Wife of Bath that my mind went tumbling backward through the years...thanks to my high school English teacher.

I can see her now. There was a sureness in the way she stood at the open door of Room 204, one hand on the doorknob, the other on her hip. A long, freshly-sharpened pencil was tucked into the twisted knot of hair at the back of her neck.

Miss Weston had snappy brown eyes that caught fire when she smiled. Her thin lips swept into a delicate v-shaped smile revealing the tiniest thread of gold on a front tooth...an under-stated touch of splendor befitting her distinguished demeanor.

She wore tailored suits and silk shirtwaists fastened at the neckline with a cameo. Her shapely legs were full at the calf, but they narrowed nicely into small ankles. Dainty feet were tucked into soft leather pumps.

And she was brilliant...freshly graduated from Milwaukee Downer College, she wore a Phi Beta Kappa key. She called it "fi-bate".

"Did you say you were fly bait?" Whizzer Wiley was the class clown; he'd say just about anything. "Didn't know flies needed house keys."

"Phi Beta Kappa is," she explained icily, "the most elite of honor societies." Any fool knew that.

How I idolized this paragon of pedagogues who knew absolutely all there was to know about everything.

One day she began reading to the class in a foreign language, "When that Aprille with his schowres swoote, The droghte of Marche hath perced to the roote..." It was Middle English, she explained, the ancestor of Shakespearean English.

We took turns reading aloud from the Prologue. When we got to the gat-toothed Wife of Bath, no one knew what gat-toothed meant. "Can anyone guess?" Miss Weston asked. She waited, scanned the class, and then looked straight at me.

"Catherine is gat-toothed," she said.

Every pair of eyes fastened upon my mouth. I found that space between my front teeth sufficiently humiliating without having the attention of the class focused upon it. Surely vanity never had a stronger hold than at age fifteen, going on sixteen. It was like having the elastic in your underpants snap and having them fall around your ankles. It was like dreaming you were waltzing down Main Street bare-naked, but this was for real.

Even worse, the footnote said gat-toothed in Chaucer's

time, was associated with amorousness and sensuality. Miss Weston had the good grace not to pursue the definition further.

I must have forgiven her and forgotten the shame because when I was in college I wrote her a letter in care of a Mrs. Weston on N. Buffum St. in Milwaukee, who I thought was her mother. I figured it would be forwarded. Instead, it was returned with a letter from a Mrs. Weston who said she never had a daughter who taught English in our town.

Maybe you think I wasn't embarrassed when I visualized a stranger reading that letter. It was all about Miss Weston being the best teacher I ever had, how she had awakened my sensitivity, had lit the divine spark—flowery stuff like that. It's just as well it came back.

Likewise, the memories.

Soren Kierkegaard reminds, "Life can only be understood backwards, but it must be lived forwards."

What are memories if not loose pieces in a jigsaw puzzle...a fuzzy squiggle here, a twisted blur there, occasionally a precise image...ultimately keys to understanding. The creative imagination crafts meaning from "emotions recollected in tranquillity." We make connections, fit fragments together...Voila! a pattern emerges. A moment of grace as we peek at the whole.

Like "Aprille schowres," revived images engendre the flour. They, too, see to the blossoming. It's a perennial chore.

***

A WALK IN WINTER

Late this mid-winter afternoon, while the sun is still on its way to meet the land, my dog and I leave the warmth of the farm kitchen, brave the zero temperature, and walk across the fields.

We pass Amigo, my daughter's horse. He decides to walk with us as far as the fence will allow, then he stands and watches, his heavy fur coat rippling in the wind.

With the delicate sensitivity of an artist, the sun makes intricate patterns of light and shade as it plays upon the waves and ripples of windblown snow. Chopped soybean stubble pierces the silver surface and casts long deceiving shadows, blue against white. My boots crumple rows of gray brittle stalks. The snapping sound syncopates the dull munching of boot against snow.

Duchess bounds ahead of me. She flattens her front legs and burrows her nose in the snow, turning her head from side to side. Her tail waves like a white flag in the wind.

Suddenly a great flock of crows make a ruckus as they alight from the hedgerow of Osage orange trees. Impulsively, I imitate their squawking cries as I stare overhead. One vibrating discordant caw from me sets a new batch of ebony birds flapping in unified and noisy protest from the trees just down the line.

I scale the fence, Duchess darts between two strands of barbed wire and we cut across grasslands. The wind has hurried the snow along this stretch; walking is easier and here and there thick brown grass is immediately underfoot.

Winter has edged the evergreens with eyelet. Stepping into the pine grove, I discover that chunks of snow have fallen from branches making craters in the snow, much like the small pox scar just above my nose.

In skirting the grove, I startle a few pheasants. They screech and, with a mighty slapping and whirring of wings, make a rapid departure. This must be their playground, for tiny tracks make coleslaw of the once untrammeled snow.

And did you know that pheasants, too, make winter angels? I notice the careful markings of tail feathers and on each side the pattern of a wing. The same impression is repeated again and again as I continue on my way. It's almost as if one used his finger and drew the pattern in the snow; a delicate arched fan at the rear and the wing feathers gently curved back toward the splayed tail.

Are they oblivious to their feathered images in the snow, or do they, like humans, delight in dabbling impressions on the soft receptive white? Perhaps all this is due to some sort of mating ritual?

Winter walks mean bird and animal tracks to study, patterns to please the eye, winds that whisper wily secrets, clear blue skies that wrap the horizon and become reflected in the mirror of snow. Sounds are intensified in the cold stillness, colors are more vibrant, outlines more clear. I experience the sensation of being an entity quite apart ...remote and observing. I exist on another strata.

As I round the hill, my tracks come to meet me and I now and then hop into the same holes in the snow, or then again, beat yet another path across the field. Duchess has covered far more territory than I with her leaping, bounding, jumping, and circling.

The trip back home is not (as I had hoped) easier than the first. The wind stings my face, bites my nose, and dulls my senses. I always hope for answers on the trip back from whence I came, but always I am left to wonder, even as I open the kitchen door to warmth and security.

***

ON WRITING MY OWN OBITUARY

I wrote the following essay in 1973, thinking I had stumbled upon a humorous topic. I scattered random notes across a blank page, as is my habit when writing—laughing at each innuendo.

The piece surprised me and turned out to be serious and revelatory. When I sent it to the editor of Spiritual Life, the quarterly of the Carmelites, he replied, "I promise not to change a word if you will permit me to change the title to "The Role of the Feelings in the Spiritual Life". I agreed, even though I felt I knew nothing about that.

Alden Whitman, chief obituary writer for the New York Times declared that "an obituary should be written with grace, capturing ideally its subject's unique flavor." Loudon Wainwright wisely concludes that "surely the unique flavor of some of the departed is best interred with their bones."

When I read the harshly naked facts of death notices, the list of dates, the names of survivors, the time of services, the place of interment, and the charities to which one may contribute, I shudder inside, particularly when the brittle notes refer to one I knew and loved. Where in that stiff parade of statistics is the essence of the person whom I once called a part of me?

Have you ever thought about writing your own obituary? Interesting idea, isn't it? What do you regard as your unique flavor? Despite Socrates' wise admonition to "Know Thyself," it does seem the quality we least possess is the ability to truly assess ourselves.

Nevertheless, I know that I possess one quality in abundance. It rules and dominates my being. It clumps my throat and makes my belly cringe with hurt and fear. It causes me to love deeply, completely, and everlastingly. Because of it, my heart leaps and pounds, or again puffs imperceptibly in quiet whispers. My blood crawls painfully up my inner arm; my feet leave the ground to tread on air; my arms ache to hold; my mind, in helpless isolation, shrieks for the comforting harbor of communication.

This part of me now and then informs me of secret hidden things; it sometimes lifts a mystical veil. Yet, other times, in quite the opposite direction, it blinds me to the infinite, imprisons my soul and denies me, too, the right to reason. It adds italics, underlines, and exclamation points to the living experience. Because it's there life is more painful, more poignant, more exquisite, and more beautiful. I feel deeply.

Feelings can't be explained, they simply are. To one who has them, one who hasn't seems cruel, cold, and quite bizarre. "The worst sin toward our fellow creatures," George Bernard Shaw observed, "is not to hate them, but to be indifferent to them; that's the essence of inhumanity."

Transcendental meditation is equated with an absence of earthly feelings, a serene union with the infinite. Certain philosophers and prophets envision the afterlife as a state devoid of feelings...the soul released from emotional bonds. If I merit blessed eternity, and such a theory is true, whatever will my simpering soul do without the feelings that are the essence of poor old me?

We are each deeply touched only by that which we are attuned to—any outward worldly happening, in order to impress us, must have its counterpart within our being. I find that as I grow older, my emotions may have become more steady, but they are also more aware. With a dispassionate disregard for our bruising places, life hurls us against her building wall of painful paradox and incomprehensible inconsistency. Inevitably, the soul absorbs along the way.

That universal bond of sympathy, that empathy which binds an infinitely loving and suffering mankind, has deepened and expanded with passing time. New depths of consciousness and sensitivity are ever wakened by the constant thirst for truth, by the everlasting search for some light to give meaning to one's existence. Man, so wise that galaxies and nuclei yield up their secrets to him, is yet so innocent that he knows not his true nature nor the purpose of his life.

My grown children have called me naive and innocent because I always want to believe the best. "Poor Mom, she doesn't know the score." In truth, I think I know a wee bit more than I am given credit for.

If when I die, someone says, there lies a silly intrepid dreamer, an impractical idealist, a stupid fool who dwelt too much upon the difference between what is and what ought to be; perhaps that someone knew me all too well, or maybe (like myself), he knew me not at all.

***

THE DAY MY MOTHER MET ZONA GALE

What tale from the Arabian Nights...is a
hundredth part as wonderful as this true fairy
story.... It is so much more heartening, too, than
the tales we invent.

...Clarence Day

It was a quiet winter afternoon. Snow had fallen through the night and popcorn flakes were continuing to refill roads as the lumbering snowplow, visible from my office window, rounded our curve. Skinny trees were fat ghosts; our fence posts wore saucy white caps.

Mother had propped pillows at one end of the sofa in my study. Her tiny frame took up only half the length. A dotted Swiss night cap covered her thin gray hair and a book rested on her bent knees. I should explain *that* in itself made this a momentous occasion. Mama often reads magazines and faithfully reads newspapers from front to back, including my husband's *Wall Street Journal*. But she never, *never* reads books.

"Don't like reading that made-up stuff," she declares. I'd rather spend my time reading what's true."

And so I must tell you how all this came about. I'd written a short piece about the Pulitzer Prize winning Wisconsin writer, Zona Gale. Thereafter, from halfway across the nation, I received a letter from Dorothy Walker, an attorney who lives in Portage, Wisconsin, and who was a very close friend of Zona Gale.

When I read the letter to my eighty-eight year old mother, she exclaimed, "Why I knew Dorothy Walker when we were young girls in Columbus." She proceeded to recall dances in the pavilion and celebrations in Fireman's Park.

Dorothy Walker was astounded and delighted, for she

276

also remembered Mother. She sent a collection of Zona Gale's short stories set in the author's hometown of Portage. It was this book that Mother started to peruse that afternoon in early December.

I watched her head move in little jerks from left to right while her nose wrinkled in a frown. I'll bet she needs new glasses, I was thinking, when suddenly Mama began chuckling softly. "Say, you know this is really good," she said, without lifting her eyes from the page.

Mother would read a bit, then be moved to comment. "She's right about small towns and rivers—they just kind of belong together. But who'd think of a thing like that? Grandma Lazers used to love living near the crick. Remember how she told you an airplane from the Old Country dropped you on a lily pad and she rushed to pick you up while her kolaches burned in the oven?"

Remember? I'll never forget. For years, I believed every word.

Zona Gale wrote about local funeral orations, most of them funny. Mother was remembering my Dad's funeral sermon. "You might say Father Adams was a stranger. He came to town three years before Dad died, but he gave such a wonderful sermon. I wish Dad could have heard it. He ended it saying, 'Congratulations, Frank!' He meant, we know you're in heaven, Frank, you made it." Her voice broke slightly.

"Can you feature that for a priest's name?" Noting my puzzlement at the sudden switch of focus, she elaborated, "Well, Adams doesn't sound like a Catholic name. It sounds Protestant. And Archie! Imagine that for a first name for a priest. They really like him in Marshall. He's into everything in town. His picture is in the paper every so often—always in a sport shirt. When I took over the money for the masses after Dad's funeral, he came to the door barefooted, wearing a bright yellow jacket that said BLATZ on the back."

A quiet interval, then, "Listen to this—here she writes about a woman calling a livery stable asking for the 'little blacks,' but they were at a funeral so they just changed them for her; hitched the bays to the hearse in front of the church instead." Mother laughed softly, "The livery man says, 'Reckon the *corpse* won't care.' He shouldn't have been too sure about that. I remember before my Dad died, he always told us, 'I don't want any undertaker's horses pulling me. I want my own gray team.' So the boys took the grays to town and hitched them to the hearse." She turned to me, "It was just like that hearse we saw in the County Museum last week, remember? That was back in 1917. Hardly seems possible."

Then she remembered a story much like the one in the book about a farmwife who didn't want her daughter to continue high school. "Mrs. Benny Schuster took her daughter out after three years. 'Margaret's gone long enough,' she says. 'One Domestic Science course and everything she makes, she needs a pound of butter.' She quit and went into the convent, you know, became a nun."

"Wasn't she a cook in the convent?"

"By Golly, you're right," Mother laughed. "I forgot that. Domestic Science was just what she needed after all, wasn't it? I bet she learned to use lard."

Speaking of village humor, Zona Gale acknowledged, "We do have our charming illogicalities." Mother was reminded of the time Tillie Haskins helped her serve at Ladies' Aid meeting. "She wanted to know what soap did I use to make my dishes so white. They were milk glass, mind you. When I told Dad, he said Tillie always did have a screw loose."

Chautauqua!" It was an awesome exclamation. "My, My! I haven't thought of that in years. One came to town in 1920. It was held in a tent behind the old school grounds."

"Weren't they religious revivals?" I asked.

"No, no, no. Well, inspirational, you might say. They had wonderful speakers. Music, plays. They were darned good. Had a different program every night of the week and they had a full house each time. My mother and Mrs. Louis Petty, Emma...Emma Petty was her name, went with Dad and me. It was shortly after we were married."

There was wonder in her voice. "I just can't get over it. I

feel like I've been reading things I saw happen in my own life."

"Even made-up stuff can do that for a person, Mama."

"Nope, I wouldn't give you a plugged nickel for those fairy tales, but this was darned good. So *real.*"

"Like reading a newspaper...of looong, long ago?"

"No, not really," she said. "More like yesterday."

***

NIGHT-TIME NICHES

Sometimes I can't sleep at night, but I have discovered there's magic in those lonely hours. My habitat grows small, secret, and silent.

Inside my dimly night-lighted house, with gossamer curtains drawn, 'they' can't see in, but I can see out. As I pass the glass sliding doors, my mirrored counterpart walks unfalteringly that narrow gap that slashes my inner and my outer world.

I study the patterns the moonlight draws. The shadow of a tree climbs the wall and travels the ceiling. I rest my head on the sofa back and watch a jet plane move steadily past the stars.

The sounds and silences are more pronounced than during daylight hours. They sing solos at night. The night defines and separates, making us look, making us listen. A cough or a snore crumples the quiet, then snuggles comfortably into the darkened corners of the hall. The refrigerator suffers from midnight dyspepsia; it belches and gurgles and its innards rumble. My electric clock grows garrulous; it gossips with a syncopated hum.

The telephone should keep its silence. A late and unexpected call is like a foot placed in an aisle, or a chair yanked asunder as one is sitting down. With ruthless glee, it jars the equilibrium.

A train whistle, a wailing siren, a truck that roars—each takes its turn echoing through the hollow halls of night.

I remember how, as a child with chicken pox, measles, or tonsillitis, I always grew sicker at night and ached for the morning sun. As a young mother, I watched helplessly as my children's ills grew in intensity and felt their fevers climb during the late and quiet hours. Dawn dragged its stockinged feet. I watched the clock...six, then seven. Could I call the doctor now?

As the children grew older, their curfew times grew later, so my anxieties multiplied with each set of headlights that turned our corner, then passed our drive. Whipping up a proper worry is harder in the sunlit hours. It takes darkness to perfect the art.

Mysteries must have been written at night, and letters of love, and formulas for magic potions. But if worry, pain, and loneliness creep into night-time niches that they may flourish there, it is yet true that stars, while *there* by day, can only live for us when sunshine hides behind the world. Unfathomable insights are born of darkness. Magical are the hours from dusk to dawn, vessels for dreaming—while we sleep, or while we wake.

***

FUNERAL BEGINS WITH F-U-N

So why should the subject be taboo? If death and taxes are inevitable, then also funeral, the ritual which accompanies the former. It's a celebration...a reunion. It's moving on or falling back into the mysteries of the universe...a rebirth.

I was, however, taken aback by the Miami funeral home that features a drive-in picture window where the deceased may be viewed at any hour by the interested, the curious, and the beloved. Not my idea of meaningful rites of passage.

Quite unlike some funerals I've attended lately which left lasting and favorable impressions. In accordance with his wishes, 30 family members scattered my brother-in-law's ashes, along with flowers, on the waters of his favorite fishing grounds in the Chesapeake Bay. The serene ritual completed, the boat rocked wildly, dashing every one off balance. "That's John registering approval," my husband said. The more literal-minded said it was the skipper's initial attempt to restart the engine.

And Lucille's requiem comes to mind. Large in body, mind, and spirit, she radiated positivism. Always late for writing class, the atmosphere came alive when she finally arrived. So lively was her manner, so varied her interests, you scarcely noticed the oxygen tank she carried, or the lifeless tufts of thinning hair. She lost her bout with cancer at age 52.

Talk about putting "fun" in funeral! Lucille's friends packed the biggest church in town. Family members wore smiles and rainbow colors. None more lively than son Eric, on leave from the Peace Corps in Togo, wearing an African robe of yellow, red, and green. He read his Mom's heartening letter, launching him on his exciting mission into the unknown. The send-off was an eerie and fitting turnabout. One daughter played the trumpet, the other shared her tribute while clasping a picture of her mother at age 16. Dad, in scarlet shirt, stepped forth to hug his offspring following each contribution.

An invitation to share feelings was followed by

momentary silence. Then the floodgates opened wide as young and old, male and female, rich and destitute, Christian and infidel, came forward one by one. It was astounding to witness the lives she touched. She rescued a young family from financial disaster, opened her home to a destitute young nursing student, even saved a child from drowning. The young mother tearfully related, "She insisted she didn't save Tommy, but she pulled him from the water. His scalp was torn back and she knew what to do. Lucille said she cried out for God's help and He gave it."

Finally, the minister had to tactfully end the testimonials. "I didn't know Lucille, but I do now," he said. Lucille called herself a born-again Christian, although she belonged to no church. Instead, she lived the holy enigma of the Christ, giving of her time, her money, and her heart. I heard many surprised attendants comment, "And I thought I was her closest friend!"

At the cemetery, across an expanse of green, the family emerged over a knoll. They came as one, arms linked, floating like a multi-colored scarf, hair blowing in the wind, laughing faces turned toward the sun. One would think they were off to a picnic, and indeed they were.

Friends gathered in the high school gymnasium (Lucille's husband is a high school teacher). A collage of memorable photographs hung on one wall. Festoons of ribbons and balloons dangled from the ceiling. There was fried chicken, and there was potato salad, and orange crush in barrels. Above the strains of her favorite music, I could imagine Lucille applauding and shouting, "Marvelous! Just marvelous!" Where Lucille *is*, there, too, is love kickin' up its heels.

When my husband's brother, Bud, went on to what he dubbed his "after-earth adventure," friends and relatives gathered at his church for a memorial service celebrating his life.

I often thought Bud was optimistic to a fault, ever looking at the bright side, refusing to see the 'real'. *"Everything* comes from God," he said. "I accept the good and the not-so-good." (He couldn't bring himself to say *bad!*) As he lay dying, he told me he felt lucky for the chance to say good-bye to loved ones. "If I'd been killed in an accident I couldn't do that."

A widower for fifteen years, Bud loved to host cocktail parties where he offered his guests fruit punch or livelier libations, finger food, invigorating conversation, and since he was a chivalrous gentleman of the old school, a rose for each lady. In the evening of the morning service—a party ala Bud—was held at his club.

"There may be some raised eyebrows," his oldest daughter said, "but I found his party guest list and this is a gift from his three daughters." There were champagne toasts of congratulations, remembrance, and bon voyage; and, of course, there were roses for the ladies. So, it was a fitting send-off for a joyous soul who loved God and Life.

Another terminally ill friend, fearing he'd not be so fortunate, left a handwritten note peeking from the pocket of his designated burial suit. "Who's planning the party?" it said.

Betsy planned her own. Betsy and I were writing a book when she learned she had a few months to live. At first, how she did "rage, rage against the dying of the light." But all that changed when she announced one day, "They're already celebrating my arrival. And I'm to have a new assignment...I'll leave on Sunday." And she did, though not in the morning hours as she planned. She had her daughter wheel her out to greet the sunrise and she died that afternoon, at age 58...a gorgeous lady who looked ten years younger.

Her own invitations were mailed to 130 friends. "Let's meet in Cheesman Park. I'll be with you," she promised. "Bring food and balloons and bring your pets." There was Irish music and dancing on the green!

It's always sad to see the young leave too soon. When Tim, a high school student, was killed in an automobile accident, friends crafted his pine box and wrote messages on the side, the way you'd autograph a cast. They pulled the coffin on a wagon to the burial ground where the lid was removed. He lay in jeans and plaid shirt with sleeves rolled

back.   His peers recalled special moments and dropped
mementos in with Tim—a flower, a letter, a key, even a pen
with his name imprinted on it—for he was a poet.

His poem was read; a keynote of the service.   It was
solemn and wise and roused feelings too deep for tears. A sage
dwelt inside a teenage boy.

So who is ready and who is not? Who is young and who
is old? My friend, Ruth, remembers two incidents that gave
her pause the day her husband of fifty years was laid to rest.
Mourners filed past the casket. One, a grandson, placed a cap
atop his grandpa's head; the one the old man was wearing
when he collapsed of a heart attack and died. The boy had
given it to his grandfather. "World's Greatest Grandpa," it
said.

A curious toddler at that funeral tugged at the widow's
skirts and asked, "What's in the box?" She lifted him up so he
could see. Wide-eyed, he turned and looked into her eyes.

"He looks brand new," he said.

***

ON SOUVENIRS

The word may be tricky to spell, but it says something about the human spirit. And it says it euphoniously. How soft the subtle sound of "souvenir." Its French root means to remember, to come to mind.

Therein lies the difference between the mere accumulation of possessions that characterizes the materialism of our age and the collection of mementos—a perennial human frailty or, as some might view it, a commendable characteristic. A grasping of "things" seems to correlate with greed and false values, while hoarding keepsakes may have greater affinity with the heart than with the hand.

Our reality is determined by that which we touch, smell, see, and hear so we hang onto happenings, pleasurable or sad, by keeping tangible reminders. They secure the experience, tuck it into an envelope for safe keeping, affording one the opportunity to relive, with feeling, berry picking in July or moonlight ice skating in January. Small wonder that tossing out those talismans borders on the sacrilegious.

I am moving my office from a remote corner downstairs to a smaller room upstairs. The necessary sorting and discarding is a difficult undertaking. It invites introspection and prolongs the task at hand.

There will always be room for a small framed snapshot, the only picture I have of my parents that was taken before I was. They were honeymooning in Wisconsin Dells. I only remember my mother with gray hair and my father weighing over 250 pounds. In the photograph, mother's hair is dark; Dad stands tall and slender.

On my parents' fiftieth anniversary, Ralph had what I regarded as a splendid idea, (particularly since they wanted no special 'folderol'). "Let's give them a weekend in Wisconsin Dells. Maybe the hotel where they stayed still exists". Mother was downright sullen at the suggestion. That dad burst into laughter and chided mother, "How about that, Annie?" only fueled the fires. I suspect that many a happy union began with a less than blissful honeymoon—especially in an era when sex was a subject more veiled than the bride.

There are diplomas, certificates, letters, postcards from faraway lands, even a few love notes my husband left in unexpected places. Books overflow the shelves. I make a valiant and ruthless effort to sort them. Nevertheless, old diaries, their tiny keys long-lost, with little more to report than "Went to a basketball game this evening," and code names I can't decipher for boys I had crushes on, get tossed onto the 'Save' pile, next to my mother-in-law's plush-covered autograph album. Manuscripts fill filing cabinets. Paper accounts for so much of the accumulated goods that I glance out my window apologetically, wondering if I worry the trees.

Speaking of paper and books, I am reminded of the day Beth cleaned my kitchen shelves. "Mom, you don't want this old beat-up cookbook anymore, do you? Twisting from her perch on the step stool, she dangled it over the wastebasket.

I swooped to the rescue.

True, the book has shed its plaid cover, the back binding is curling to reveal a glued piece of crinoline, the pages are torn, taped and tattered. The paper has yellowed and several pages are loose. Pages bearing favorite recipes are splattered and stained where a whirring mixer sprayed bits of batter. Eggs and milk have signed the guest book.

A special green section labeled "Wartime Supplement," contains information on saving waste fat and tin cans; pointers on food rationing, sugar substitutes; and canning information. Special notes pepper the pages: "increase the sugar," "add vanilla," "very good," and sometimes "Yech!"

This treasure traveled from army base to army base and is directly responsible for helping to build a happy marriage. Flipping its pages, revives memories of our first company dinner, the raves of Ralph's boss when we served grilled trout with almonds and lemon butter, and our first anniversary dinner—roast chicken, candlelight, and one rose in a crystal vase.

Get rid of Old Faithful? Never!

Back to sorting tangible chips of time and place residing in my office—a shell from Hawaii, driftwood from our Wisconsin cottage, an embossed clay cup from Greece which holds my pencils. My "pen cup" bears a picture of excavating machinery designed by my husband.

I smile as I glimpse my carved apple head which is mounted on a chunk of applewood. Therein lies an interesting tale.

A Chicago psychiatrist carved apple heads for a hobby. He became upset when a patient copied his process and of all things, God forbid, was interviewed on a local television station!

More than a little piqued, the doctor approached my brother-in-law, a patent attorney, to see what legal recourse he had. He was told he had none since apple carving was an ancient folk art. "However, I may be able to get you some publicity too," my brother-in-law suggested. "My sister-in-law is a writer."

I did the story, sold it, and as an added bonus received an apple head from a shrink who shrinks heads as an avocation as well as a profession.

Most treasured are the handmade gifts from our children when they were small—a mosaic of family hand-prints made by Anne, a clay beast shaped by John, a rather crude clay head fashioned by Beth when she was in kindergarten. The latter holds my rubber bands around its neck. The lavender glaze, the bulging eyes, the gaping mouth turned out to be exactly right—never has form better fitted function.

A whimsical yellow polka-dot dragon, a gift from my granddaughter, holds a pen, while a cracked ebony bowl holds paper clips and rubber bands. I was about to dispose of the latter, when my husband dashed in to rescue the bowl. "You wouldn't throw *that* away?" There was genuine horror in his tone. He remembered it as a permanent fixture in my parents' home, where it sat on a kitchen shelf and held needles, buttons, thread, thumb tacks, some Lincoln pennies, and a few

Canadian coins. Pieces of costume jewelry with missing stones or broken clasps found their way into the bowl.

Occasionally, there have been times, most of them long ago, when I regarded the man I married as taciturn and insensitive. The latter accusation melts when I recall the things he saves. What reason, other than sentiment, for keeping a curry comb? (Our dog died in 1979.) Or bulky boxes of love letters from WW II, or a picture taken when I was 18...with a lock of hair stashed behind it? A box contains bombardier wings, pictures of his B-24 crew, and ribbons from the Air Corps. Yet he never talks about those years and is disgusted when he meets a man who does..."All he was interested in was reliving the war."

He hoards handcrafted ashtrays made by small, loving hands, although he doesn't smoke. He has his father's company badge and my father's watch—his grandfather's straight edge razor and his grandmother's tea strainer. A hefty suitcase in his closet contains arrowheads his dad collected as a boy.

When our children sort the remnants of our lives, they'll find more packets of love among their father's things than my own. However, they'll also find more worthless junk hoarded by a pack rat.

Secrets sing out from souvenirs. They harbor surprises. I found a few when the home place was sold. I was astounded to find a book of serious poetry among my father's things. His handwriting filled the margins. He never seemed a man who cared for poems, except the one he lived...with exuberant and joyful abandon.

Mother kept a toy tractor that was to have been her son's Christmas gift. Three year old Jackie (with the golden curls), died of Spinal Meningitis before Santa could make the delivery. Whenever Ben Voelker came to hang wallpaper, he'd leave bare the space where my brother had scribbled on the dining room wall, and then frame it with a border. Mother pushed a small desk in front of her sacred secret.

Wallace Stegner wrote a poignant reminiscence about the town dump in Whitemud, Saskatchewan. He said it held far more poetry and excitement than did the people of the town. Stegner recommends sociologists go to rubbish heaps to study the life of a community. "For whole civilizations we have sometimes no more of the poetry and little more of the history than this." Quite often it is enough. From potsherd, stone weapons, chiseled tools, and brittle bones, archeologists rebuild entire social structures.

What we throw away says much about who we are. Yet, I move that what we hang onto (those foolish treasures we *deny* the refuse piles) says more about the poetry that is the human soul, for what are souvenirs if not the loving residue when lives are seined? And they are most often found in the home.

***

SAD FATE OF THE WISH BOOK

I have several friends who each day faithfully check the obituary pages of their daily newspapers. While I've not taken up the habit, I did take to heart the recent death notice of an old friend featured in a national news magazine.

The Sears and Roebuck catalog (or "Sears and Sawbuck" as we dubbed it when I was growing up), has bit the dust. Sears catalog and the Bible were once the mainstays of every Midwestern American household in the late 19th and early 20th century. (And lest we forget Montgomery Ward and Company, affectionately known as "Monkey Wards.") Today's specialty catalogs fill America's mailboxes and are cited as devilish competition for the old and dying wish books.

It's interesting to note that the two mail-order approaches also catalog the changing American lifestyle—indeed map the leaps and bounds we've made soaring toward the Good Life.

Once the American farmer, eager to avoid the expense of the middleman, and unable to make trips to distant cities, relied on Sears catalog as a lifeline to the hinterlands.

In 1893, the catalog had 196 pages advertising sewing machines, saddles, bicycles, and musical instruments. The following year, it expanded to 507 pages and the copy was written almost entirely by Richard Sears. In its heyday, the catalog contained 1,500 pages, weighed six pounds, reached 20 million people, and offered 100,000 products. You name it, they sold it. Sears literally helped build America. By 1927, more than 35,000 people constructed Sears kit homes.

An Ohio woman in my writing class sold her article (with snapshots) of their Silverdale No. 2011 farm home chosen from the 1919 Sears catalog and costing $1,623.00, to a nostalgia magazine. The two-story, seven-room house remained lived-in and unchanged until it was modernized in 1984. In 1989 an Ottawa restaurant purchased rights to reprint the reminiscence on their place mats.

If you've been around for more than half a century, and grew up on a farm or in a small town, you remember the thrill of paging through the new Spring and Summer or Fall and Winter catalog. As well as I remember Decoration Day parades and May baskets, I remember that exciting day in the postoffice lobby when townsfolk got a deliciously fat catalog to carry home.

I was quick to pick out a plaid skirt and sweater. Maybe a wool cap or a pair of oxfords, and surely a sled, a doll, or a game of checkers. A letter to Santa was a letter to Sears & Roebuck.

In summer, I sat on the porch floor and cut up the old book, making paper dolls from the models in the corset and underwear ads, then dressing them in flared skirts, fancy blouses, and wide-brimmed hats. Or I made doorstops by folding every page in a certain pattern, until a lovely circular whirl with pointed top took shape before my wondering eyes.

Can today's swanky catalogs build such a treasury of memories? They rarely feature those necessities of life we ordered from Sears, like galoshes and long johns, corsets and cough syrup, tools and Tinker Toys. As for sparing the expense of the middleman, the higher the price, the more enticing the unique, imported, luxurious gadget...sure to delight Milady, or her significant other, guaranteed to tickle the fancy of the executive who has everything. And the higher the family income, the more varied and abundant the catalogs from which to choose.

There is, however, an obvious advantage known to ritzy modern-day catalogs. They face a fate far less humiliating than the Sears and Sawbuck or Monkey Ward wish book of yesteryear. The worst that can happen to Lands' End is landfill—the best is recycling to live another day. If you grew up on a farm in rural America, you remember the sad fate of an outdated catalog. It was the "in thing" in the outhouse.

***

CAN YOU BEAT THAT?

Buildings of reflecting glass
make us catch our breath,
Computers dazzle us.
If we're lucky, we have a friend, more or less
Our own age, to whom we can say:
"Can you beat that?"
And the next day somebody does.

.....Elise Maclay

Grandparents, and parents too, can forget those old tales about walking three miles to school in three feet of snow. Announce a simple truth that today's kids may find even harder to fathom: "We learned to write!" Do you ever wonder about the second 'R'? What in the world happened to Penmanship?

Palmer Method books were opened to specified writing exercises. Pens were dipped into ink wells. The pen rested lightly against third finger and was held in place by gentle pressure of thumb and forefinger. Arms rolled rhythmically.

The teacher counted as we made connected ovals. Great coils wormed their way across the page, slanting to the right. The next exercise squished the coils. Rows of uniformly slanted lines (push-pulls) began with a single swish and ended with a flourish. Capital letters and specific words were copied from the book. The finished page was mailed in for a Palmer Method pin.

My nasty suspicions regarding the death of penmanship were vindicated by a recent announcement in *The Boston Globe:* "People are beginning to question whether it's important to learn long-hand. Nearly 40% of U.S. households have computers. Increasing amounts of work and communication are done on a keyboard."

A Cambridge, MA, mother complained that her fourteen-year-old son "never really learned how to do cursive, but segued right from printing to the computer."

At its convention in Washington, the National Association of Elementary School Principals found no time for sessions on handwriting. "Too many other more pressing education topics." Some parochial schools lack funding for computers, so cursive writing is part of the curriculum. I look at my refrigerator door. A handmade picture and message by granddaughter Katie (age seven), who attends private school, and a computer colored picture with keyed message from grandson Aaron (also seven), whose parents are computer experts.

Here's an interesting twist. For $99.95, an Oregon software company offers a computerized font that duplicates a person's handwriting! No need to hand sign a document.

Even more intriguing, a *New York Times* article featured Benedictine monks in Abiquiu, NM, who pray, garden, carve icons, bake bread—*and* design sites on the Internet's World Wide Web.

A thirty-year-old monk, a former systems analyst from Denver, sees the work as a return to the ancient tradition of scribes working in sixth century monasteries creating illuminated parchment manuscripts from the *Bible*. "In a sense," he says, "the Web and what will happen in the next decade is a return to that tradition." The lettering is done by hand on canvas. Illuminations are then scanned into computers before being incorporated on Web pages.

Brother Aquinas is the director of the scriptorium, an adobe building with a hard-packed earthen floor and rough-hewn tables. A wood crucifix hangs on the wall; hand-painted illuminations share shelf space with Windows 95. Aquinas explains, "twelve new brothers joined our monastery. We needed more income."

Getting on Internet filled that need nicely. Solar panels generate power for 12 personal computers. Hand-printed and illuminated Web sites are offered at $65 an hour for programming and $110 an hour for artwork. Annual income has jumped from $48,000 a year to "probably $200,000 this year," Aquinas says.

Cursive writing to computers. Illuminated parchment manuscripts to clean interface design via computers. Isolation to technological communication. Poverty to economic ecumenism.

Can you beat that? Oh, what a tangled Web we weave!

***

FULL CIRCLE

We shall not cease from exploration
And the end of all our exploring
Will be to arrive where we started
And know the place for the first time.

T. S. Eliot
Four Quartets

I began this collection with "Once Upon A Rainbow," epitomizing the wonder of childhood. Although we "see" an arc (because the world is in the way), the rainbow, viewed from a higher vantage point is a circle. Traveling its under-belly to complete the circumference is no easy journey.

Increasing numbers of our population are pursuing that pain-filled, joyous exploration—like ancient holy men and women circumambulating sacred places, like monks spinning prayer wheels and nuns whirling rosaries in the outward search for the inner source.

Recent statistics reveal that each month the world's population aged 55+ gains 1.2 million persons. At this hour, no doubt the figure is even greater. In the United States alone, the Census Bureau reports that between 1960 and 1994, while the total population grew by 45%, the population aged 65+ climbed 100%!

There are city, state, national, and even congressional committees on aging that won't let you forget you're part of that burgeoning statistic. Senior centers, retirement organizations, and prime-time publications offer the latest advice on taxes, health care, medical insurance, and retirement housing.

As a septuagenarian, I'm eligible for the information, but something inside me rejects all that guff about old age and what to do if it strikes. Pablo Picasso put a positive slant on the aging process, when he said, "It takes a long time to become young."

Frankly, I don't think my attitude is all that unique, nor do I think it's entirely a matter of wearing blinders or kidding myself. Attitude matters in matters of age. And kidding oneself is not all bad. Humor is a compensatory tempering of the dawn of consciousness. Making a joke of life's absurdities makes them bearable. What's more absurd than wrinkles, forgetfulness, and sensory deterioration, when you know full well there's still marvelous stuff inside you haven't even tapped yet.

Then too, you've no doubt noticed those insightful Aha's you found so enlightening have dropped the big A. The divine ha-ha means *letting go*.

Small wonder a recent poll maintained, "the older people get, the happier they are ...nearly two-thirds of Americans 65+ are pleased with their personal lives...and a happy marriage enhances your chance for a long life." I'll go along with that 100%. "But how can that be?" you ask. "Who would *enjoy* being old?"

My granddaughter understands. There's a kid with savvy. Because I take continuing education courses, she wants to know what I want to be when I grow up. I'm not sure I want to be grown up, that is. I think once I was but now I'm not, and I like myself better now.

It's downright refreshing *to be* who you are, to tell it like it is, to do your own thing in your own good time, and not mind a bit that someone is watching. It's what I tell myself when, upon impulse while taking my daily walk, I slide down the slide in the playground, without even a tagalong kid to make it legit.

My daughters, successful professionals themselves, remind me that now I have the time to expand my horizons and explore my talents (inasmuch as I wasted my own productive years producing, then tending, the crop).

How many times have you been told tremendous rewards will be showered upon you if you give of your time and your self? In the glorious golden years, opportunities abound. Your mail burgeons with requests for dollars; you can canvas your neighborhood for March of Dimes, Cancer Fund, or the Heart Association; or give time to the hospital, hospice, or community center.

Be honest now. Haven't you had this volunteer bit tossed in your face once too often? I never was a Mother Teresa or an Albert Schweitzer, so it's not easy to shift gears now. However, my best friend's mother, age ninety-two, is proud to volunteer each Thursday at her local senior center..."to help the old folks." That's what really convinced me there must be something in it.

I plan to give it a try. I just signed up to teach writing classes at the elementary school just up the road. (I can tell you right now who'll end up teaching whom!)

We're constantly told age is no deterrent to accomplishing significant things. Look around! George Burns kept us laughing until the final curtain. Bob Hope has slowed down, but he hasn't given up. Colonel Sanders, Grandma Moses, and Winston Churchill came into their own after 65. Betty Freidan, past 75, writes, and lectures, about self-fulfillment and conscious aging. Julia Child, 10 years older than Freidan, is still chopping, mixing, baking, and sipping wine. Hugh Downs, as Barbara Walters reminds each week on "20/20", manages to "stay in touch" at 76.

Keep busy is the perpetual admonition. Eat well. Exercise. Keep mind and body alert. Try aerobics. Ride a bicycle. Square dance. Swim at the rec center. *Run!*

Listen, when your 1976 Oldsmobile breaks down, you don't take her out on the Interstate and open her up with your foot to the floor. Glory be! The rat race is over. Sure, *move*, but relax. Enjoy! The work of the world, thank God, is no longer your primary responsibility.

A Denver teacher asked her first-graders to imagine what life would be like at age 100. A six-year-old sage named Michael Gordon said, "I think I will become humble and stay home a lot."

Here in the magnificent Rocky Mountains, I walk a lot

and I catch my breath when I come upon an elk or a deer, or a herd of either. It's a thrill that never wears thin. I have a fox that visits each day and even naps upon my deck. My neighbor watered my plants when we were on vacation. "Your little fox came and peeked in the door," she said. "He smiled, I swear— probably thought you were home again."

Reminds me, several years ago a young visitor was overwhelmed when he saw my fox (different generation, I'm sure), look in the door. "I *never* in my life thought I'd ever live to see *this!*" His proclamation was a solemn prayer. His nine-year-old twin brother stood by, not the least impressed.

A few months ago I ran into the lad's mother, whom I'd not seen in years. She rushed over and said, "Kyle never forgot that day when he saw the fox on your deck. Guess what? He's in Wildlife Management now."

How about that? No wonder he was impressed with the little fox. A hidden counterpart lay deep within his soul.

To *be* who you are, to really *look* as if for the very first time, to explore, to speak truth—simply, to marvel at trifles, to enjoy the right-now laughter of a child, or rosy streaks across the sky, to think the eternal *now* instead of time—Hey! That's like taking a hot bath after a week at a cabin without plumbing. It's also what being a second-time kid is all about. You might call it living with reverence and a sense of wonder.

According to an ancient Hasidic story, just before a child is born, an Angel whisks away 'memory and knowing' with one flick of a finger beneath the nostrils. Thus, the small cleft between nose and upper lip is formed. And thus, we spend our lives seeking wisdom, groping desperately in our perpetual becoming, in our eternal quest for being.

Invisible flecks of wisdom may remain if you catch a kid that's young enough, for it is true those remnants may well be lost, twisted or mislaid during the earthly journey.

It's nothing personal. It happens to all of us. The false belief of separateness and limitation is given freely, blithely, to all who enter the world. We are like the eaglet raised with a flock of barnyard chickens. One day, fully grown, he envied a magnificent eagle soaring on high and had no idea that he, too, could fly. A birthright unrecognized!

The good news is that the gift of not just looking, but seeing, may descend now and again in its own good time. And seeing, when it happens, is beyond believing. One way to speed the process is to give careful notice to the wee ones among us, who, at the most unlikely moments, still speak the forgotten language of the flowers. In small, clear voices they awaken us to the song of God...if we take the time to listen. And paying attention heals.

The pain you thought you could never endure, the paradox that constantly hit you in the gut, ultimately fostered a rebirth and transformation...a peaceful acceptance of, an abiding love for, a childlike intimacy with, all that is. One hopes the bitter winds blew away the chaff and left the grain. That's not to say there aren't blue days, rather a wider perspective has robbed them of their power to debilitate. Those times when hope scurries into a corner leaving the door open for acedia, I question the wisdom of listening to the news.

Ashley Montagu had it right. "The trick in life is to die young as late as possible." His idea must have caught hold— more and more people are perfecting the art.

***

EPILOGUE

CANCER AWAKENS THANKFULNESS

My husband, Ralph, retired from his engineering career in January, 1991. We reveled in our new freedom. How often, with swish and swagger, he would bow and offer his arm as we headed up or down our winding driveway to fetch the newspaper or collect the mail. With mock pomp and circumstance, he'd issue his usual wry invitation, "Come, Milady, travel with me the steep road of life." As we fell into step. "Together forever," he'd proclaim to the Ponderosa pines.

On just such a day I had warned, "We must stay well and enjoy these so-called 'golden years.'" You might say we'd been spoiled. We've both been exceedingly healthy, so it seemed not the least important when Ralph suggested in April that we attend a Health Fair. It went in one ear and out the other, but during the final weekend of the fair, Ralph renewed his suggestion.

A prostate examination and a prostate specific antigen blood test (PSA) revealed problems that warranted a biopsy. Malignant was not the report we anticipated, but it was the word we were given. How could it be? He'd been so healthy, no symptoms whatsoever.

Reading about prostate cancer was encouraging. The outlook was good. Unlike many other cancers, it does not spread rapidly, but if let go, it may metastasize, attacking the bones. (A bone scan proved negative.) "If discovered when you are over 60." the book said, "you may outlive it and die from an unrelated cause. By age 80, virtually every male has prostate cancer, although it is only visible when looked for with a microscope."

So we were very optimistic. However, driving home from the doctor's office, the sky was bright blue and the sun shone on our mountains as Ralph reached for my hand and touched it to his lips. "Whatever happens, Katie, we had a good time in a beautiful place." That was about as dramatic as things got.

The urologist outlined options: 1. Do nothing, but watch it carefully. 2. Radiation of the general area. 3. Surgical removal of the prostate gland. All cases are different and even doctors' opinions vary.

I'm sure you noticed the part synchronicity plays in lives. Once consciousness is concerned with a problem, relevant issues pop up all over the place. By chance, as we were considering a course of action, Ralph tuned in to a 20/20 show that suggested surgery is often the best choice in the early stages of prostate cancer. Bobby Riggs refused surgery early on and he related his disease progressed mercilessly thereafter.

We opted for surgery.

"I don't expect the cancer has spread to the lymph glands," the doctor said, "but we won't know until surgery. If so, the horse is already out of the barn."

Although cancer had not spread into the lymphatic system, the pathology report revealed another previously undetected malignant tumor in the prostate.

Following surgery, Ralph came home to our house on the hill. We were thankful for early detection and steady recovery. Each evening, we watched the news and followed, with elation, the failure of the Soviet coup. The outer world goes on, even as inner worlds take powerful precedence. In the cyclical patterns of the earth, we take turns. One person's pain is ever another's complacency.

Nevertheless, a new awareness has become a kind of celebration. The voices of our kids and grandkids on the telephone, the morning sun glistening on the pine needles, the gray quiet that settles each evening on the shoulders of Double-header Mountain, our gift of added time with one-another—ordinary miracles we no longer take for granted.

Ralph says he looks forward to twenty more years. I'm all for it. As the TV ad reminds, we got here the old-fashioned way; we earned it—via forty-six years of sorrow and joy, despair and elation, acting and waiting, doing and letting go. That's what golden means. It's a vibrant, mellow place that has taken on the patina of age, while recapturing the magnificent wonder of a child. It's a far fry from those brash beginnings when you *knew* what life and love were all about.

***

Acknowledgments

It would require another three hundred pages to thank the souls who reached out in kindness and caring.

To my family whose faith, love, and support were never influenced one whit by editorial acceptances or rejections; to my publisher/editor, whose gentle guidance put this book into my hands: and to dear friends, neighbors, and writers who blessed my life with living stories, loving hearts, and invaluable lessons for a floundering pilgrim. Thank you.

Lest we forget, holy solitude, which taught me to love myself.

Catherine Lazers Bauer

Additional Books from Cosmic Concepts

Copies of **ONE DAY ON EARTH A Third Eye View** ($15.95 plus shipping) and the other books from Cosmic Concepts press listed below can be purchased from the Holistic Alliance.

Jesus and the Message of Love by Ronald D. Pasquariello $12.95
A contemporary narrative celebrating the love of God.

Your Life and Love Beyond Death by David Hyatt   Hard cover: $20.95
A compelling account of documented evidence   Soft cover: $11.95
proving beyond a doubt that life and love await you
on the Other Side.

The White Stone by Alcott Allison $8.95
A mystical novel of 4th century Ireland, this moving story in
total physical and psychic vitality puts our current times to shame.

Benny the Lazy Beaver by George Fisk $10.99
Illustrations by Scott J. Barker. Benny helps children gain self-esteem,
as he gathers some himself in his transition from lazy to altruistic beaver.

A New Sense of Destiny from Ancient Symbols by George Fisk $9.95
The author explains how we of the 20th century can find renewal
of vision and vigor for living by immersing ourselves in the powerful
language of symbols drawn from astrology and alchemy.

Searching for Home by Laurelynn Martin $11.95
Laurelynn's near-death experience changed her life, and it can change
yours. "Many books have been written about such encounters, but this is
surpassingly rich in the spiritual insights it offers." Kenneth Ring, Ph.D.

Brand New Me by Herman Aaftink $14.95
A step-by-step guide that will show you how to take hold of your
situation, develop your ultimate potential and change your life forever.

For More Information and Wholesale Orders Please Contact:

Cosmic Concepts press
2531 Dover Lane
St. Joseph, MI 49085
Phone: (616) 428-2792
Fax: (616) 428-9671
Email: Sales@CosmicConceptspress.com
Web: www.CosmicConceptspress.com

For Retail Orders Please Contact:

Holistic Alliance
100 Church Street
St. Joseph, MI 49085
Phone: (888) 870-4555 or (616) 982-0900
Fax: (616) 982-1887
Email: CosmicConcepts@HolisticAlliance.com
Web: www.HolisticAlliance.com